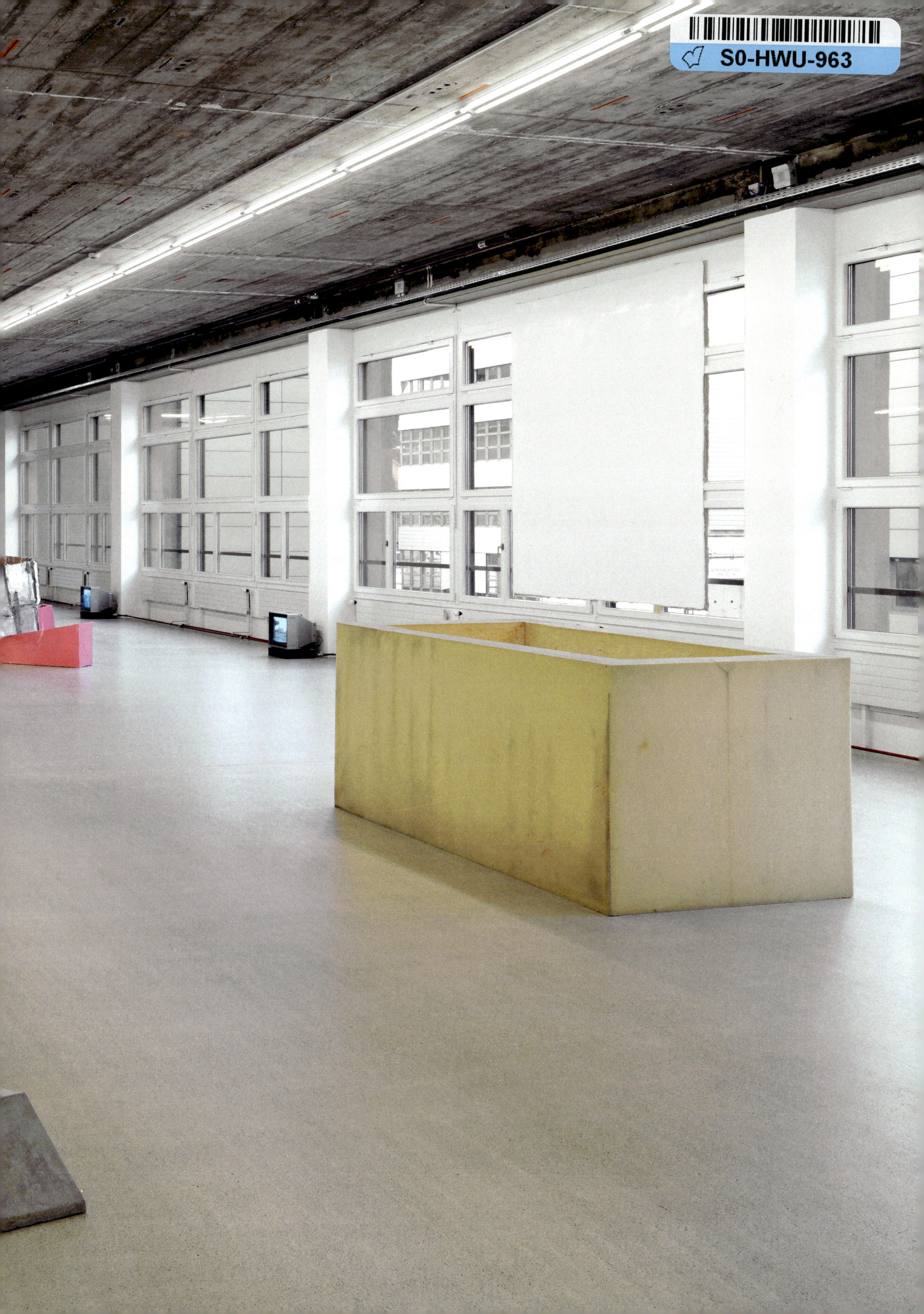

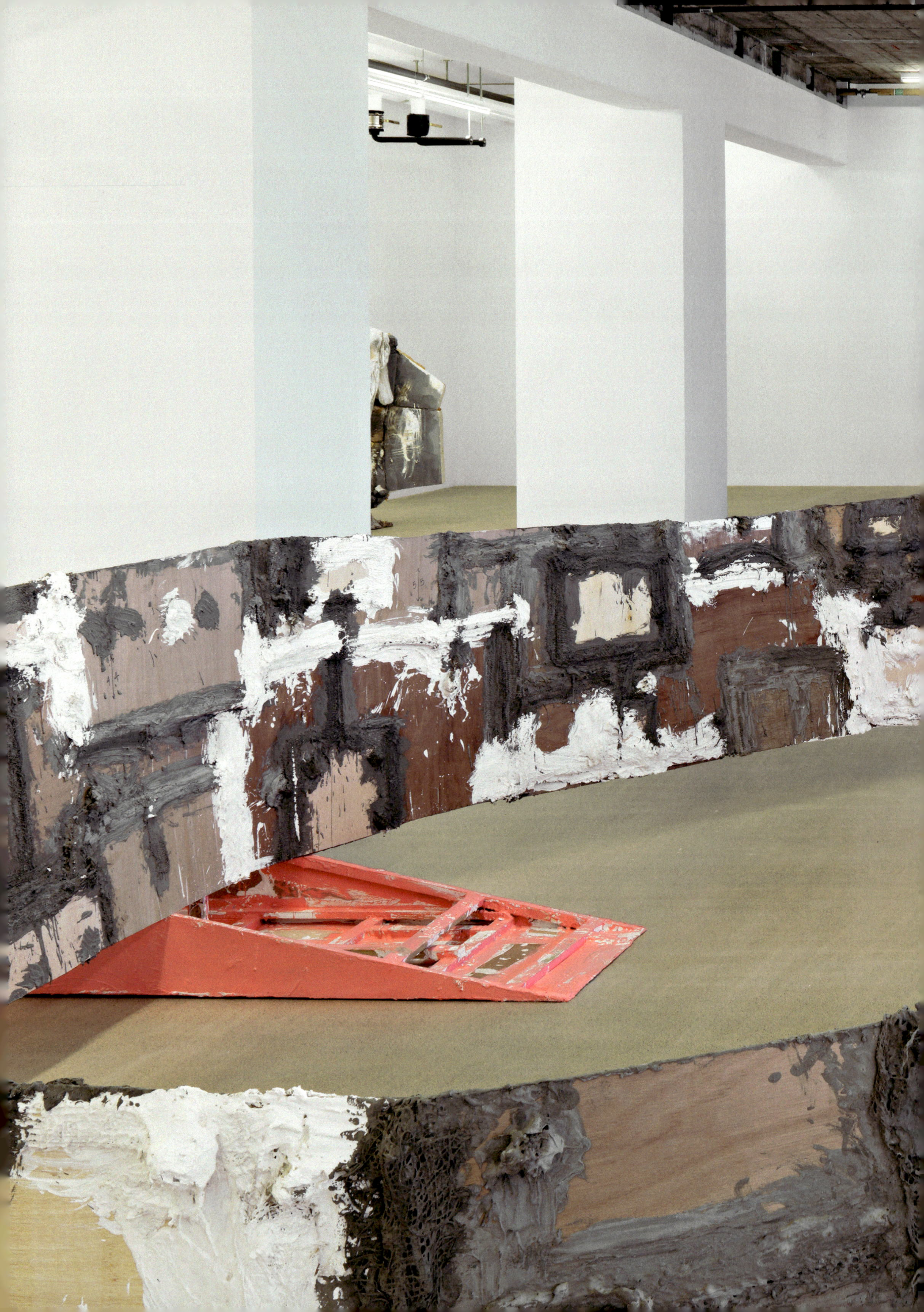

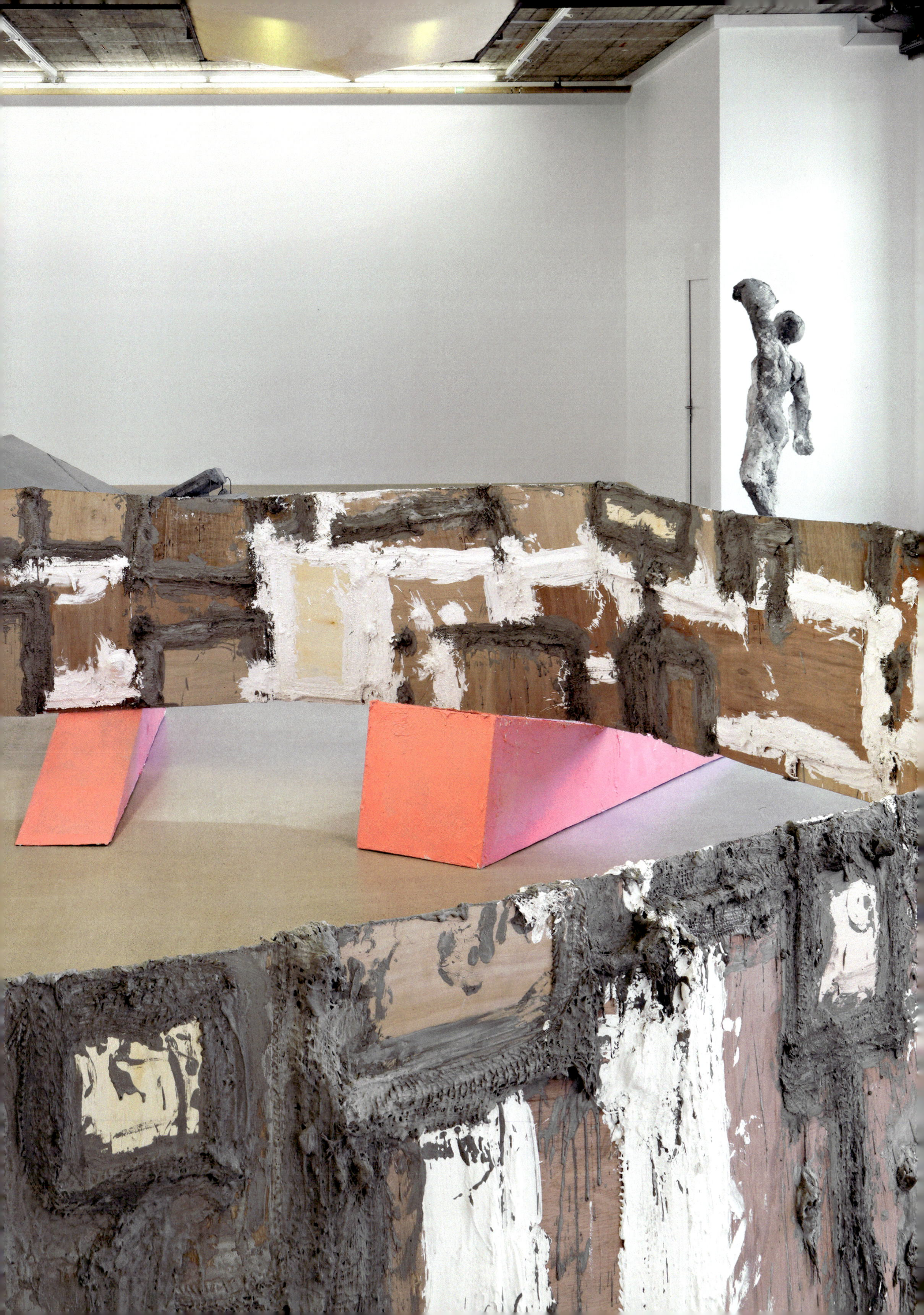

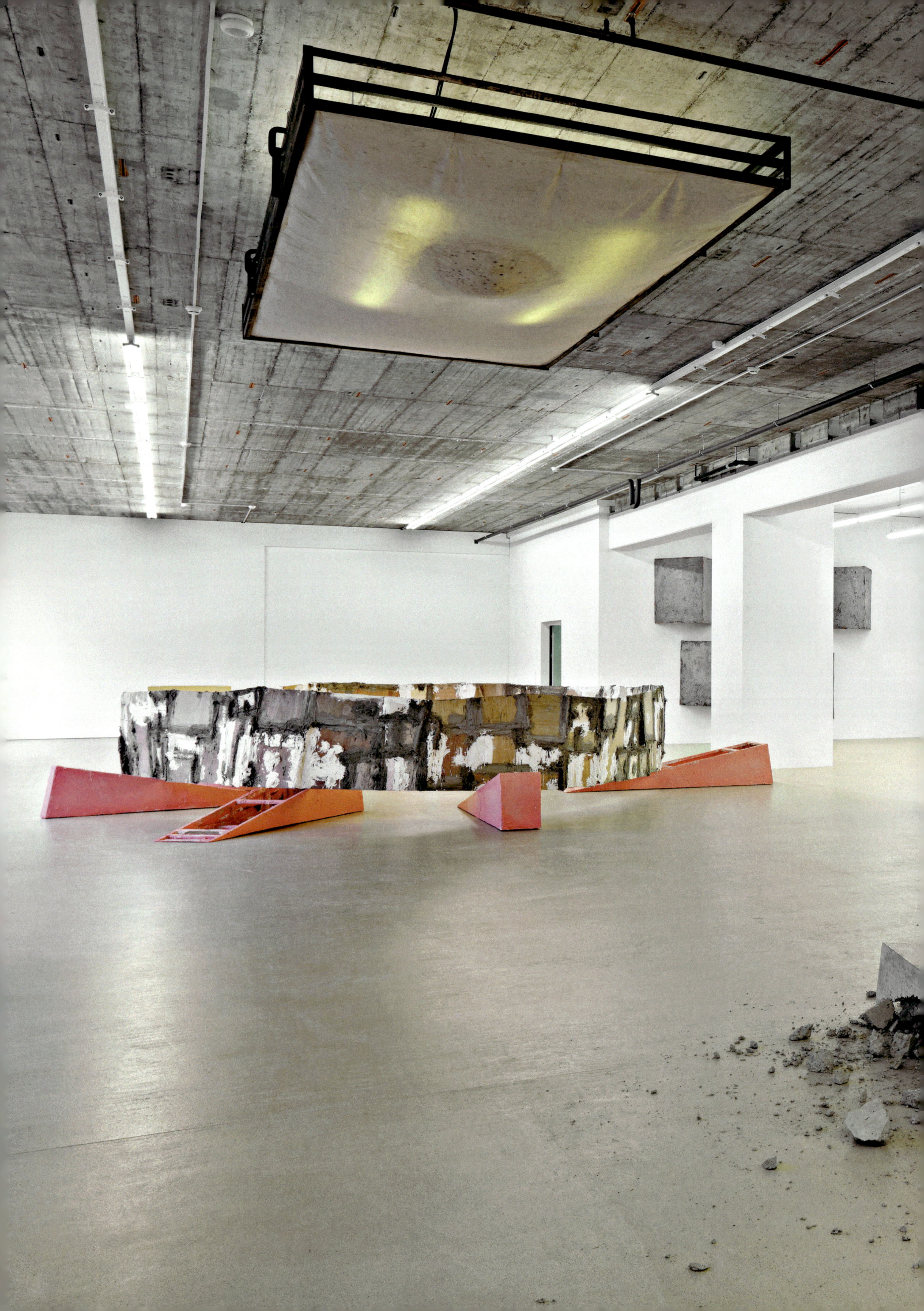

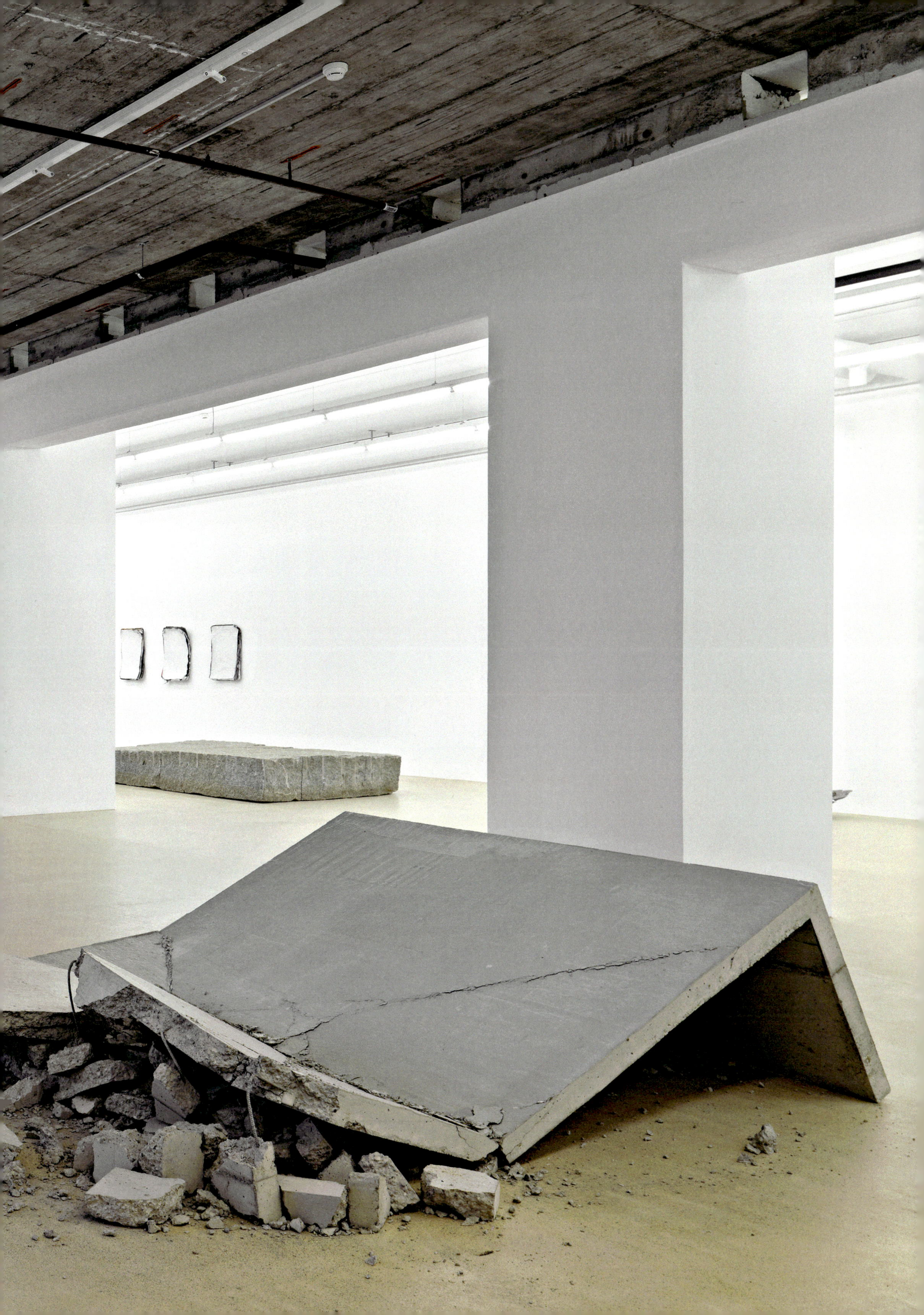

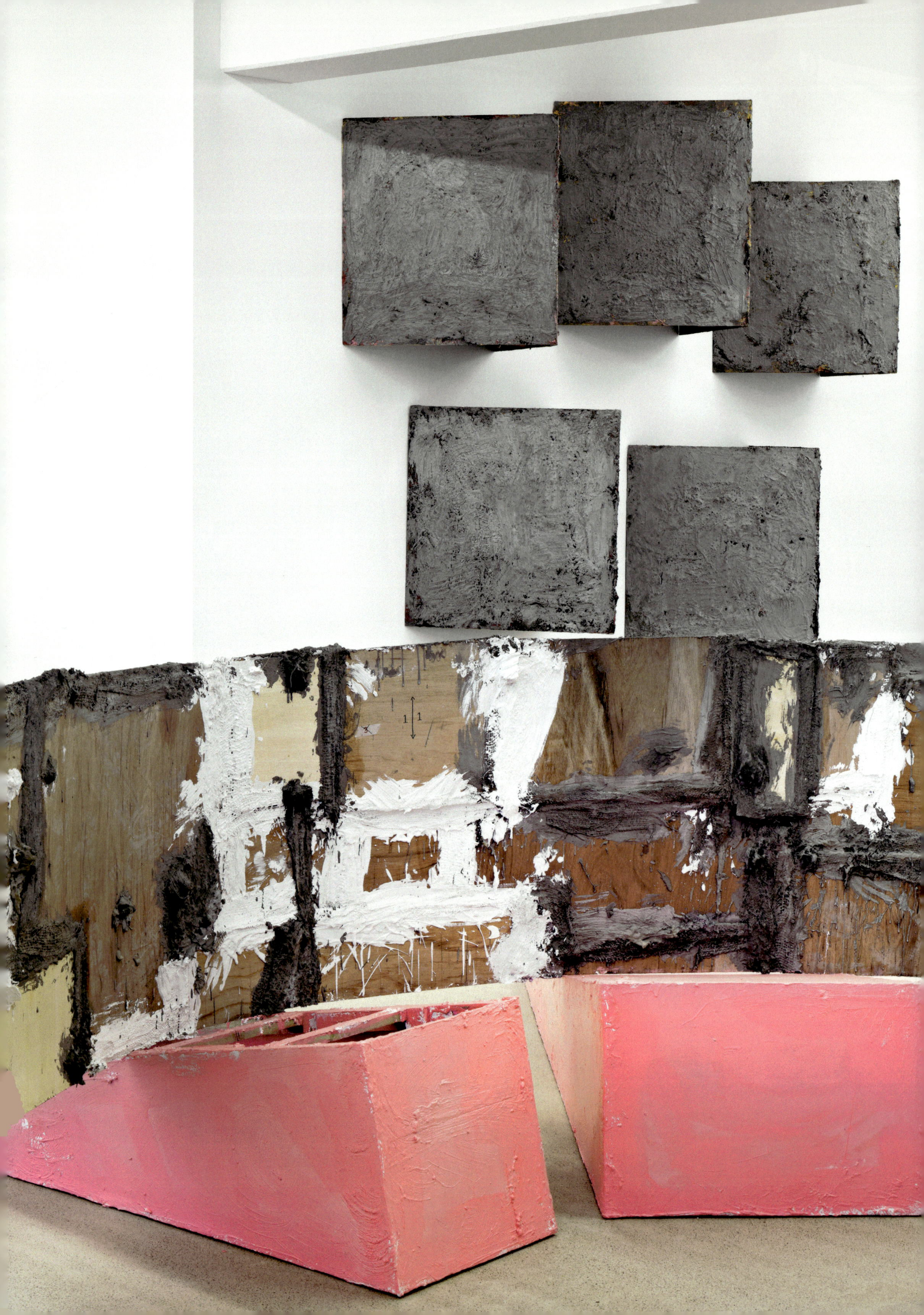

On the Break
Lines of Architecture
and its Bodies

Displaced Fractures

Über die Bruchlinien
von Architekturen und
ihren Körpern

Edited by
Heike Munder/
Thomas D. Trummer

Published by
migros museum für
gegenwartskunst Zürich
& Siemens Stiftung

Distributed by
JRP|Ringier

TABLE OF CONTENTS

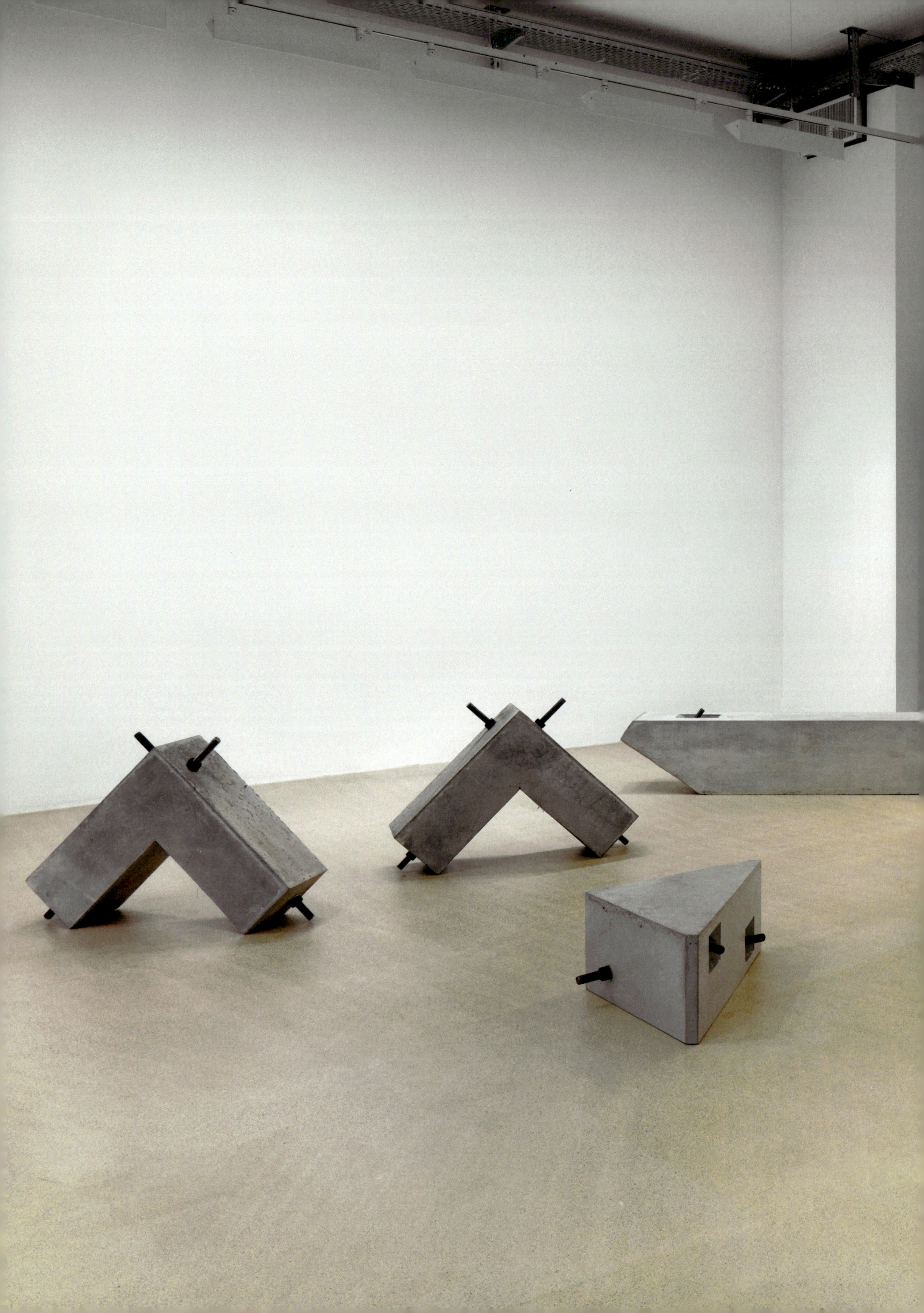

ERASED
2008–2010

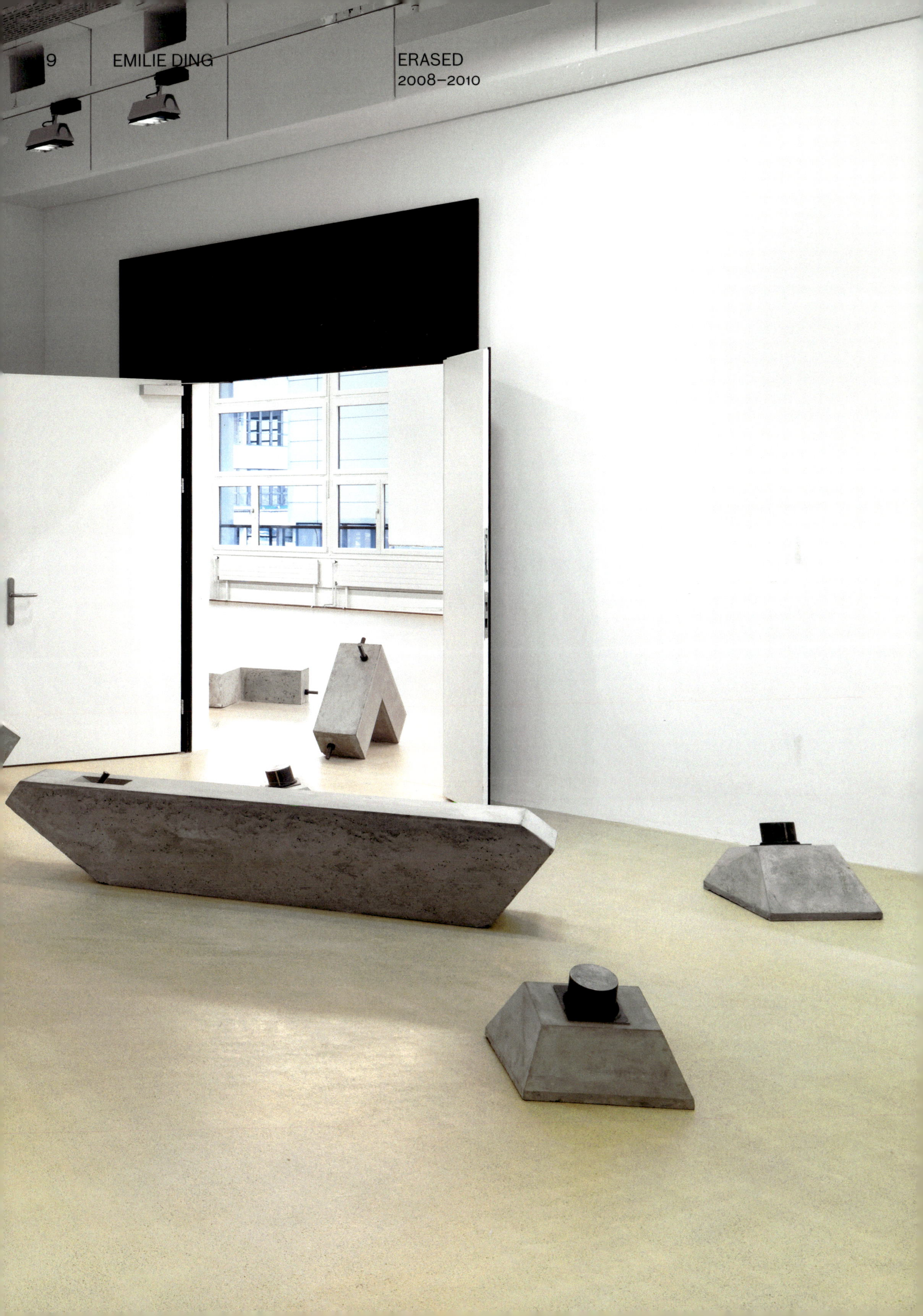

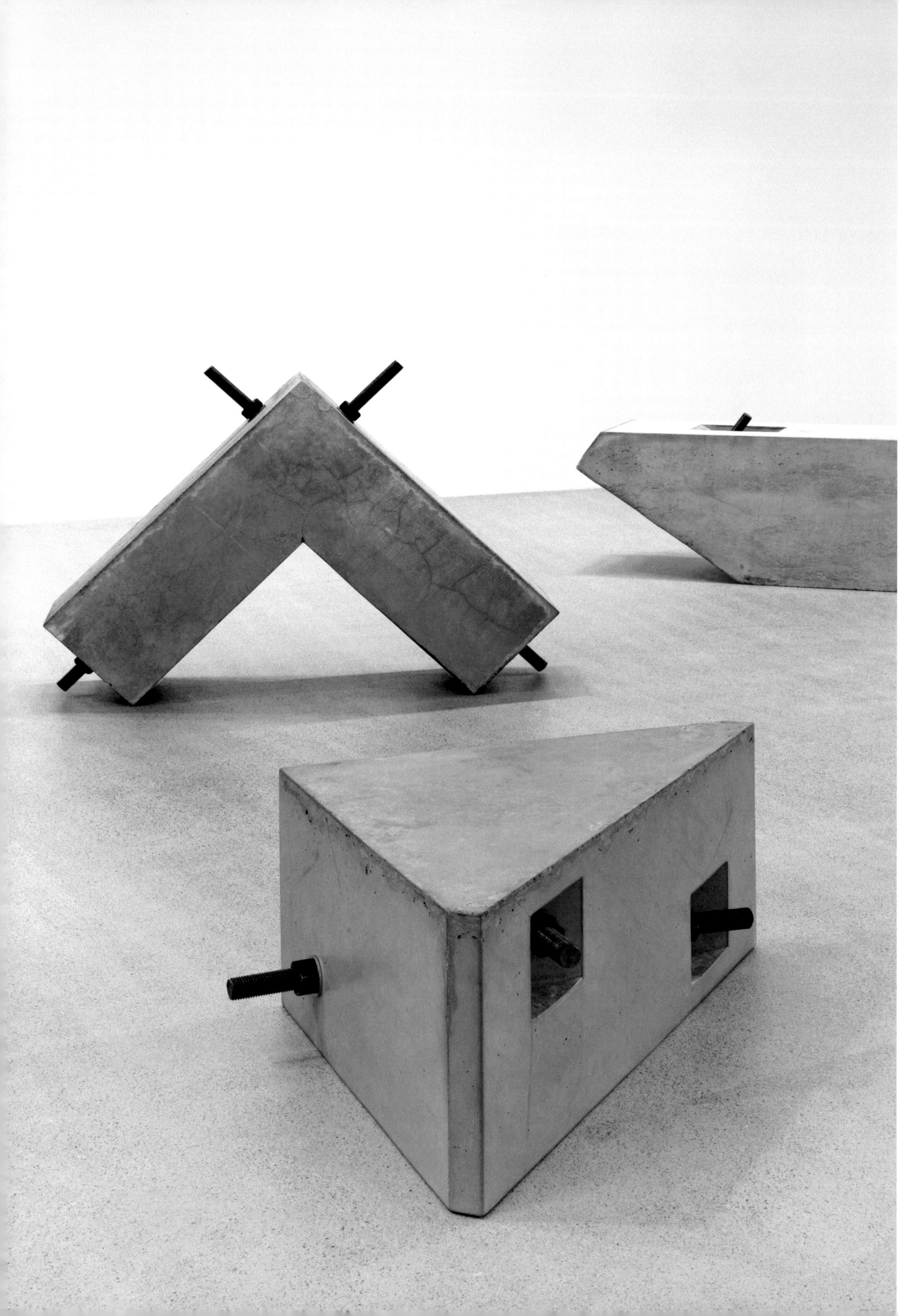

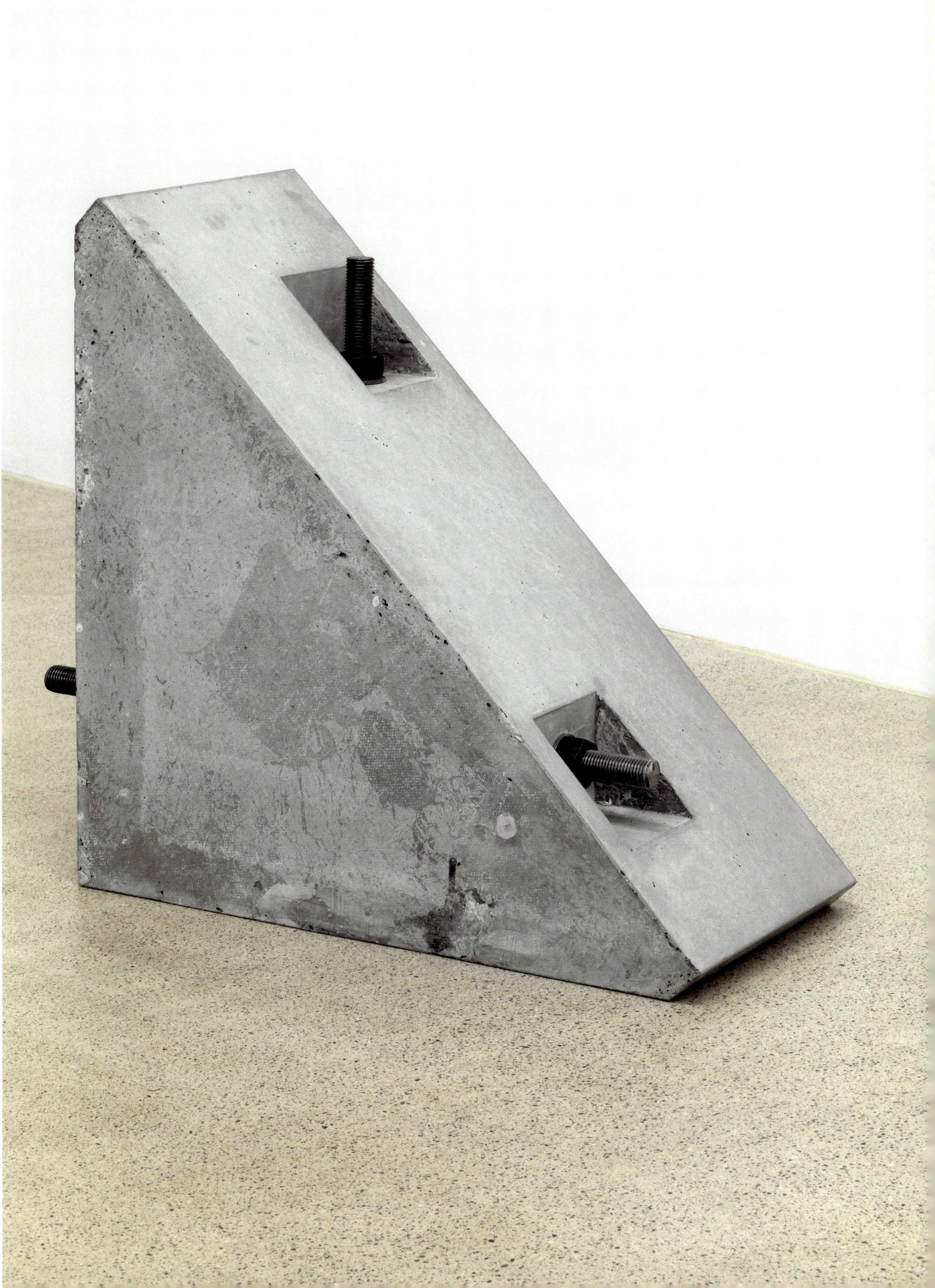

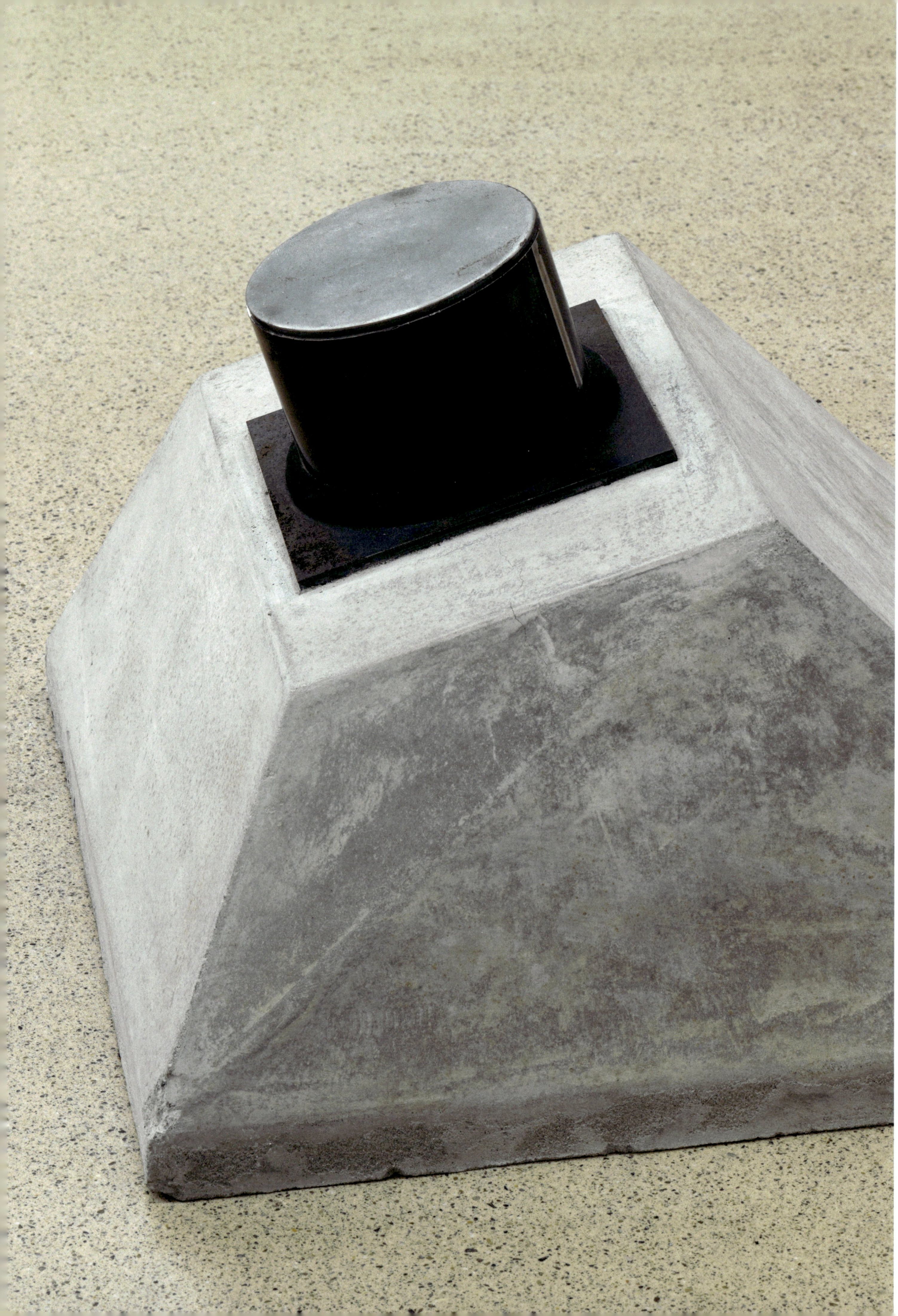

KILIAN RÜTHEMANN

OHNE TITEL (SARKOPHAG)
2009

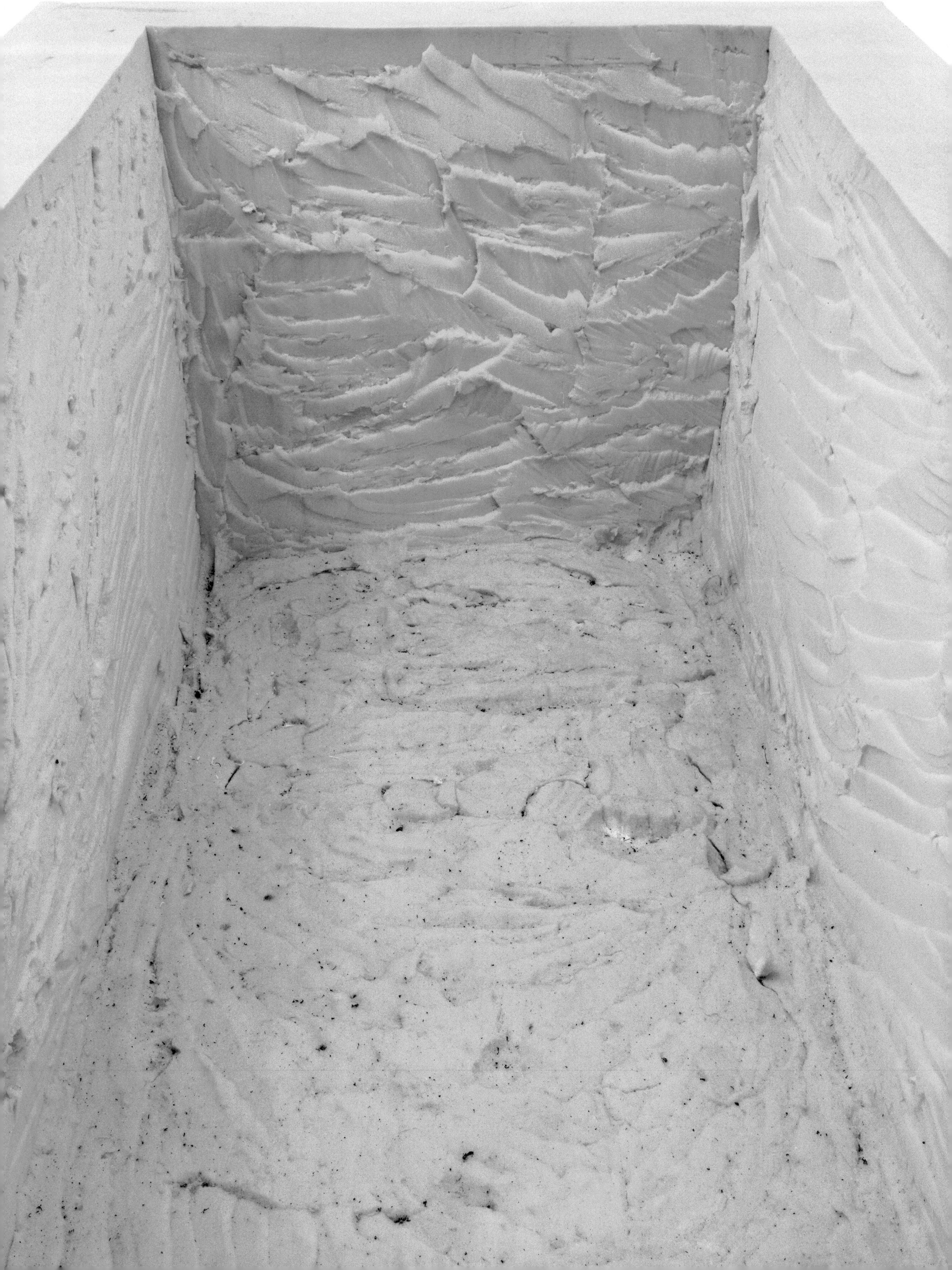

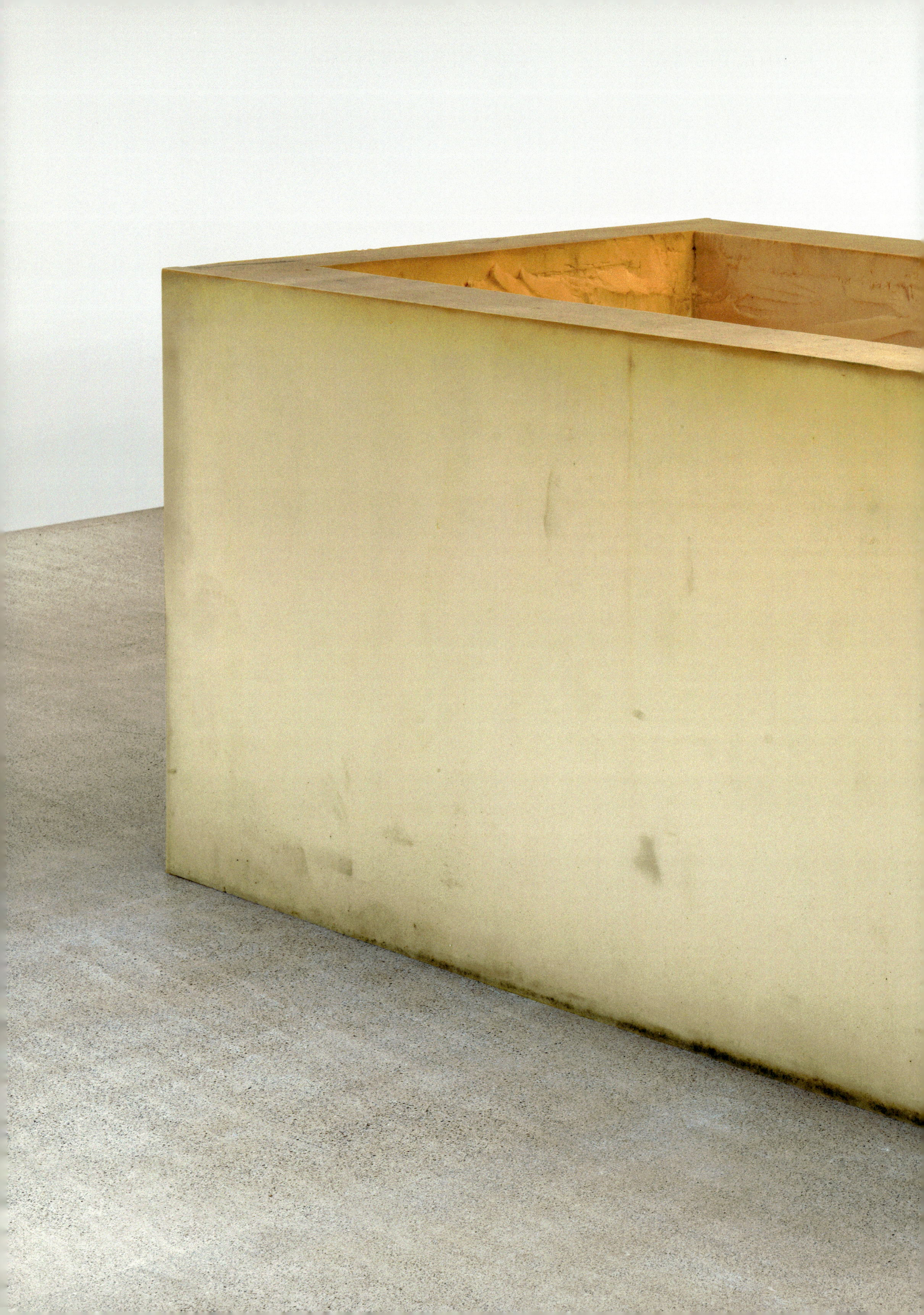

15 KILIAN RÜTHEMANN

OHNE TITEL (SARKOPHAG)
2009

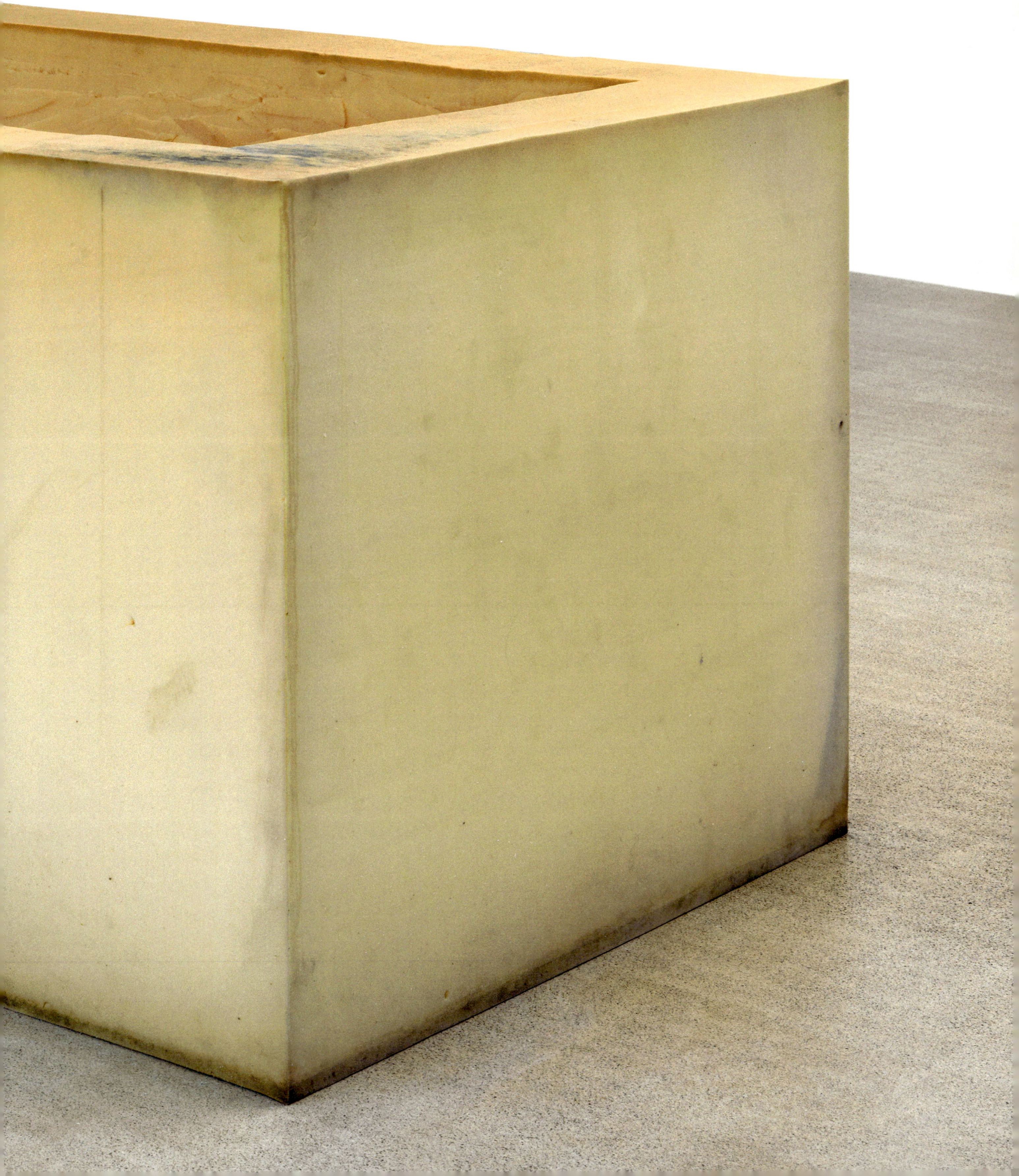

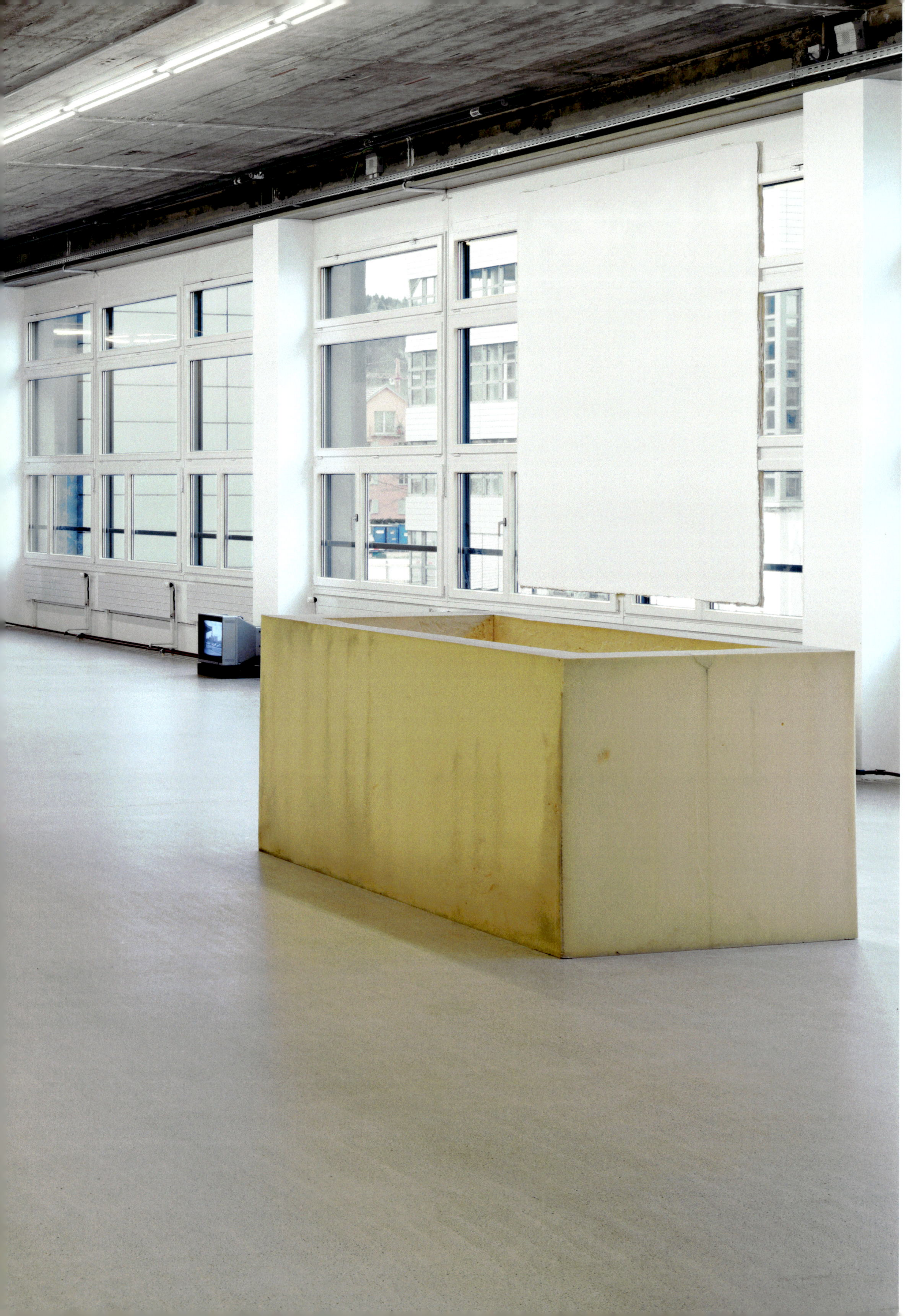

THE TRUTH WILL ALWAYS HAVE A HOLE IN IT
2010

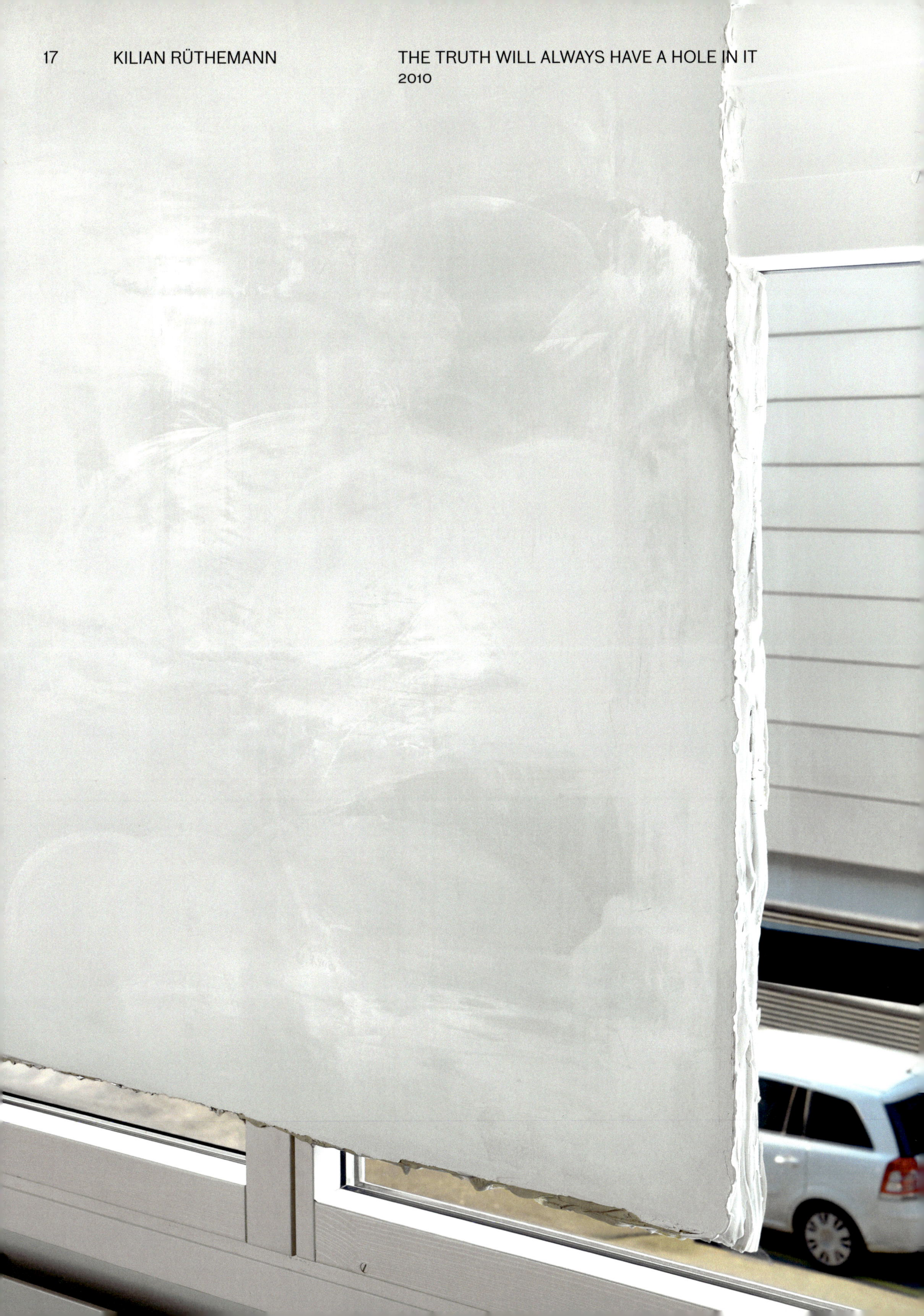

POSITION 0310
2010

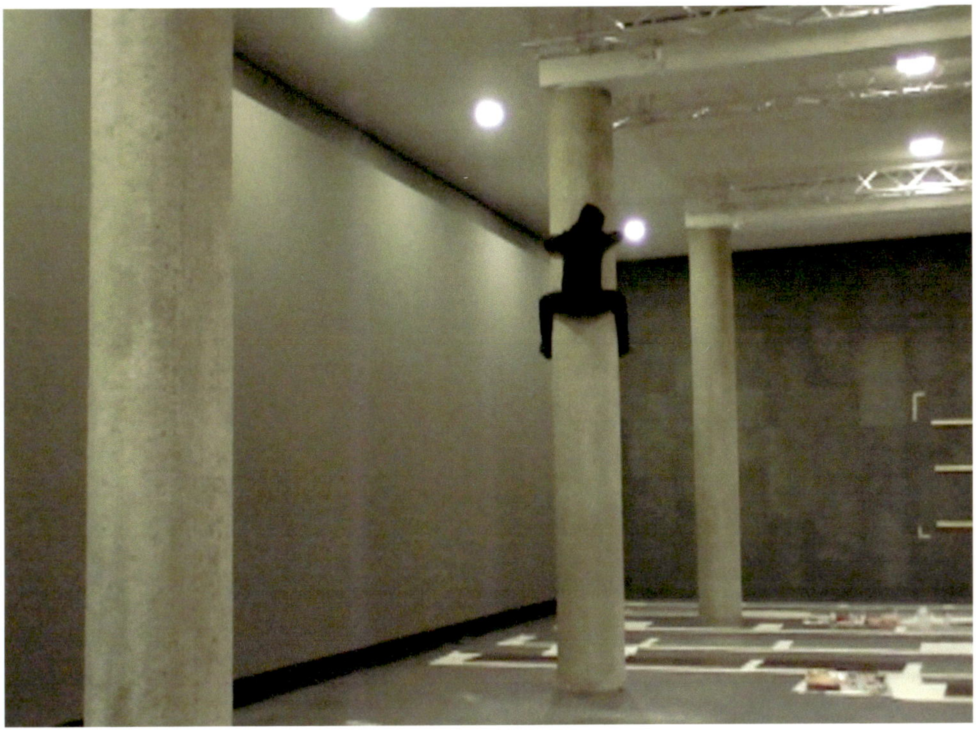

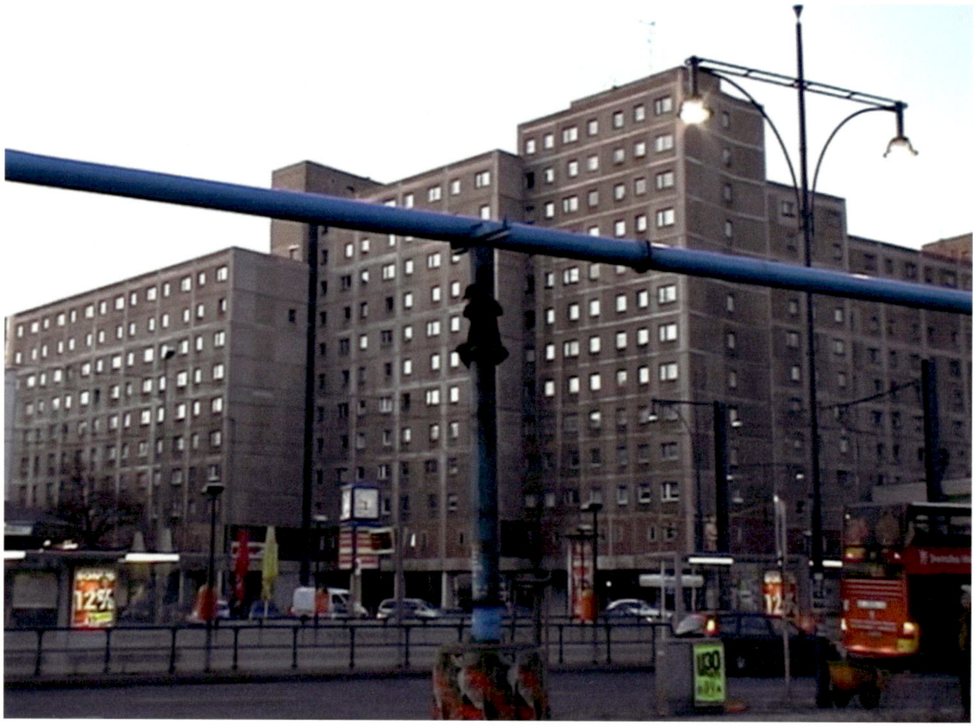
12%

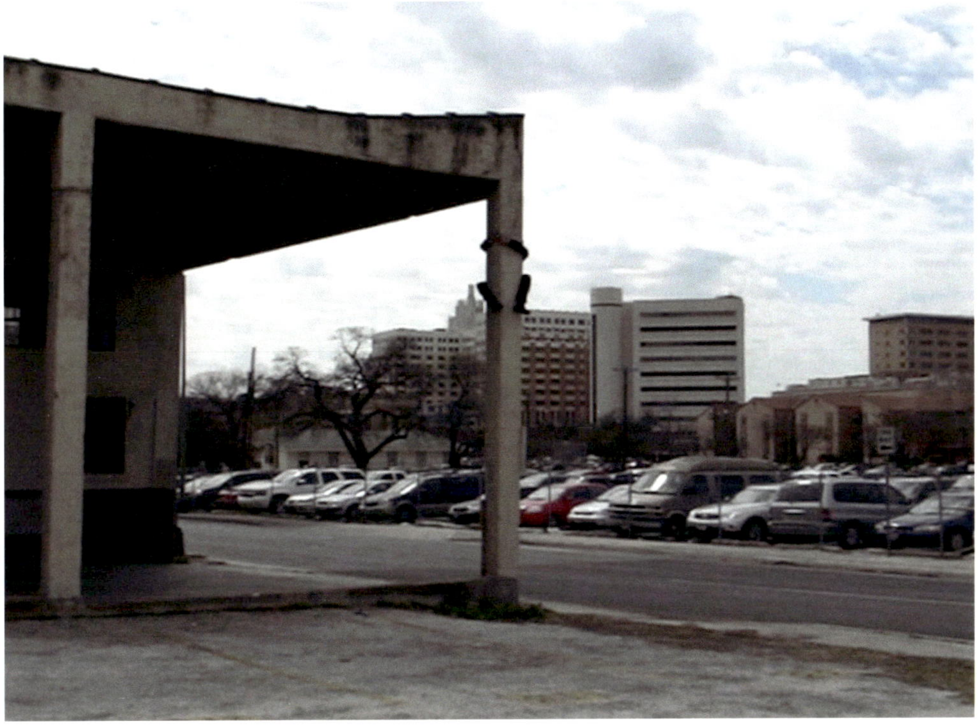

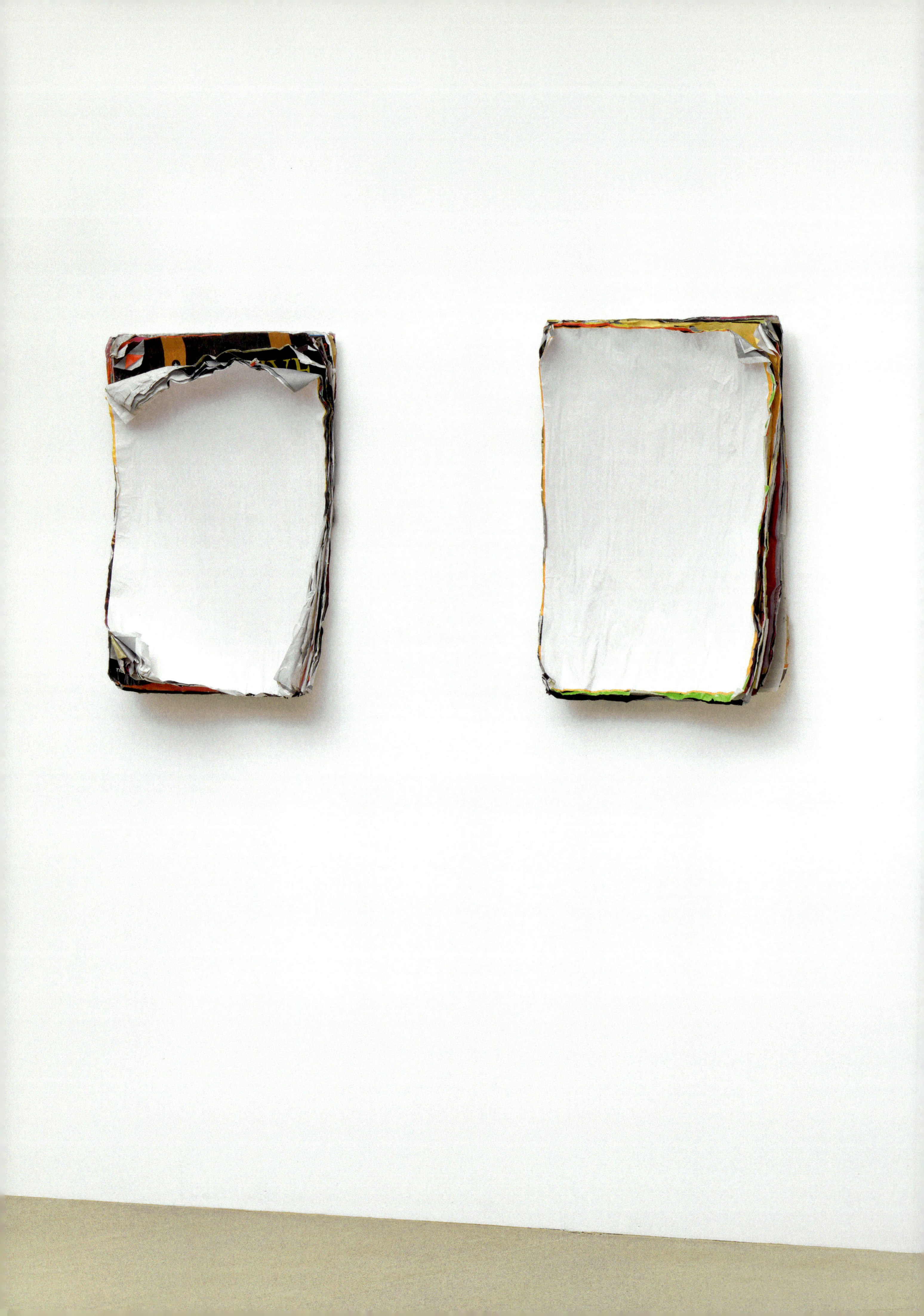

23 KLARA LIDÉN

UNTITLED (FROM THE SERIES "POSTER PAINTINGS")
2010

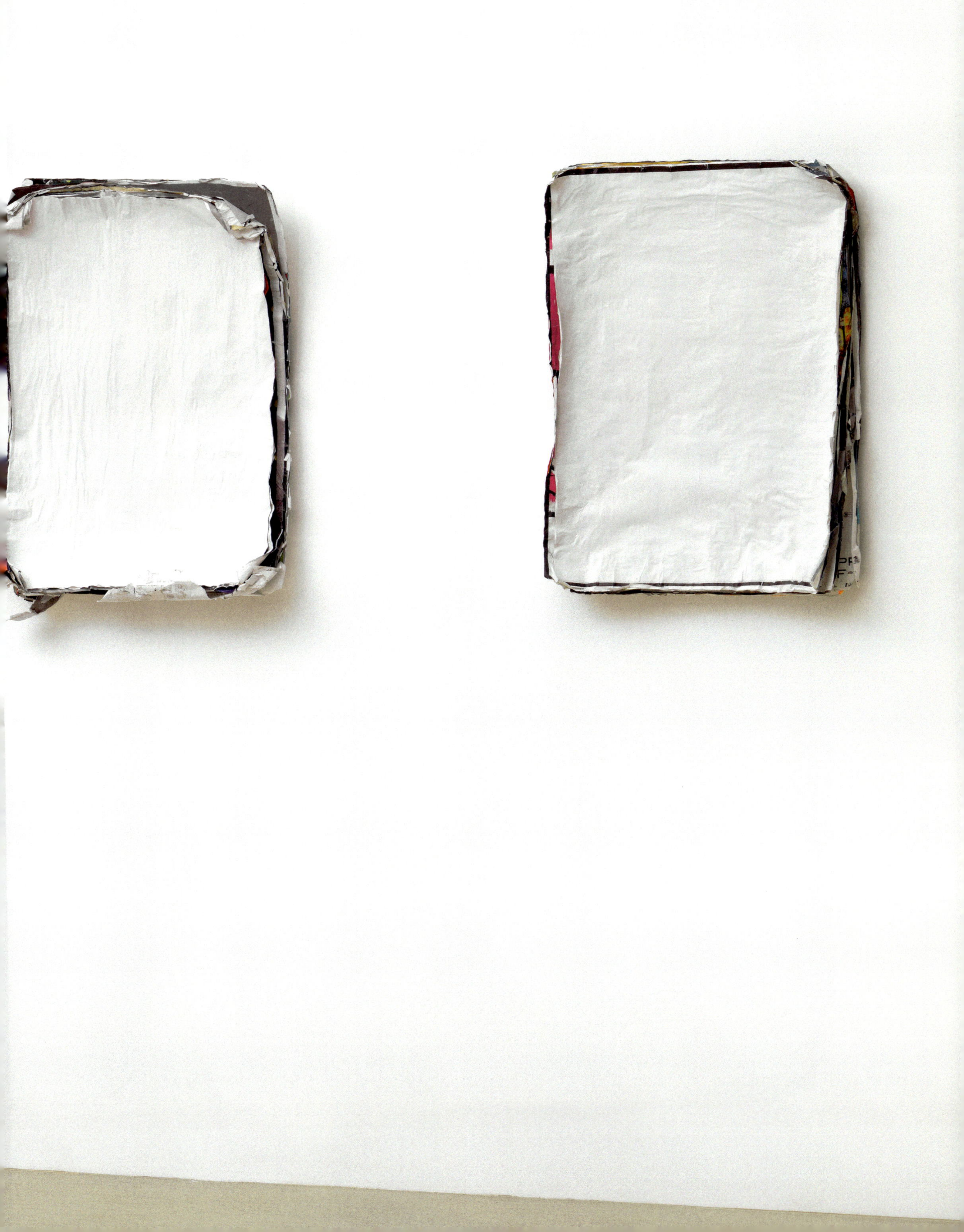

HEIKE MUNDER / THOMAS D. TRUMMER

Displaced Fractures

I

Fractiousness is part of human nature, and probably an element in all cultural activity. Upon closer inspection, it even constitutes the core of the cultural. Someone who shows recalcitrance is not just being unruly, he is also engaged in a particular form of cultural activity. Around 80 years ago, early in 1930, an academic publishing house in Vienna released a book by Sigmund Freud that gave the phenomenon a name; its title, *Das Unbehagen in der Kultur* [*Civilization and Its Discontents*], subsequently inspired numerous theorists of modernity to ever new adaptations. To date, minds as different as Jacob Taubes and Charles Taylor, Judith Butler and Nina Hagen have proffered their own variations on the theme of discontent. The wealth of allusions threatens to obliterate the original and the ideas it pursued. Freud's book in fact represented the continuation of his long-lasting efforts to illuminate the interdependency of individual and collective neuroses. Freud's innovation, which has lost none of its explosive force, was to complement the conventional interest in the individual neurosis by outlining the project of a "pathogenesis of cultural communities": individuals are not the only ones to suffer from repression—so do social communities. Freud's use of the term "*Unbehagen*" follows a history of terminological precedents with whose general lines he must have been familiar. As early as the late 17th century, the English philosopher John Locke had spoken of "uneasiness," in which he believed he had identified the energy driving human action. Why do humans do anything at all, rather than nothing? Locke's answer was built on a combination of myth, Puritanism, and anthropology: because they feel uneasy doing nothing. Man is never at one with his situation, and he is forever incapable, as Locke's contemporary Pascal wrote, of remaining idle in his room. Uneasiness or discontent is the motivation for all human action; it is its ultimate and most profound reason. Freud's book takes up this history, but, inspired by Nietzsche, the thinker of the will, inverts its moral meaning. On the one hand, culture is an aberration of humanity because it dissociates us from the world of wayward drives; yet it is at once also the fulfillment of humanity, because it highlights the unconscious quality of this waywardness. Culture, Freud argues, tames the individual's articulations of will and simultaneously foments new forms of resistance. Culture, in this context, would be an institution under threat from its own center, an institution that poses a challenge to itself and regards itself as profoundly questionable; and art is nothing other than the insurrection against its own establishment.

II

Art has always possessed a keen sense of what is brittle, porous, and fragile in man. The artists represented in this exhibition, however, negotiate humanity's fault lines not directly on the body, but instead in architectures that stand in for it. The fractures and sutures of buildings serve as metaphors for the rifts that run through human existence. The concept expressed in the title, "displaced fractures," shifts the idea back to the body; it comes from medical terminology, where it describes the phenomenon whereby a bone fracture may appear in a place that is different from the site of the main stress. A displacement takes place, cause and effect dissociate, because energies as much as symptoms become visible in strange places. The same idea is also expressed in psychology, where the term "displacement" designates a transfer, repression, or sublimation, as well as a psychological defense mechanism that helps an individual cope with menacing tendencies that result from drives and desires.

The installations, spatial interventions, and sculptures in this exhibition work with this displacement of symptoms on a variety of levels. A major area of tension unfolds between designs that reject form and monumental conceptions, between subjective and rational-formal gestures. In this analogy to the concept of the "displaced fracture," the materials of architectonic construction, stable in themselves but also subject to change over time, serve as projection screens enabling artists to act out existential mental and emotional states and questions regarding human existence. Even a fleeting glance at the works reveals that antipathy, antagonism, and energetic refractoriness are at issue, expressed in communicative and sculptural processes of formal creation, in which the transitions between states of the material and dimensions of the sculptural come to light. Everything is laid out before us in reality, and prompts us to reactivate in new ways our submerged experience and sensory perception of what material is and what symbolic functions it may fulfill. In transposing subjective questions of our time onto what is ostensibly solid, this sculptural discourse allows the precariousness of the present age to become visible and palpable. The refusal of form, the frequent formlessness, in which Rosalind Krauss and Yve-Alain Bois already recognized a synonym of the repressed, becomes a central theme in the exhibition. The works on show display the structures of the architectonic as well as the traces of the personal. They are precisely delineated postures lending concrete shape to moments of formal crisis. The dynamic use of color and the employment of free form are particularly distinctive in these interventions. They attest to the presence of the human in order to ultimately suggest, through the free and defiant use of such features, the vulnerability of the present and of memory.

III

Something all works have in common is that they take up space, performing an expansive occupation of the room, and that they tend to invoke subjective states by way of objects. The work of Phyllida Barlow offers an exemplary illustration: raw materials are heaped up in towering dense clusters of forms. Sometimes bundled to form dwellings, they always evince a raw physical presence that for a long time presented a counterpoint not only to the smooth aesthetic of Minimalism but also to the polished look popular in the 1980s, for instance in the œuvres of Jeff Koons or Haim Steinbach. In Barlow's work, art is presence and a site of conflict, grand architecture and simple model, monumental form and subjective inscription at once. Concepts such as "existence" and "endangerment," "I" and "other," "existential state" and "being" are brought to actuality. Yet despite their massive sizes, Barlow's sculptures are always suggestive of bodies, and hence anthropomorphic. They are formal inventions between urban props and autonomous shapes, between architecture and surface. We see self-contained sculptures resting in their own presence, in which tensions rooted in human experience are placed in parallel with those inherent in the material. We might speak of a repositioning of the construction of the individual subject within the sculptural discourse that allows sculpture to become thematic again by uncovering categories such as size, shape, form, and formlessness. All these concepts are subject to a radical interrogation; the artists discussed here seek out an individuation in the objective, in order to give adequate form in their work to personal as well as universally human conditions, to life and the will to live.

IV

Oscar Tuazon's work negotiates the tensions between architecture and nature that emerge in the disintegration of public space. Using a reduced architectonic language, he transfers the essence of this engagement into the exhibition space, relying on simple construction materials placed in relationships of physical tension. The rectangular sculpture bearing the speaking title *I want to put something inside my body and carry something in it. I want to get inside my body and get carried in it, I'd like to get buried in it, put my head in it and get in it, I'm not scared of it.* (2010), which consists of a metal frame across which a tarpaulin has been stretched, is suspended just below the room's ceiling. Composed of easily available materials, the object looks functional and yet is out of its element: it has been installed in an exhibition space to cause irritation by its mere presence. Different elements are always wedged into each other in a theatrical fashion, creating a stage-like situation in the room in order to direct our attention to details that would otherwise be invisible. Tuazon raises a second internal structure within the exhibition space, generating a confrontation between two planes: that of the interior, something that settles in, and that of the exterior, something that envelops.

Revealing the fragility of existence requires its translation into the material. That is most evident in a heavy table made of concrete bearing the poetic title *I use my body for something, I use it to make something, I make something with my body, whatever that is. I make something and I pay for it and I get paid for it.* (2010). One of the legs supporting the table has buckled, and it is falling apart, disintegrating into rubble and sand; it is just holding itself upright on one side. The crumbling material it is made of is a leftover from the archaeology of industry, and hence a component of the typical architecture of everyday life, a lifeless body that stands in for a living one. Model structures that here represent the analogy drawn between the "thing" and the "I" serve to test the metamorphosis of the objective. For the aim is to show the damage, the patent disintegration of the artistic assertion, the material's resistance to the artist's control, in order to reveal affectivity and physical objectification. The title repeats and elaborates what is alluded to in the material. The artist's own physical activity is incorporated into the everyday circulation of capitalist value-creation and exploitation. Physicality, subjectivity, and society are thus condensed into a poetic but also laconic and refractory representation of social structures and the consequences inherent in them. Some of these sites of artistic concretion accordingly seem to be aggregators for the ego's pain, others, evacuated ruins of collectively dissociated longings, achieving an unfinished and undecided state—and hence also the form of determination of purpose. Hence the conspicuous effort to let things be, in an artistic method that emphasizes the process and seeks to bring out the material's own dynamism.

V

This sort of treatment of the material can be read as an impulse activating the forces inherent in the substance out of which art is created. In Klaus Winichner's works, the material serves to give the artist's consciousness an outward form so that it can acquire three-dimensional extension. By heaping up materials, Winichner also highlights the ruinous aspect of the now. Working in different genres such as sculpture, painting, and drawing, Winichner fuses the human portrait—his own or that of acquaintances—with the sculptural discourse. In his critical engagement with sculpture, he often employs industrial construction materials or construction debris. The emblematic portraits are the products not only of figuration, but also of fragmentary architectures representing the human. They are abstract assemblages composed of objects the artist has sometimes also manipulated individually: mattresses, books, flower pots, and amorphous materials. These conglomerates, often expansive enough to occupy an exhibition room by themselves, look like the vestiges left behind by human existence. The distinctive feature of this critical engagement with form is a *terror perpetuus*, an unceasing restiveness and inner irritability that refuses to release the finished work of art into a freedom promising autonomy. Any conclusion, any perfection would imply the victory either of substance or of the force that shapes it. It is characteristic of Winichner's art that he seeks to avoid both—also avoiding the ascendancy of his own hand. To have command over the material would mean precisely to put an unsatisfactory stop to the process that defines art, its living and refractory evolution.

VI

Winichner's work relates to early sculpture, to the pre-Socratic mode, as it were, of the form. At issue are static structures, the statuary's power, autochthony, authority, and realism. The worn and dusty books Winichner buys at flea markets, many of them treatises on the Classical figure, indicate to what extent he sees what he does as part of both a sculptural and an intellectual tradition. In his œuvre, these books serve as a commentary on the long history of sculpture, on the uses of the statue and the public monument, on their representative function and their service as objects of veneration. Ulrich Rückriem chooses a very different avenue: his work, in which monumentality and formalism are the defining visual parameters, is the product of precise craftsmanship and a highly developed awareness of plastic form. Taking up ideas and methods of American Minimalist and Concept Art, Rückriem has nonetheless created a very distinctive œuvre. He saws compact blocks of stone to pieces or drills holes into them, in order to render memory and historicity legible in the fissures, cut faces, and rupture lines of sculpture. Central to Rückriem's method are the process of work on his materials and the concept he has laid out in advance. What the violent acts of cutting, breaking, and drilling indicate is also true of language and its meaning. By presuming to make these silent volumes speak, we would arrive at an understanding—but at the price of violence to the meaning their idiosyncrasy intends.

Many of Rückriem's sculptures have been installed on public squares—they have long become a part of postwar German identity. Often conceived as memorials or monuments, these stones speak of a history of social action—and yet lie in our path as utterly rigid blocks. In fact, these sculptures draw their aesthetic force from the sole presence of a disquieting power. The resistance the stone offers remains visible and physically palpable.

VII

Kilian Rüthemann's works engage the architectonic attributes of the exhibition site. The aesthetic of his œuvre is defined by his efforts to uncover structures and his quest for the unstable and fragile in what appears solid and immutable. In his attempt to tease a previously unseen poetic quality out of the spaces he works in, he employs radical means—for instance pouring an additional concrete floor on a flight of stairs, making walking up and down much less comfortable. Rüthemann's works are studies in his materials that bring their refractoriness to the fore and explore their particular nature. Form, in Rüthemann's works, is subject to rigorous organization. The unrestrained forward push is not his mode; instead there are kinetic moments and hence also shifts and "displacements." In 2009, he designed a sarcophagus made of rubber foam for the Instituto Svizzero in Rome; it was on display in the Institute's grounds and will now be part of the exhibition at the migros museum für gegenwartskunst. Exposure to the weather has adulterated the material's formerly uniform color, making it look like a piece of ancient heritage. Rüthemann thus plays with the effects of the material's erosion. At the same time, this process releases the work from the authority of its creator. In the growth of moss and the brownish damage due to damp, the weather has left its mark on the object. The material thus released into its autonomy generates idiosyncratic responses. The tomb is the epitome of culture, of the presence of humans and their ability to believe. The synthetic material accordingly seems to become nature, and the contemporary object the emblematic relic of the venerably ancient history of Roman heroism.

Like Rüthemann, Emilie Ding tests material situations in a minimalist language; the way in which she works is akin to Rüthemann's ideas about art. Where the latter plays with the resilience of the material, Ding values and employs the edge. Things that are defined by their cuts continue the discourse of American Minimalism. Ding places distinctive formal elements, the *Erased* (2008–2010), which always faintly suggest that they are destined for use, on the floor of the exhibition room. They are pieces of concrete that, with angular shapes and studded with steel bolts, look like hinges, supporting elements, or movable pieces of architecture. Not only are the connections between them missing, their function, too, remains mysterious. The arrangement of these blocks and the shapes in which they are cut constitute a critical engagement of formal discourses. Ding thus combines a discourse about human existence—disparate, isolated, endangered—with a technical debate that transcends existence and individuality, and calls them into question by virtue of the massive materiality and size of her concrete sculptures, as well as the suggestion of a forever unfinished serial production. The original aggression of the concrete sculptures is neutralized as the individual objects integrate, in a seemingly natural fashion, into the existing space, only thus making the discourse on an abstract and intellectual level possible.

VIII

Architecture could be said to come into being when objects attain dimensions that enable them to enclose spaces we can enter and inhabit. Unlike sculpture, architecture can be walked into, conveying a sense of protection, abode, cover. In her 16-mm film *Palast* (2004), Tacita Dean presents shots of Berlin's Palace of the Republic. Without offering a view of the building as a whole, Dean focuses on the phenomena that play on its surface, on the sensual and poetic qualities of its appearance. Reflections in tinted windowpanes, a golden sheen, and the warm light of the evening sun contrast with the cupola proudly towering above the neighboring cathedral. Dean films a palace whose demolition is imminent; today the building has gone, to be replaced, the city's government has decreed, by a reconstruction of the Wilhelmine *Stadtschloss*, or city palace. Like many others, Dean has ambivalent feelings about this new claim to political power, whose manifestation will rise on this site. In her contemplation, we can sense a sort of presumptive work of mourning unfolding in slow sequences of shots. The awareness of the impending loss and of historically significant decisions being made, gives rise to the characteristic uneasiness that befalls culture, not by virtue of its mere existence but because of the inscrutable power of a decision that, in order to engender something new, reconstructs and modifies the old, necessarily preferring it to the more recent. The building has an expiry date. In this respect it resembles a consciousness perceiving itself in a state of inexorable decline. The motif of antipathy appears here as nostalgia as long as it is oriented in a forward direction that, in sentimental recollection, is still aware of the now. It appears as indignation once it turns against a future that is inevitable. Yet Dean realizes her assessment of cultural history as a political sign not in the form of a vociferously demonstrative work; instead, her film is a quiet elegy.

IX

The explosive power refractoriness can develop is most distinctly apparent in the work of Klara Lidén. Architecture is a power of order, and the artist conducts a contentious engagement with its functioning as well as its failures. It casts the ethical and the conventional in cement, obliterates the passionate and the human. In contradistinction to the picture Dean paints of it, architecture, for Lidén, is not an abode or a shelter but an alienated *horror vacui*. Lidén occupies public space by means of bodily postures that seem strangely misplaced; she dances into a subway car or performs a "moonwalk" in the streets of New York. In her work *Position 0310* (2010), a series of four videos, the artist clings to public columns or gas pipes like an animal, pausing in deathlike stillness. Only the traffic around her tells the viewer watching the videos that these are not freeze frames. Irritation with and rebellion against the regulations governing public life are perennially characteristic of these acts. Lidén creates installations out of found materials such as cardboard or the paper from posters that have been torn off. The compositions resemble the historic *déchirures*, speaking a language of insurrection against the material as much as the environment. Anti-authoritarian, appellative, unflinching, the artist fights the superiority of what is, of the ostensibly real, putting the disastrous aspects of the modern urban world to the test on her own body.

X

Art, held back by tactics of objectification that have grown brittle, is currently giving free reign to pent-up expressive energies, and it is these energies that this exhibition wants to make room for. Instead of presenting the language of things *as such*, these things are to speak *for themselves*—that is the reformist call of the present. The point is neither to incorporate art into the sciences in order to heighten their prestige, nor to meticulously drain things of their sensual qualities in order to point up the merit of words. Instead, this art wants to enable the discharge of different, more varied, burning productive energies. Art wants to posit gestures of indignation, to point out contradictions, perhaps even to compel actions that damage things or the self; in any case, to bring matters to a crisis, to precipitate a decision. This art invokes expressionistic heights and the depths of agony, the great and the small, the social and the elemental, the preservation of the self and its abandonment, yet in doing so it does not strive for balance between them; it stages their dramatic contest. Accordingly, these sculptures display what the concept of fractiousness describes more clearly than any other. By building, we embrace the disintegration, by setting upright, the decline, by unfolding, the erosion of our endeavors. The works reflect fragilities, fractures, and precarious states of affairs, courage as much as resignation, fortitude and the confession of weakness, the urge to give shape and the experience of destruction. Relics of Classical sculptural art become an unconscious-conscious sign that places our own associations and moods in well-founded interdependence with the structures and entities of our world.

KARSTEN HARRIES

On the Ill Will Against Architecture or The Antinomy of Beings

The title demands an explanation: how is this ill will against architecture to be understood? We are given a first answer by the title of this exhibition, *Displaced Fractures – Über die Bruchlinien von Architekturen und ihren Körpern*, and by the work of the exhibited artists: again and again we meet with intrusions into and attacks on the pre-given architecture. What shows itself here is a discontent with architectures of all kinds that, especially today, is widespread.

Why such discontent? Do we not all dream of a comfortable home? Isn't it the task of architecture to help us to so transform this world that it better answers our needs? And is this not also true of the conceptual architectures that language and reason build for us? Kant took our reason to be, by its very nature, architectonic. Why then this seemingly unnatural ill will against architecture, this attraction of the fragile, this play with tears and ruptures, especially in this age, which has allowed deconstruction to become an academic fashion, a fashion that has spread from philosophy to the humanities and to art and, surprisingly even to architecture. Of special significance here was the Museum of Modern Art's 1988 exhibition "Deconstructivist Architecture," curated by Mark Wigley and Philip Johnson. (1) The catalogue spoke of "the emergence of a new sensibility" fascinated by possibilities of contaminating, disrupting, violating, subverting architecture. That sensibility led to an architecture that self-consciously calls traditional architecture into question, that is to say, an anti-architecture, which in today's architecture world, both in theory and practice, has played a significant role, for example in the work of Frank Gehry, Zaha Hadid, Peter Eisenman, Daniel Libeskind, Rem Koolhaas, and Coop Himmelb(l)au, the architects celebrated in that exhibition.

Are we dealing perhaps with a fashion that will soon be a thing of the past? Why especially today? But that is to say also: not just today! Is not Cain said to have built the first city, and is not the Tower of Babel the first work of architecture discussed in the Bible? Here already we sense something like an ill will against architecture, which may seem especially of today, but possesses a history that shows that it is nourished by something that concerns us human beings as human beings.

1 Philip Johnson and Mark Wigley, *Deconstructivist Architecture*, Museum of Modern Art/Little Brown and Company, New York 1988.

From the very beginning architecture has been shadowed by protest directed against it. Paradise had no need for a house: in this garden Adam and Eve were already at home. To be sure, the Fall, this liberating awakening of our freedom, cost us human beings this home. But is it not precisely this reason that promises to more than compensate us for what has been lost, to build us a new home? And thus Bacon and Descartes, these founders of our modern world, dreamed already of a science and a technology that would allow us to return to paradise. This remained the dream of the Enlightenment, and it is this dream that has shaped our modern world. Is there a reasonable alternative?

But do we not ask too much here of reason? In keeping with the lesson of the Tower of Babel that no human willing will be able to build us our true home, painters like Hans Baldung Grien or Albrecht Altdorfer thus placed the Nativity in some fantastic ruined architecture. Is a ruin not a more fitting place for the birth of the redeemer, who is to deny time its sting, the devil his victory, than any architecture that reason is able to build us?

The conviction that the house that reason has built us does not allow for a genuine dwelling did not disappear with Nietzsche's proclamation of the death of God. Something deep in us is dissatisfied with the spiritual and built spaces that our reason has furnished for us, and experiences attacks on architecture so understood as a liberation. And such discontent appreciates what is fragile and disintegrating, feels at home in ruins that let us experience the *mysterium tremendum et fascinans* of nature, of space and of time. Significant is the decision not just to paint ruins, but to actually build them. An early German example is the Magdalenenklause in the park of Nymphenburg (1725–1728) with its faux tears and falling off plaster. Just as the 18th century, this age of the Enlightenment, loved such ruins, as deconstruction and this exhibition show, the ruinous retains its seductive appeal. How is it to be understood? Is what shows itself here something like the bad conscience of our life-world, shaped as that has been by our architectonic reason?

Such distrust of an architecture ruled by an architectonic reason let the Viennese painter, and soon-to-be architect, Hundertwasser call for its destruction. Here are a few words from an exhibition pamphlet, directed against the "90-degree angles of Vienna": "In 1920 the pavement and the walls of the houses had to be constructed smooth, but in 1957 this is an insanity I cannot understand. The air raids of 1943 were a perfect automatic lesson in form; straight lines and their vacuous structures ought to have been blown to pieces, and so they were. Following this a transautomatism ought normally to have occurred [...] But we are building cubes, cubes! Where is our conscience?"(2) In this admittedly rhetorically overblown and playful affirmation of the destruction of architecture by the bombs of World War II, the ill will against architecture, especially the functional architecture of postwar Europe, is evident. Hundertwasser wants to call us back to a more natural life. And so we read in the "Mould Manifesto against Rationalism in Architecture" that he read in 1958 in the abbey of Seckau: "When rust settles on a razor blade, when mould forms on a wall, when moss grows in the corner of the room and rounds off the geometric angle, we ought to be pleased that with the microbes and fungi life is moving into the house, and more consciously than ever before, we become witnesses of architectonic changes from which we have a great deal to learn."(3) Has our reason not estranged us from ourselves? Here the ill will against architecture turns against rationalism. A longing for home feeds it, that finds in tears and ruptures, rust and mould, traces of the lost paradise.

But the ill will against architecture is also fed by an opposite longing that dreams of distant, open spaces, that wants to open the built environment not to nature, but to freedom. The work of the architect Lebbeus Woods offers a good example. Woods turned his back on the presumably promising career that his association with Eero Saarinen had opened up, to make "anarchitecture" his own, appropriating a term first used by the English architect Robin Evans, and that I had come to associate with Gordon Matta-Clark's cutting of an abandoned building, and with the group of artists he had gathered around himself in 1973 in New York. And are the artists exhibited in this exhibition not also anarchitects?

Woods is a creator of spatial fantasies that attack the architecture familiar to us, for example by allowing fantastic formations to enter or attack them, as if they were polyps or parasites. Today such fantasies are not unexpected. Has Bataille not taught us to associate Architecture (with a capital A) with the commanding voice of those in authority: priests, kings, burghers, capitalists, and policemen? Here it is not thoughts of an all-too-often violated nature that feed the ill will against architecture, but thoughts of a freedom, made possible by the long unthought of possibilities technology has opened up. Has it not become possible to create an environment that answers to our ever changing needs and desires in a way denied to us by the all-too-ordered environment that is our inheritance? The utopias that promise such possibilities have to reject the call for a place-bound architecture that accepts without protest the primacy of nature or of the embodied, gravity-burdened self and its life-world, as unbearably retrograde, all too ready to content itself with lifeless imitations of the place-establishing architecture of a not-to-be-recovered past. And thus Woods calls himself the enemy of gravity and declares war on it, opposing to its arrogant claim to rule his life his own claim to be a free, autonomous, self-determining spirit.

Woods is not the only one to have made such claims. In his declaration of war, a desire already known to the Enlightenment finds expression. Thus, with his spherical house Ledoux shows himself to be an enemy of gravity. The enthusiastic embrace of the sphere by the architects of the Enlightenment belongs with the enthusiasm that greeted the first balloons, which promised a godlike freedom from the tyranny of place, promised to fly across boundaries and whatever false walls separated human beings. Heralds of a freer, more genuinely humane, because truly cosmopolitan world, "these balls of air are"—for Helmut Reinicke—"the first invention linked to the concept of world revolution. The balloon rises into the sky, —as a sign that reason on earth is extending its sway. Such a revolution [...] has this subjective aspect that human beings want to find themselves, want to give themselves a human countenance. Such a revolution has this subjective aspect [...] This subjectivity is the divinity of religions. The attack on the latter is the greatest presumption and thus liberation. The airship is a practical presumption of that sort."(4)

2 Hundertwasser, "Mould Manifesto against Rationalism in Architecture," Ulrich Conrads (ed.), Michael Bullock (trans.), *Programs and Manifestoes on 20th-Century Architecture*, MIT Press, Cambridge 1975, p. 157.

3 *Ibid.* pp. 159–160.

4 Helmut Reinicke, *Aufstieg und Revolution. Über die Beförderung irdischer Freiheitsneigungen durch Ballonfahrt und Luftschwimmkunst*, Transit, Berlin 1988, pp. 76–77.

Related ideas were to help shape the architectonic practice of modern architects. Thus architects such as Theo Van Doesburg, Le Corbusier, or Mies van der Rohe demanded of architecture a floating or airborne look. To the extent that construction allows it, the building should appear to defy gravity. Computer-aided design today allows us to satisfy this demand in altogether unsuspected ways. A state of mind that would free human beings from all place-assigning architecture finds its expression here.

Clothing itself in ever different images, the dream of the lost paradise refuses to disappear. But just such modernist dreams invite objection. Do we not all dream, as Gaston Bachelard thought, of an oneiric house, a happy house that promises physical and spiritual shelter, of a natural life, of a home that sometimes calls us in our memories and that yet, as remembered, never existed, even though we may perhaps experience its metaphor in a farmhouse from the 18th century? To the oneiric house corresponds the oneiric city, envisaged perhaps in the image of Messkirch, with shady oriels, images of the Virgin on the corners of houses, murmuring fountains. We are not done with this dream: it continues to inform our building and dwelling. Examples are easy to find—in America too. Consider for example, the way the successful and influential Robert Stern with projects such as Celebration in Florida would let this dream become reality. And it is to this dream that the, at least financially, perhaps most successful painter in America, the self-styled "Painter of Light," Thomas Kinkade owes his success. Not only does he show us in his paintings that recall Christmas cards, houses that promise happiness, but a builder today promises to translate that dream into reality and satisfy our longing for authentic dwelling.

Kitsch is relatively harmless as long as it remains a matter of pretty pictures in which individuals who find reality lacking can find a refuge to which they can escape from time to time. But Kitsch ceases to be harmless when it attempts to embrace reality, as when an architect attempts to translate Kitsch visions into built architecture. And Kitsch becomes really dangerous when it becomes a power that forms our life. What is shortchanged here is our freedom. The longing for home here threatens to suffocate the opposed longing for open spaces and with it our humanity.

Freedom, to be sure, is often difficult to bear. And just this leads to dreams of an architecture that will assign us our place. The Kitsch artist and architect Adolf Hitler once promised to liberate such dreamers from the fear of freedom weighing on them: "Providence has destined me to become the greatest liberator of humanity. I free human beings from the coercion of a spirit that has taken itself for its end, from the dirty and humiliating self-tortures inflicted by a chimera called conscience and morality and from the demands of a freedom and personal autonomy only a very few were ever able to meet."(5) As the aesthetic practice of many an art and architecture school of those years can show us: this was no solitary or vain promise. Nietzsche's dream of an architecture strong enough to establish a community is a dream of architectural practice as the raising of a new Tower of Babel. The Bauhaus knew this dream. Heidegger, too, dreamed it. He, too, like National Socialism, thinking of the Greek example. And was it not, from the very beginning, the task of architecture to provide not only the body, but also the soul with shelter, and to assign human beings their places? Is this not the ethical function that raises all architecture deserving of the name beyond mere building?

Faced with architecture that would thus assign human beings their places, the ill will against architecture becomes understandable. In the desire to contaminate, disrupt, violate, subvert architecture, a freedom announces itself that refuses to submit to any order, be it ethical, moral, religious, or architectonic. It is thus hardly surprising that to the rediscovered surrealist Georges Bataille, the prison should present itself as the paradigmatic work of architecture. Architecture here comes to stand for an order that imprisons us and that therefore should be destroyed, even if such destruction threatens chaos and bestiality. "It is obvious that monuments inspire social good behavior in societies and often even real fear. The storming of the Bastille is symbolic of this state of affairs: it is hard to explain this mass movement other than through the people's animosity (animus) against the monuments that are its real masters."(6) But if we admit that monuments sometimes inspire good behavior, perhaps even real fear, is it also obvious that they there-

5 Hermann Rauschning, "Gespräche mit Hitler," *Die Bildenden Künste im Dritten Reich. Eine Dokumentation von Joseph Wulf.* Hamburg 1966, p. 12.

6 Denis Hollier, *Against Architecture*, p. ix. Quoting Georges Bataille, "Architecture", *Œuvres Complètes*, 12 vols. Gallimard, Paris 1971–1988, Vol. 1, pp. 171–172.

fore deserve to be abolished? Does this society, does the world, suffer from a surfeit of "good behavior"? Should we, for the sake of greater freedom, let loose the minotaur? A deep self-hatred betrays itself in such a conviction. As Bataille recognized, this ill will against the monuments that are said to be our real masters easily turns into an ill will against reason: this is precisely, according to Denis Hollier, what Bataille intended to show with the mythical figure of Acephalus: the only way to escape from the fetters of architecture is to lose one's head. "This self-storming of one's own form requires, in fact, an infinitely more underhanded strategy than one of simple destruction or escape. The image of Acephalus, thus should be seen as a figure of dissemblance, the negative image of an anti-monumental madness involved in the dismemberment of 'meaning.' The painter André Masson drew this figure and Bataille wrote an aphorism to go with it: 'Man will escape his head as a convict escapes his prison.'"(7)

We were shown what such a storming of one's own form might look like by the French artist who calls herself Saint Orlan, when she attempted, with the help of plastic surgery and psychoanalysis to make herself into a legally different person, i. e. to be reborn. Today this is more than just an idle dream. Is not our body, too, material to satisfy natural and unnatural desires? And does not technology provide freedom today with long undreamed of possibilities? Once the artifice of Daedalus, Greek archetype of the architect, is supposed to have allowed the Cretan queen Pasiphae to satisfy her desire to make love to a bull. Saint Orlan appears driven by a still more obviously unnatural desire: the dream to be like God, author of herself. And thus this saint declares God to be her enemy.

But what is this "I" that here attempts to become, with the help of technology, another person? Does it not have to lose all content? And with this does such an undertaking not lose measure and direction? Thus what pretends to be autonomous action comes to be ruled by all too timely fashions. Here freedom undermines itself, as the ill will against architecture awakens a longing for home that calls us back and lets us look for shelter.

We are amphibians. Again and again the snake's promise, *Eritis sicut Deus*, tempts us and, succumbing to that temptation, we lose another paradise. And again and again we are tempted by thoughts of returning to some lost paradise. The interplay of the pull of distant places promising greater freedom and the longing for home determines our existence and will not be resolved dialectically. This interplay, pulling us in opposite directions, feeds the ill will against architecture. This interplay of opposed desires offers itself to us as a mirror of the antinomy of being.

But how is this antinomy to be understood? The word "antinomy" invites thoughts of Kant's four antinomies and of what these antinomies were supposed to prove: the necessity of understanding every thing in two very different senses: as an appearance dependent on our human understanding and the architecture it imposes, and as a thing in itself. The antinomies thus attempt to tear open a depth dimension passed over in our everyday dealings with things, ruled as these are by our understanding and its preconceptions. But why is the loss of this depth dimension, if it can even be understood as such, of existential import?

When I am speaking here of an antinomy of being I am thinking not only, indeed not even in the first place, of Kant, but of Heidegger. Not that Heidegger speaks of such an antinomy! But his thinking of being leads him and us into such an antinomy. What matters here is not Heidegger: our thinking gets caught in some version of this antinomy whenever it attempts to construct a conceptual edifice that assigns being its proper place. Every such attempt to grasp the essence of being falls short. We need to experience things in their concrete thingliness, to tear open the world that our reason and language have built and furnished for us, so that tears and ruptures let us find a more immediate contact with reality, contact that our everyday dealings with persons and things veil and obstruct again and again. Only such contact allows for a life that does full justice to our humanity. But "find contact" cannot mean here "master conceptually": reality cannot finally be comprehended any more than the lost paradise can be regained. The essence of our reason denies this.

But why this talk of an antinomy of being? In *Being and Time* Heidegger speaks of the dependence of being, but not of beings, on our human being. A strange assertion! Can beings be without being? How can Heidegger insist on the dependence of being on human being and then deny that beings are similarly dependent? Does Heidegger not contradict himself here? In the *Letter on Humanism* he gives us his answer: "Only as long as Dasein is, 'is there

7 *Ibid.* p. xxi.

being'? Indeed. This means: only as long as the clearing of being happens, does being present itself to human beings. But that this 'there,' the clearing as the truth of being itself happens is the gift of being itself."(8) But this being that only is as long as there are human beings is difficult to understand as the being, to whose gift we human beings owe our own being. Two aspects of being, or two conceptions of being, here oppose one another, where Heidegger at times distinguishes between *Sein* and *Seyn.* This seeming contradiction is the expression of the antinomy of being. But how is it to be understood?

Heidegger's determination of language as the house of being here provides a key. In order to be for us, things have to find their place in that house, i.e. in language: "Kein ding sei wo das wort gebricht," "No thing be where the word is lacking," as Heidegger could read in a poem by Stefan George. Pursuing the metaphor further, we can ask: but is being really at home in this house?

In this connection a picture is helpful, which Wittgenstein uses to explain the language of science in his *Tractatus* (6.341): "Let us imagine a white surface with irregular black spots. We now say: Whatever kind of picture these make I can always get as near as I like to its description, if I cover the surface with a sufficiently fine square network and now say of every square that it is white or black. In this way I shall have brought the description of the surface to a unified form" (trans. C.K.Ogden). The empty page here stands for the space of all that is possible. It is a picture of our freedom. Only part of this page is occupied: the spots represent the real. They could be different. There are infinitely many possible worlds. But can the spots in the picture ever be described adequately with the help of the geometrical nets that our reason furnishes? Then the spots would have to possess a corresponding form. But suppose that these spots were formed arbitrarily out of circle fragments. A completely adequate description of the spots with a geometrical net would then mean the impossible squaring of the circle. Our sight here exceeds our reason, which wants to represent the relation we see as the relation of two whole numbers. The Greeks are already supposed to have been profoundly disturbed by their discovery of the irrationality of the square root of 2. First attempts were made to keep this sad discovery secret and the unhappy person who betrayed the secret after all is supposed to have drowned in the sea. A tear had opened up in the conceptual architecture in which we thought we dwelt securely.

Let us return to Wittgenstein's picture. Does it not invite us to think of the pictured reality as transcending the reach of logic and in the *Tractatus* that means also the reach of language? Reality will not be imprisoned in the house our reason builds it. To experience reality is to experience transcendence.

But this, too, must be said: everything that is to mean something to us, must be sayable. And is this not also true of reality? Reason, and that is to say also language, builds being its house. So understood, reason and language transcend reality. Possessing reason, the human being is the animal that has lost its secure place in reality, the animal that, while still part of reality, yet also transcends it. That fall out of reality is inseparable from our freedom. The antinomy of being belongs to the essence of being. That was what so disturbed the Pythagoreans.

With the poet Stefan George, however, such disturbance goes in the opposite direction:

"Thus I sadly learned the renunciation:
No thing can be, where the word is lacking.
What does the poet have to renounce?
A wordless understanding of things?"

This much we have to admit: what we encounter, what we recognize and understand are always only appearances mediated by language. But such an admission forces us to think of the reality that, though mediated, yet inevitably refuses to be completely comprehended. Nietzsche knew about the loss of reality bound up with such mediation. "Every word becomes immediately a concept in that it is not supposed to serve, say as a reminder, the unique and entirely individuated original experience, to which it owes its genesis, but at the same time has to fit countless, more or less similar, that is to say strictly speaking never equal, thus all unequal cases."(9) With this loss of the unique we purchase the possibility of subjecting reality to our reason, of building

8 Heidegger, "Brief über den "Humanismus", *Gesamtausgabe*, Vol. 9, Frankfurt am Main, 1976, p. 336.

9 Friedrich Nietzsche, "Über Wahrheit und Lüge im aussermoralischen Sinne," G. Colli and M. Montinari, *Sämtliche Werke. Kritische Studienausgabe*, Munich/Berlin/New York 1980, Vol. 1. pp. 879–880.

a house for being. But is this house a prison or a cage? Does truth, with this, turn into lie? This question presupposes a "truth" that eludes our comprehension and that we yet draw on to measure what we generally call truth and find it insufficient. An antinomy of truth corresponds to the antinomy of being. Again and again this antinomy tears apart all attempts to build a house in which being could be said to really dwell.

In "The Origin of the Work of Art" Heidegger speaks of the *Riss,* the rift or tear that separates world and earth, and demands of art a tearing open of this *Riss*. "World", so understood, and language are related concepts. The opening up of a world in the artwork furnishes the space in which things and persons have to find their place in order to be for us. "Earth", on the other hand names what again and again eludes our attempts to grasp it with our concepts, and yet touches and claims us whenever we experience a person or a thing in its uniqueness: the transcendent ground of our dwelling. Only such experiences can give meaning to our lives. Architectonic reason is in its essence nihilistic. Thus, especially today, the ill will against architecture is the beginning of an effort to tear open the house that our instrumental, calculating reason has built us too firmly, to allow transcendence to blow into it.

The Torn Temple Curtain
—
Notes on Cracked Bowls and Loose Screws

The Time is out of joint:
—O cursed spite,
That ever I was born
to set it right!
(Hamlet I 5)

Displacements, fractures, and ruins are emblematic of a structural theme in art. They indicate the time span that extends between our consciousness of the past and our perspectives on the future: the present is a caesura of sorts between these two lines of vision. On the one hand, our gaze wanders into the past, selecting from traces and recollections what appears to be meaningful in the present, where it defines our identity. On the other hand, the decision to focus on certain historical information bears within it a sense of responsibility that points to the future. Whether we accept or reject it, the "legacy" of the past becomes the standpoint from which the next steps must be taken. The definition of such a position always goes hand in hand with a critical engagement with ideals, those of the past as well as those of the future. It is virtually impossible to regard ruins without a view to moral meaning; they turn out to be a focal point of social ideologies. In the following considerations, an image from cultural history will serve as a point of reference for questions regarding the "displaced fracture": the temple curtain that is torn apart at the moment of Christ's death. This subject amounts to a displacement in turn—it takes us into the philosophy of religion. In addition, the image contains a displacement, a fracture, which represents a metaphorical interweaving of different symptoms.

The temple curtain

The first and most immediate response to the death of Christ on the Cross is the tearing of the curtain before the Holy of Holies in the temple at Jerusalem. Three of the four Gospels mention both events in the same breath and describe a causal relationship between them (New Testament, Matthew 27:51, Mark 15:38, Luke 23:45). A sign at once follows upon Christ's physical death that indicates the divine nature of the Son of Man who has just died. To quote, for example, Mark: "With a loud cry, Jesus breathed his last. The curtain of the temple was torn in two from top to bottom" (Mark 15:37–38). (1)

The connection between God and humankind, manifested as God become human in Jesus Christ, is torn apart. The torn curtain symbolizes the end of the Old Covenant. It is the visible sign that God is no longer present in his temple.

There are several allusions in the New Testament to an analogy between the body of Jesus and the temple. (2) In John, Christ himself says this: "Destroy this temple, and I will raise it again in three days" (Jn. 2:19). The words are to be understood as symbolic. The destruction of the temple represents the crucifixion, and with it the destruction of the Son of God's human body. The promised reconstruction is a reference to the Resurrection. Mark conveys a comparable message: "Do you see all these great buildings? Not one stone here will be left on another; every one will be thrown down" (Mk. 13:2).

Christ's use of the temple metaphor refers to the idea that the "new" Kingdom of God is precisely "not of this world" (Jn. 18:36) but divine in origin. Seen in this context, the torn curtain also articulates the break away from the material world: in its disintegration, it reveals the invisible divine presence. In Jerusalem, the center of the world, in the Holy of Holies in the city's temple, something stands concealed behind the temple curtain whose radiance is so bright that it is the focus of religion even though—or precisely because—it is inaccessible.

The rupture described by the authors of the New Testament most importantly fulfils a symbolic function: the temple curtain is a central interface, a membrane between this world and God's. It separates the sanctuary, containing the table of showbread, the menorah, and the incense altar, where only priests were allowed to enter, from the Holy of Holies, to which only the High Priest had access, and even he only once a year, on Yom Kippur. In purely factual terms, then, no one outside the priesthood would be able to notice a tear in the temple curtain. The tear becomes the object of a public glimpse into the Holy of Holies only by virtue of being mentioned in the Gospels. The narrator of these Biblical passages is omniscient, expressing an encompassing view not tied to a specific standpoint. An observer of Christ's death on the Cross would have been incapable of perceiving both events, the death

1 All Biblical quotes from the New International Version translation of the Bible (NIV).

2 Cf. the Reverend Ralf Krust, sermon on Jn. 2:13–22 for the tenth Sunday after Trinity Sunday (http://www.predigten.de/predigt.php3?predigt=916).

and the rupture of the curtain, at once, since, according to Biblical topography, they were separated by a significant physical distance. Both moments differ widely in the possibilities of perception they allow. The crucifixion itself is an event that is performed in public in order to send a political signal. The tearing of the curtain in the inaccessible temple sanctuary is not properly speaking a visible event. As an "explicit" metaphor, it is a linguistic rather than a real event. We should note, however, that the Bible ascribes no less real power to words than to deeds.

The tear marks the space traversed by the displacement. It is the transition from "I" to the "other", from the beholder to what he beholds. What stands between them is torn apart to create the possibility of seeing the other. Beholding is a form of grasping an object that enables the beholder to absorb through his gaze what he beholds. The displacement is the consequence of recognition. What is seen draws its value from the attention accorded to it. In being beheld, the thing is isolated from the continuity of its existence and acquires the clearly delineated boundaries of an object. The latter does not remain in the totality within which it has functional meaning; my beholding it lends it a "new" meaning dependent on my understanding. This meaning-generating grasp offered by beholding is impossible until the curtain is torn apart. The relationship of an object to a usage, originally implicit in its form, that is withdrawn by the object's displacement, or to the simulated usage present, in allusions, in the form given to it by artistic fashioning, is an essential feature of the works assembled in the exhibition *Displaced Fractures*. Emilie Ding's objects are scattered across the room, like movable architectonic pieces waiting to be employed in construction or to serve as foundations supporting other structural elements. Sometimes they appear to be integral pieces of the existing architecture, which is why it is easy to overlook them. The "compound pieces" draw our attention because they are inexplicable, raising the question of whether and to what extent the purposiveness of an object is recognizable in its shape. The concrete objects' threaded bolts and screws suggest connections between the individual objects, but they do not make good on this suggestion. The connecting pieces seem to be signs indicating possible points of contact whose function is limited to their being optional.

Ding's objects appear strangely irritating in the places they occupy, perhaps even a little neurotic, if their being in a museum and the power of the institution, did not identify them as works of art. Klara Lidén cannot rely on this interpretive pattern when she uses the vertical shafts of pillars or masts in the urban landscape, climbing up and then pausing above, tightly holding on to her support. From a psychological perspective, her behavior shows the traits of an obsession. This changes fundamentally, however, once we understand the compulsiveness of the symptoms, of the architecture in our cities, which seems so self-evident to us and which yet determines our behavior.

A glimpse inside the body

As a wound, the torn temple curtain is also an expression of destruction. It breaks with the idea of the perfect body. It represents an involuntary gaze into the inside, through a painful incision inflicted upon the body. As we see through its surface, the body reveals its other, concealed existence. The gaze discovers how the body is composed on the inside. In the case of living beings, there are blood, muscle fibers and bones. Constructed bodies reveal their material qualities and technical structures. Concrete or wood become visible beneath the structure of the façade or the colorful coat of paint covering the surface. Trestles, steel beams, or reinforcement steel come to light. The gaze into the inside seems to satisfy a certain need in us, a desire to understand how a form is able to maintain its shape. The glimpse through the tear satisfies this desire for a look at the constructive principles.

The torn curtain, then, is a "displaced fracture" in the truest sense of the term. The suffering and death of the Savior on the Cross is the site of the greatest burden. Yet its theological dimension is revealed elsewhere, at the central site of the manifestation of faith in this world, in an inaccessible room where, according to ancient Jewish belief, God sits on his throne. The range of the narrative, and of the narrative perspective in particular, is no less striking than the idea that the Son of God is condemned to what was at the time the most ignominious form of execution conceivable. The spatial displacement between the event of the death and its symbolic analogue in the tearing of the curtain distinguishes it from the wound in Christ's side, where sign and body coincide. The lateral wound, like the other wounds, expresses the violation of the human body God has taken on in his son Jesus. The wounds become a central topic in the Gospels, where they allow the disciples to recognize

Jesus after the Resurrection. Body, appearance, and violation become identical.

Such concurrent action is also evident in the traces of workmanship, boreholes, and clefts in Ulrich Rückriem's boulders. The boulder has been removed from the larger solid mass of rock of which it was originally a part; isolated, it acquires individual shape. A sort of violation of the mountain turns it into a body that can be perceived as such. The technical realization, the labor of removing it from the quarry, is still evident in the block. We can recognize traces of the bores that have made it possible to blast off the block. In many instances, the block itself is cleft. Rückriem arranges the two split halves as a single block despite the crack between them so that, strictly speaking, there is no gap separating them. In purely visual terms, they still cling together, but their union is threatened, like a cracked porcelain dish that is only just holding together. The crack is nonetheless clearly visible, like a seam, marking the block as "damaged." Rückriem's cracks gesture beyond the block into the material world, where we can think of them as continuing ad infinitum. They become a metaphor for the fact that all things have been torn from a continuum. From the perspective of this philosophy, any object is the result of a fracture.

In his *Untitled* work (2008), Klaus Winichner fills such cracks. He has grouted the tears and holes in three mattresses with a variety of materials, including foam insulation, concrete, and artificial flowers. Against the expansion of cracks in Rückriem's work, Winichner offers an ironic alternative, a mundane solution to the problem of fragmentariness in the here and now. The technically unsuitable additions open a new and critically reflected narrative space. They tell the story of a different kind of use, partially undoing the focus of the gaze on the qualities of media by using materials in descriptive ways.

Ruin and fragment

Our world seems fragmented in manifold ways when we isolate things within it. These things do not become meaningful until we behold them. With the onset of modernity, objects that had been peripheral moved to the center of attention. The first indication of this shift may have been as early as 1503, in Dürer's *Great Piece of Turf*, a masterful drawing of a few lowly blades of grass; it continues today in objects created by artists that look like chunks of concrete ripped from buildings destined for demolition. Gordon Matta-Clark was among the artists who, in the early 1970s, turned such fragments into respectable works of art (which is to say, persuaded museums to show them).

Such fragments represent the culmination of many different themes in the histories of art and culture. That they are regarded as objects of art is a consequence of the possibility of isolating them and of the fact that they are perceived in this form as the traces or relics of something larger. Concrete, reinforcing steel, and residues of paint speak of a specific form of construction introduced in the modern era that has now reached an age where it is in turn exposed to decay or demolition and, most importantly, to a critical theoretical discourse. Kilian Rüthemann, for instance, examines the modernist architecture of the exhibition spaces. He does so by reduplicating steps in raw concrete or dismantling the ceiling structure of a skylight. The result is a makeshift arrangement that raises questions regarding the space. As though in a research laboratory, the structural components are temporarily laid out on the examination table. The glass panes of the skylight are propped up on carefully arranged stilts, lending them a graphic-plastic form that —minimalist in itself—paraphrases existing structures and claims to share their validity.

Our present age is defined, in particular, by the achievements of classical Modernism. We possess highlights of a rationalist way of thinking about architecture, design, and art in the architecture of Le Corbusier, the designs of the Bauhaus, and the works of Schlemmer, Mondrian, Albers, and others. The particular focus is on the adequate preservation of this cultural heritage, which by now shows significant traces of wear. The complexity of the endeavor is apparent, for instance, in the restoration of the Masters' Houses in Dessau. During the very first years of their existence, differences between the views of individual teachers and residents led to variations in the execution of the building phases, with some buildings subject to modification immediately after completion. The question as to which point in time and which state of a building should be considered as manifesting the ideal, and hence the goal of a restoration effort, becomes so important because it in turn articulates what the present age considers worthy.

The often rather incompatible sutures that stand out as cracks or displacements in the resulting reconstructions resemble those that appear time and again in the works of Phyllida Barlow. In their patent ineptitude, Barlow's crudely puttied seams, unevenly spackled surfaces, or wedges on which entire forms stand precariously tilted render the fractures only more clearly visible, elevating them to the status of the central event in the artist's sculptures and installations.

In art-historical terms, they stand in the tradition of the Romantic attraction to ruins. The longing gaze, in the era around 1800, at dilapidated buildings, preferably churches, or the half-eaten apple in Baroque still lifes, proclaim the relativity and transience of everything that exists, in contrast with the timeless validity of "eternal values." In the Baroque tradition, they indicate the relativity of earthly things, against which they posit religion or the spiritual. Mundane pomp is a seduction. When it shows cracks or other traces of decay, such symptoms of decline open the door to creeping doubt about its validity. Metaphorically speaking, the beholder here seeks to see through the cracks, aiming at the core of things, where he hopes to glimpse what holds the whole together.

The frisson we derive from the contrast between our awareness of being alive and watching as something dies seduces us into looking at ruins, as Tacita Dean does in her video about the demolition of Berlin's Palace of the Republic. Here, too, we can overhear the call for a critical engagement with the ideals the ruin communicates, with their collapse and their perspectives.

Particularly in works that have been destroyed, ideological issues time and again catch our eye. Ideology becomes especially interesting when it fails. Accordingly, the perfection of an ideal, be it architectonic or artistic, acquires decisive significance in the fragment. The possibility of this inversion is rooted in a sort of dissolution of the ideal in its destruction. The fragment manifests the ideal as something that has been overcome. At the same time, any fragmentary work contains the ideal of perfection. Even recognizing that an object is a fragment requires an idea of the whole. This idea itself need not necessarily be complete. It is enough that the fragment bears traces indicating that the object is damaged at this point, that it originally was more than can be seen at the site of fracture. There are two complementary attitudes we can take to such a fracture. We can consider the fracture itself to be meaningful and hence satisfactory, or it can spur us to complete the object; to make it whole in the imagination or in material reality. In doing so, we draw on patterns we derive from our experience with comparable objects.

What distinguishes the artistic approaches in the exhibition *Displaced Fractures* is the fact that rather than *being* readymade ruins and architectural fragments—found movable pieces from the realm of the forgotten and neglected zones of our cities and architectures—they imitate their aesthetic. This approach represents the fusion of two strains in art history: the European tradition of the Romantic attraction to the ruin, and the political commitment of the art of the 1970s, when artists went out to the fringes and transitional zones of the cities to observe and analyze marginalized social forms, spaces, and architectures. Artistic interventions brought these peripheral phenomena into public view, rendering them visible in photographs or collecting fragments from these areas and then transposing them into a gallery, thus moving them from their marginal locations to a center of cultural attention.

With their sculptures and sculptural interventions in space, by contrast, the artists included in the exhibition *Displaced Fractures* create visual foci that are perhaps better compared to the "Follies" of the landscape park which, in the 18th century at the latest, could also take the form of artificial ruins. From this perspective, ruination and decline appear as inevitable processes in the natural cycle of becoming and passing away. Cultural achievements rise and fall, just as cultures themselves pass through a zenith before entering a period of decay. Gothic architecture, preferably in a state of ruin, appears as the cultural flower of medieval Europe, and after its decay, its surviving remnants came to be read as signs, serving as a backdrop for a present age that measured its own worth by their standard. In this regard, the Gothic ruin is comparable to the decaying industrial compounds that are slowly crumbling and rusting in the marginalized zones of our cities, eventually to disappear beneath sprawling spontaneous vegetation. They represent the economic development of society in the era of industrialization. Their architectonic structures are no longer adequate for today's purposes, or their location is not attractive enough. In this form, some of them have now embarked on a remarkable second career as cultural sites. The marginal locations of such buildings makes them seem appropriate at a time when culture is being crowded out of the centers and into the periphery.

In an art that takes up decay as a structural principle and implements it in its sculptural practice, destruction becomes the foundation for construction. That is, in a certain respect, a paradox. Devastation is in a way conceived as a means to visual creation. On the other hand, this view can also lead to a different perspective on the sculptural treatment of material in general. The way a block of marble is treated in the creation of a Classical sculpture then appears as a destructive act as well, a practice that cuts the original marble out of a larger mass of solid rock in order to fragment it. This line of thought brings us back to Rückriem's work.

Our identification with the sculptural body leads us to understand the body created by the sculptor as a counterpart or transfiguration of our own self. Ding, Rückriem, and Winichner likewise work with the principle of transference in creating forms that we can take in as a whole. In their dimensions or their anthropomorphic shapes, these works refer to the quality of being self-contained that we perceive as a defining feature of our own bodies. Oscar Tuazon explicitly points to the interrelation between the sculptural process and the body in the titles of his works.

In fragments isolated from larger ensembles, architecture becomes comprehensible, individualized into an object that hence also lends itself to anthropomorphic animation in the imagination. The violations inscribed upon these bodies become painful to their beholders as well. They thus allow us to understand suffering in quite classical terms, through compassion—Aristotle would describe it as a "cathartic" experience. Projection and displacement are joined on a metaphorical level, just as the death of Christ affects the temple curtain, and only the rupture of the latter reveals the true magnitude of the death of Jesus.

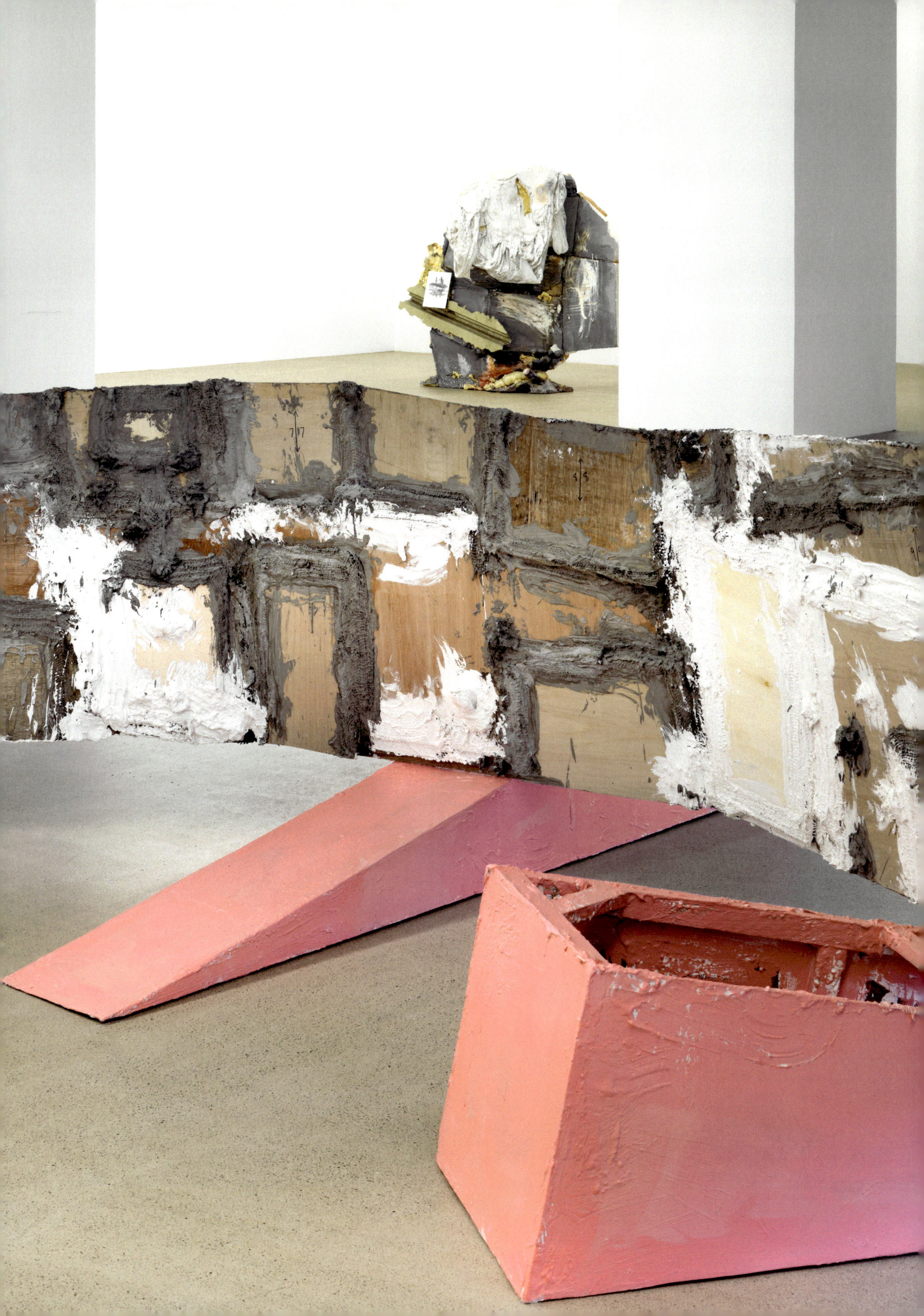

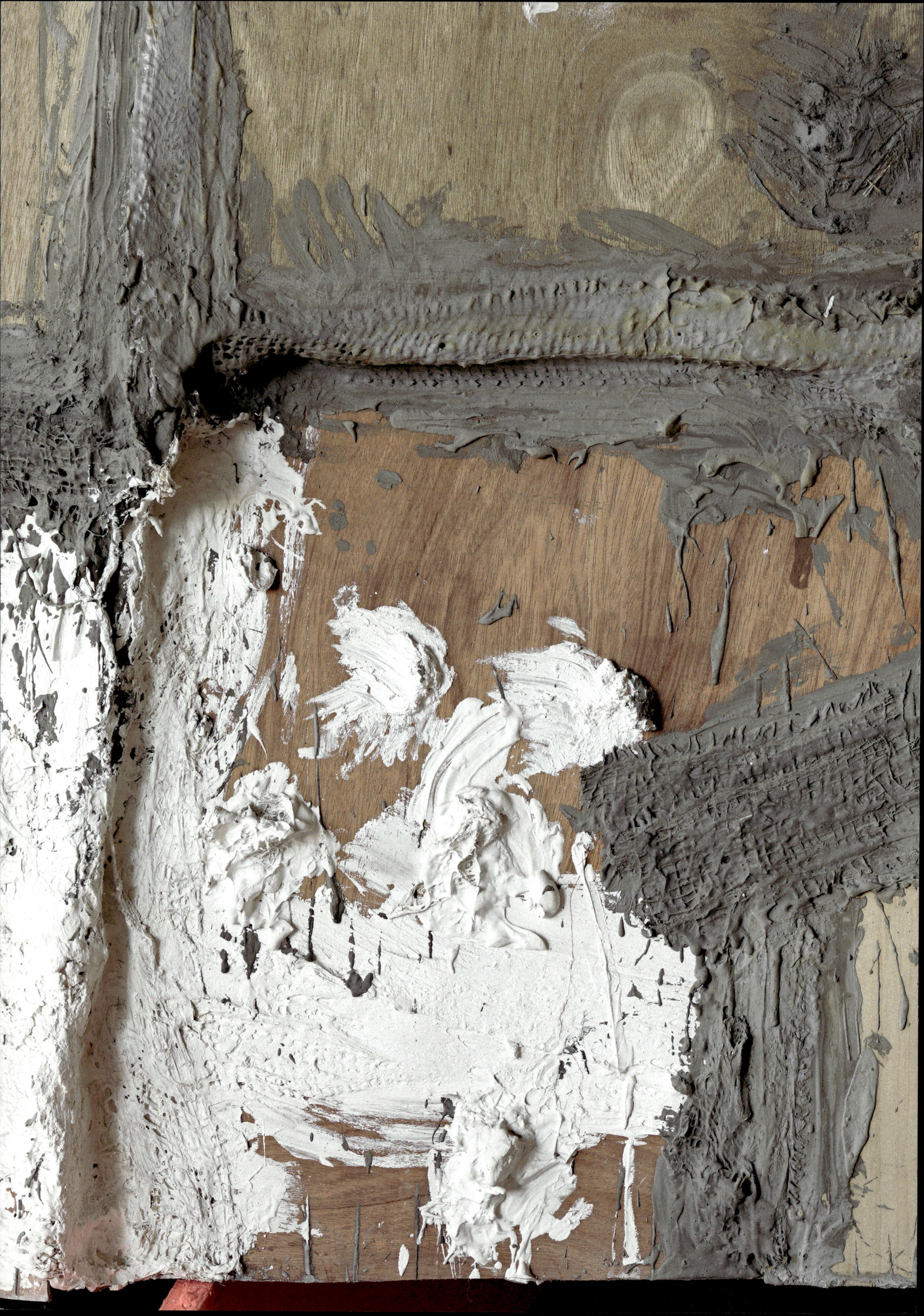

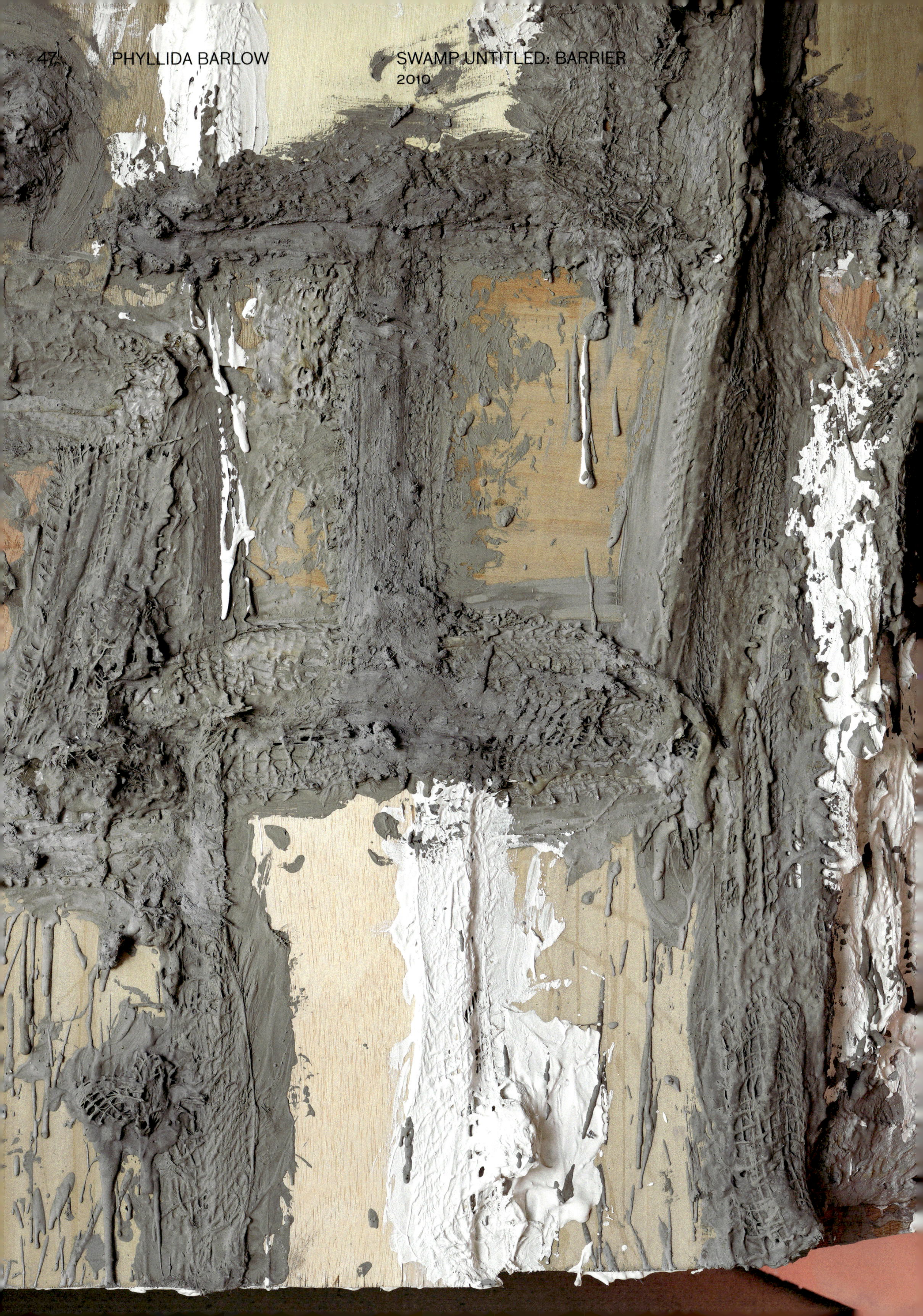

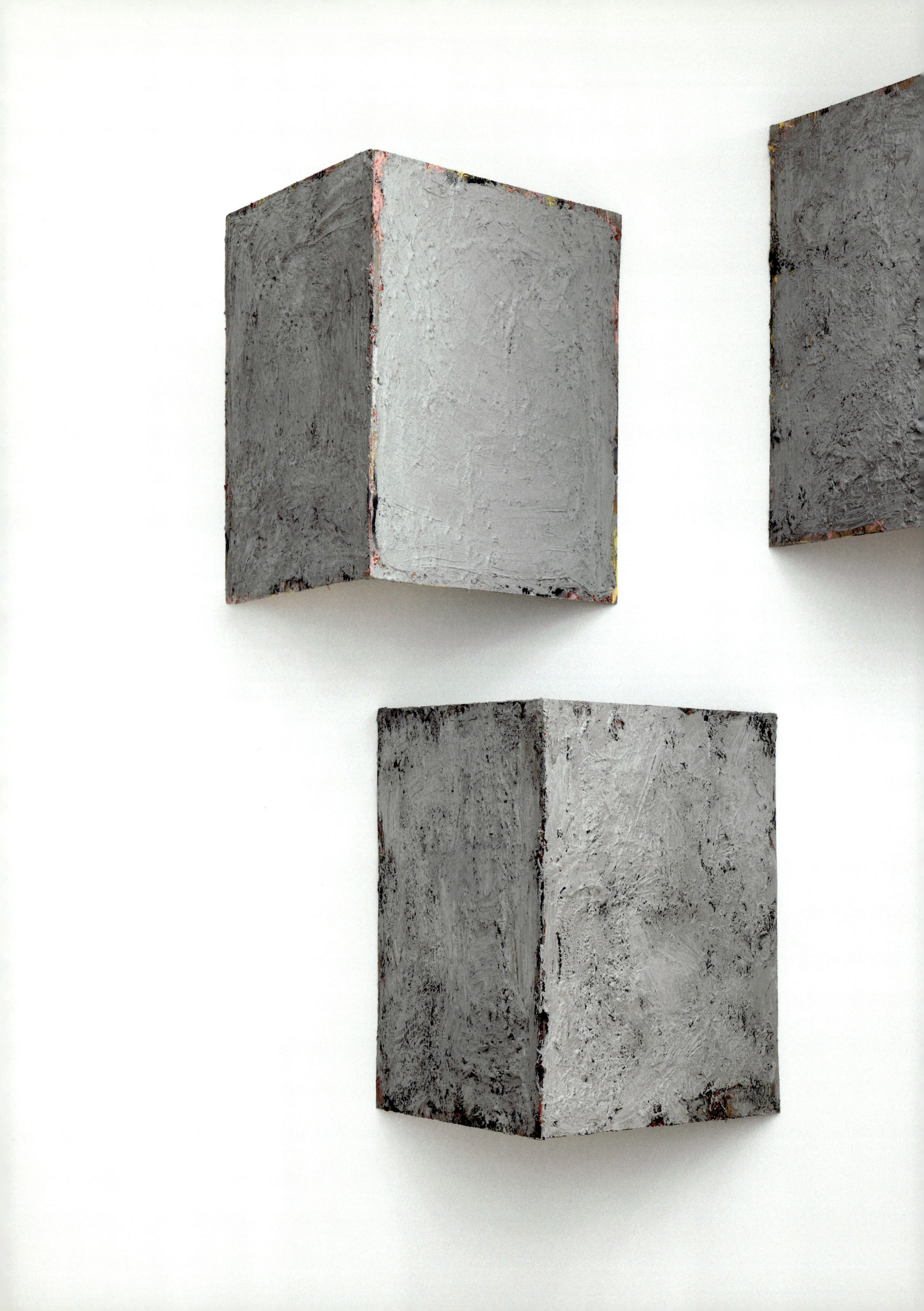

UNTITLED: SIGNS
2010

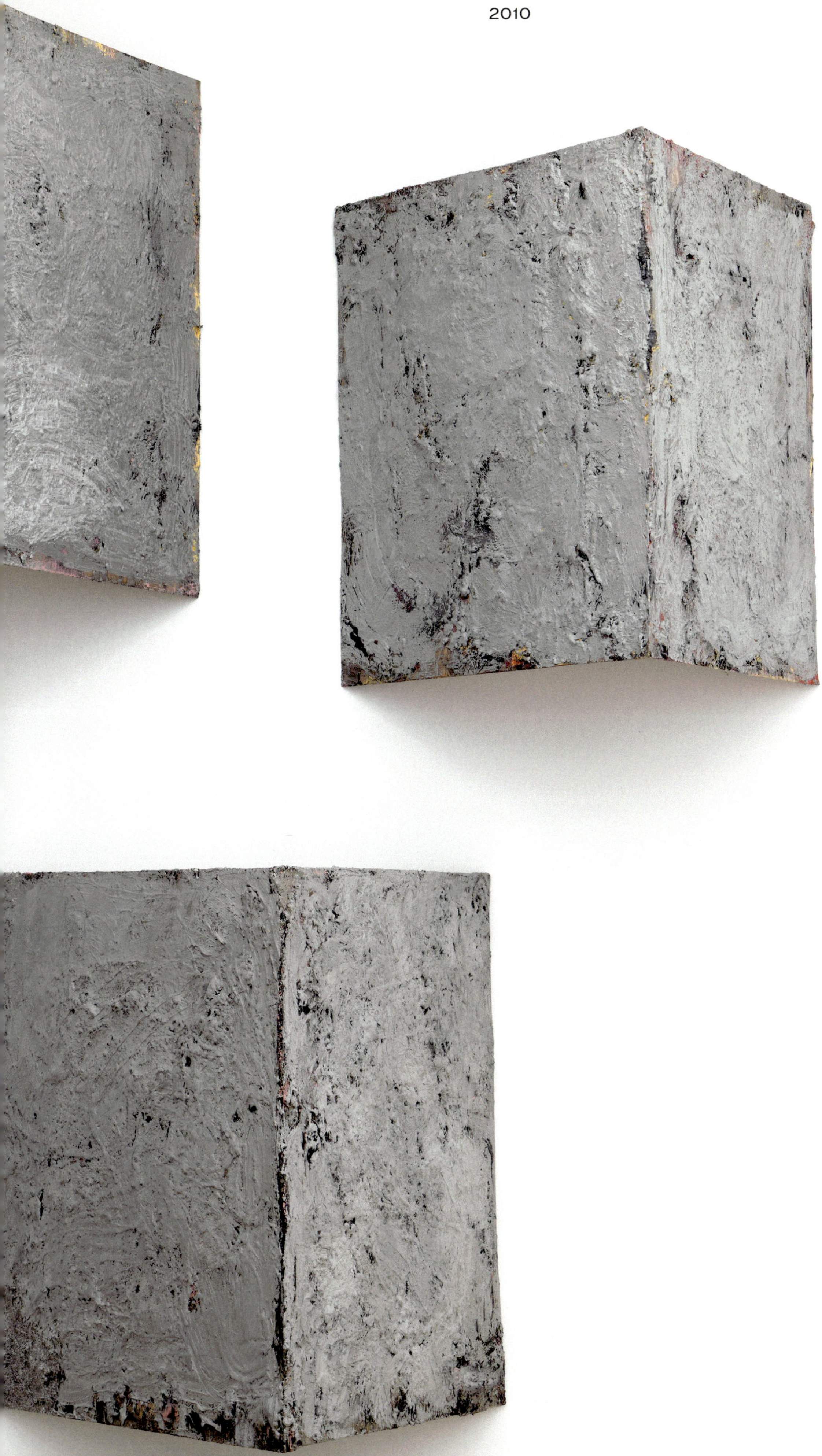

PHYLLIDA BARLOW

UNTITLED: SIGNS
2010

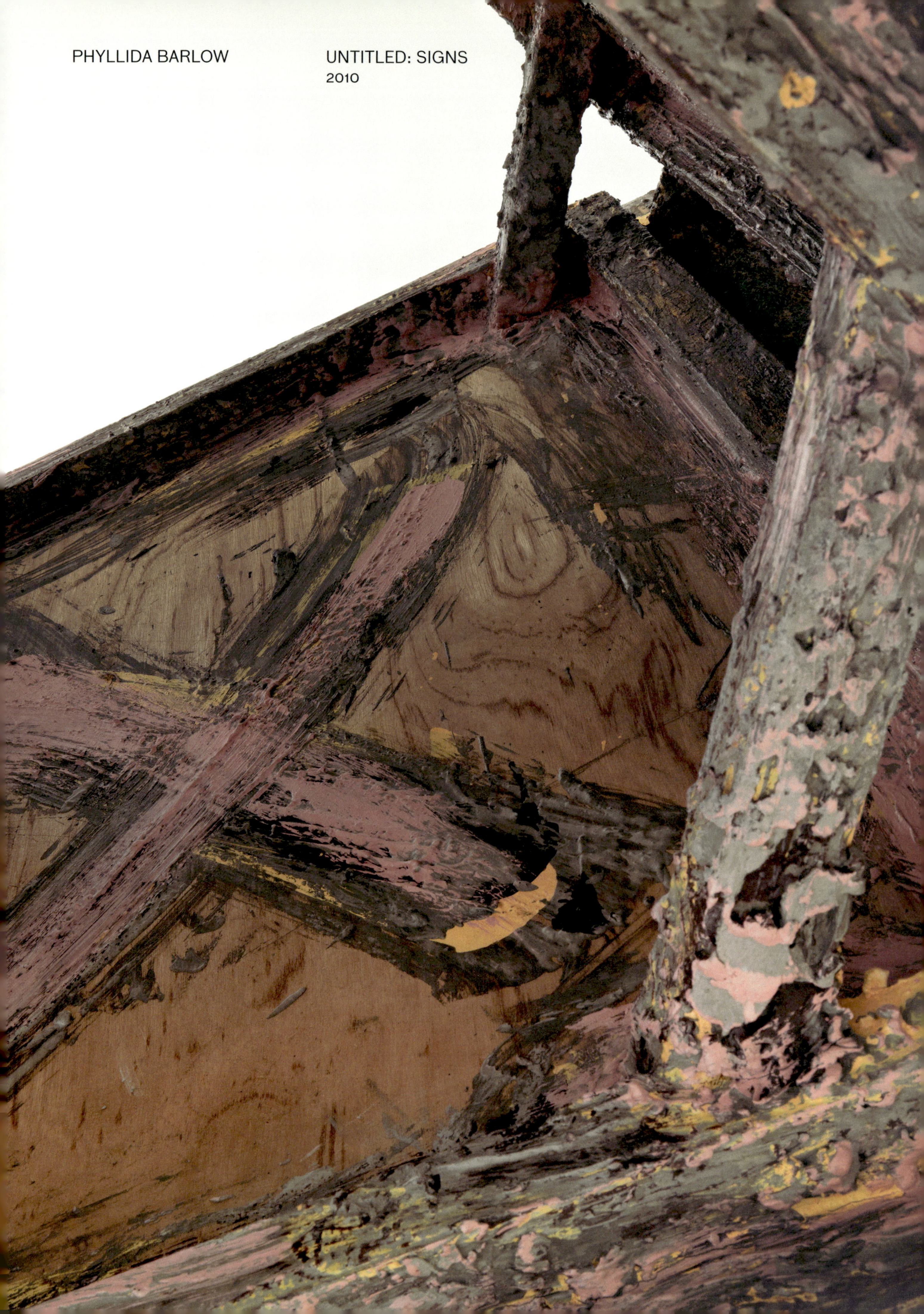

ORANGENPFLÜCKERIN
2010

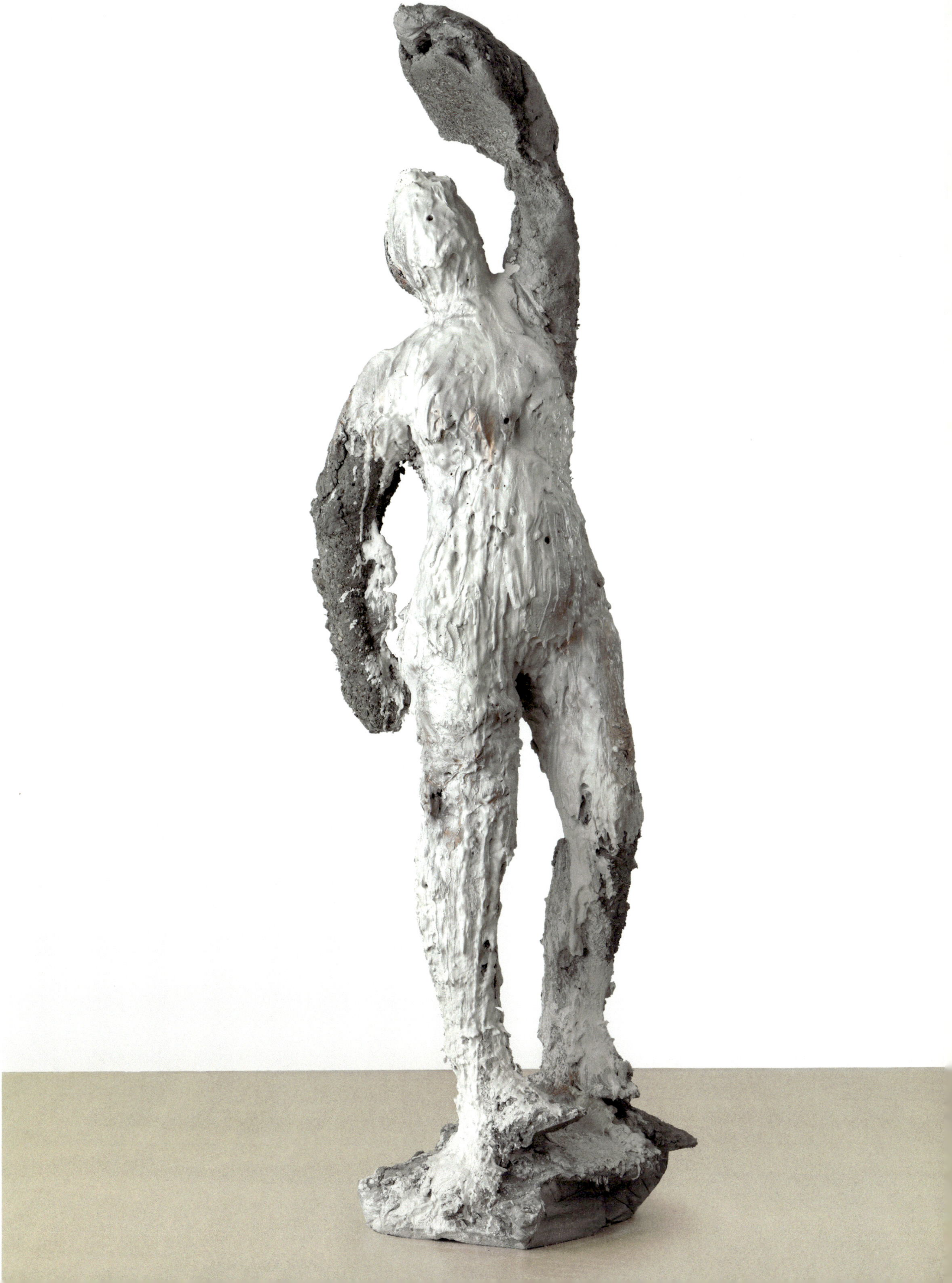

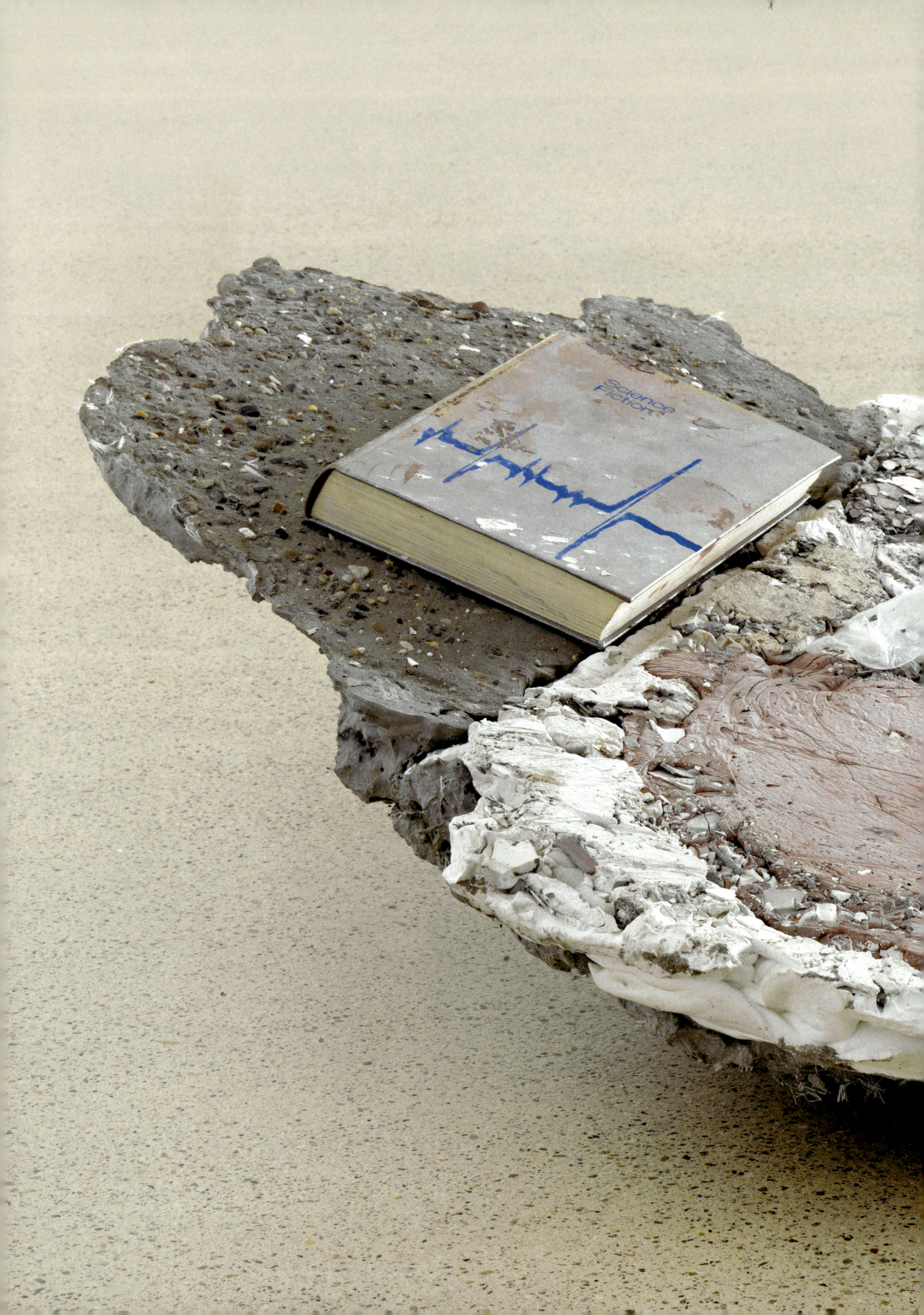
Science
Fiction

KLAUS WINICHNER

SCIENCE FICTION
2009

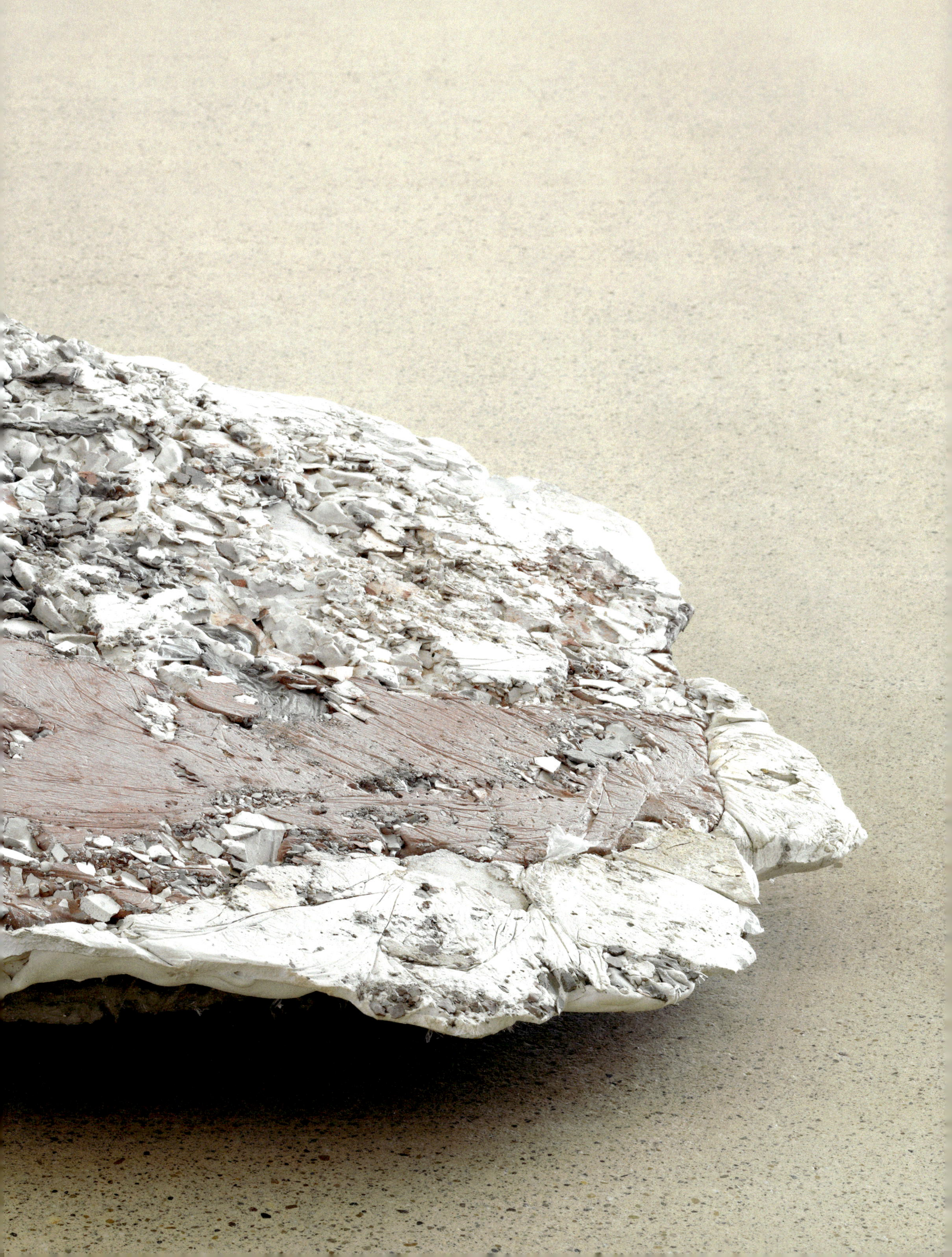

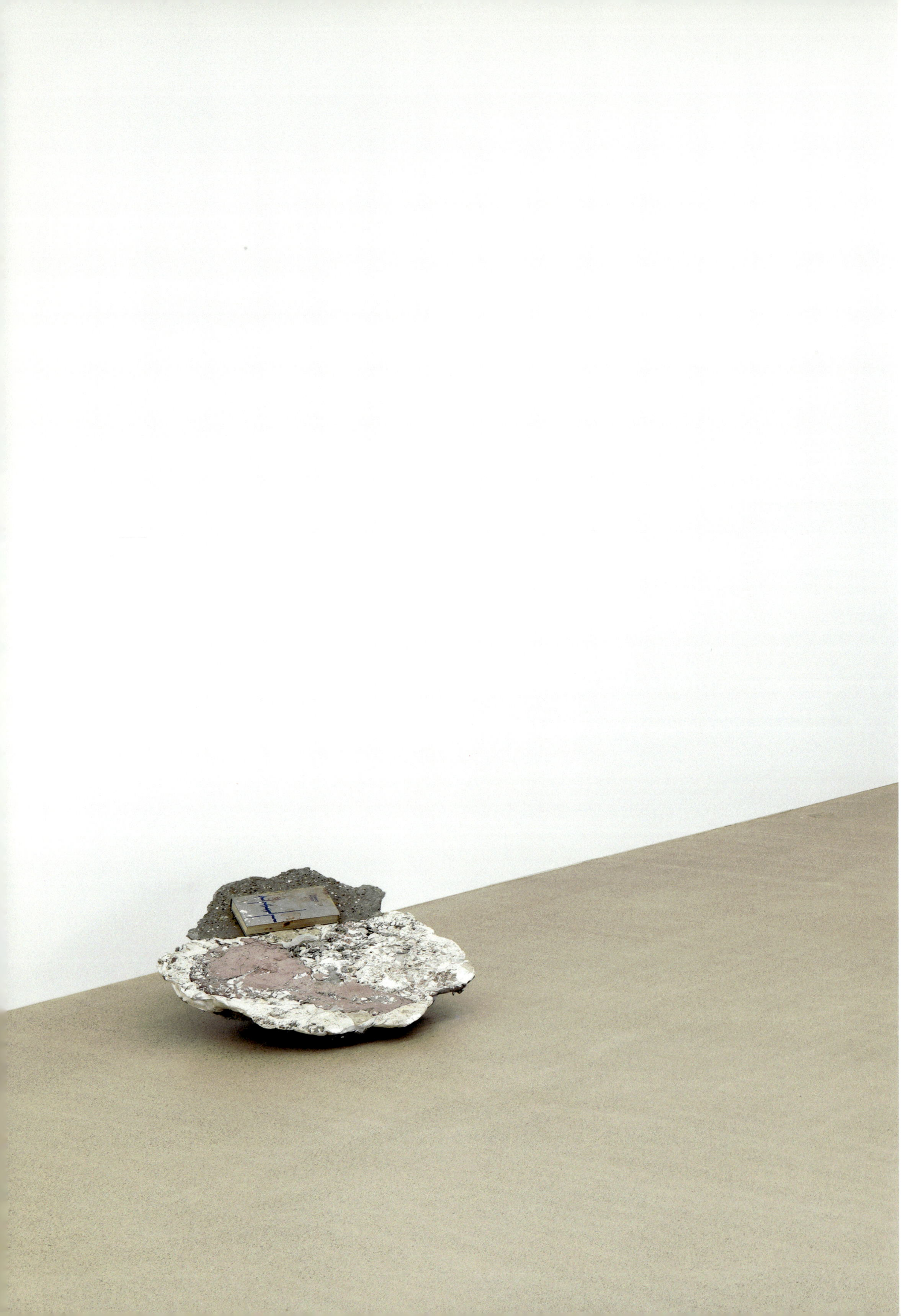

KLAUS WINICHNER

VOM GRUND UND SEINER URSACHE
2008

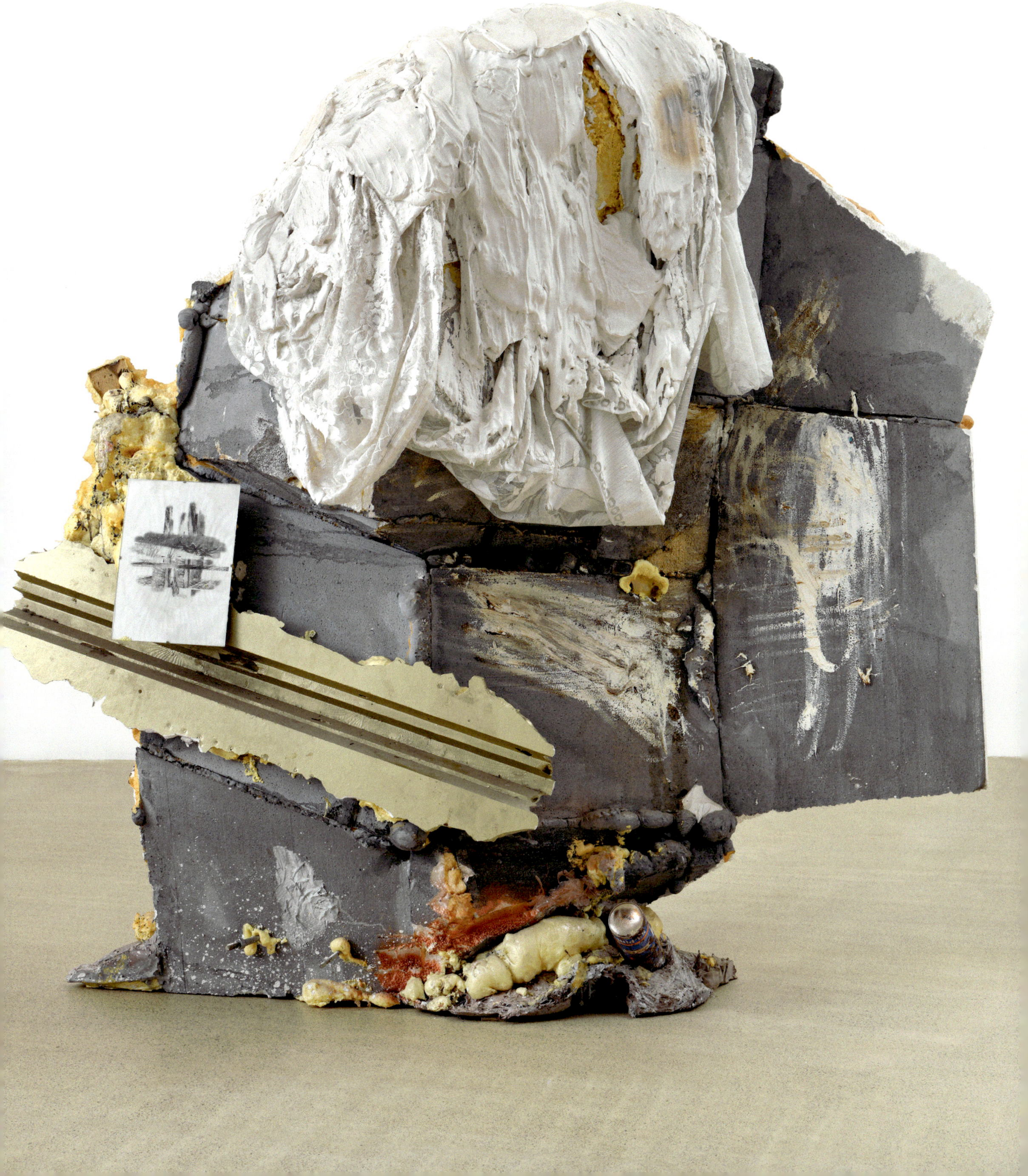

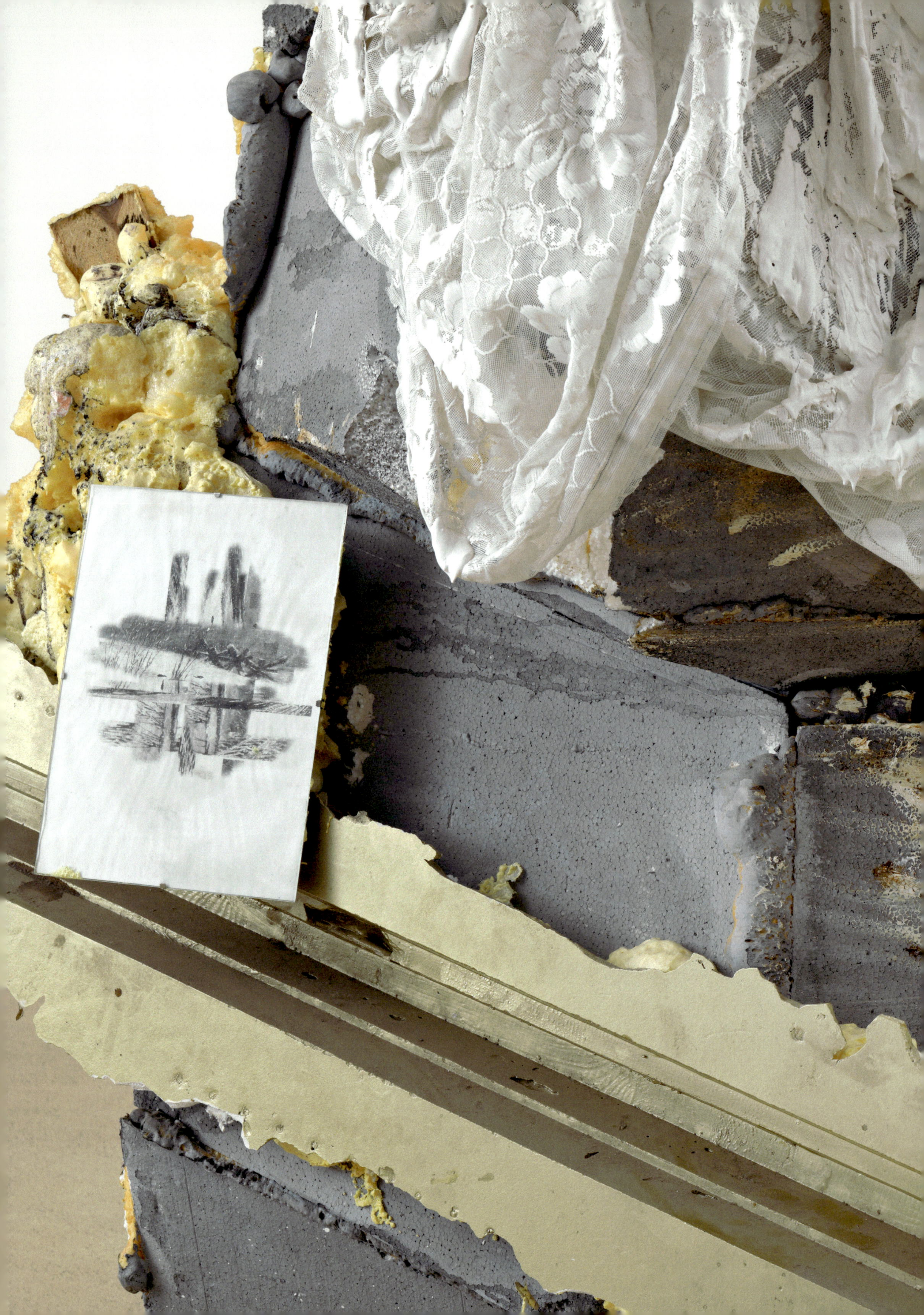

2008

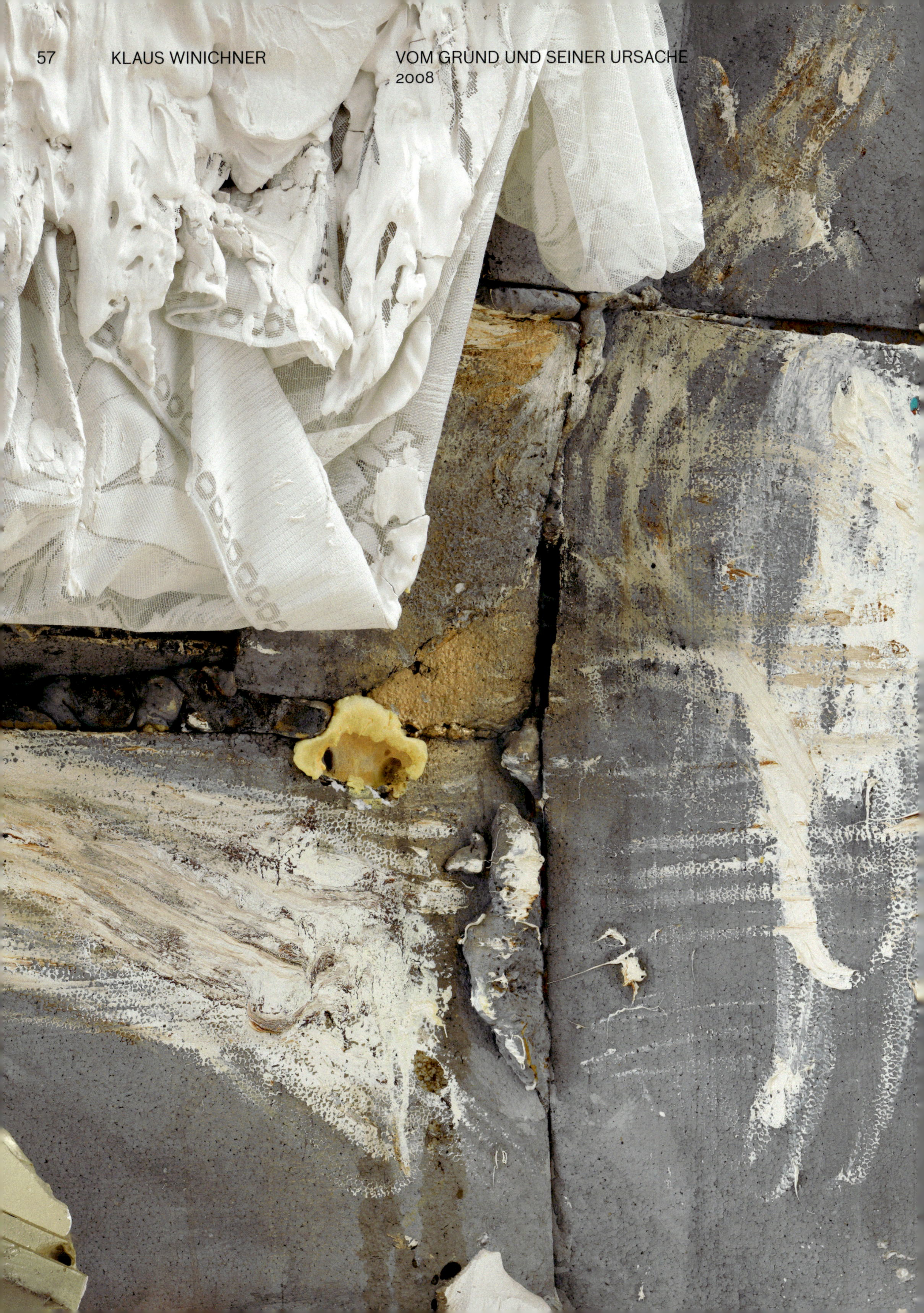

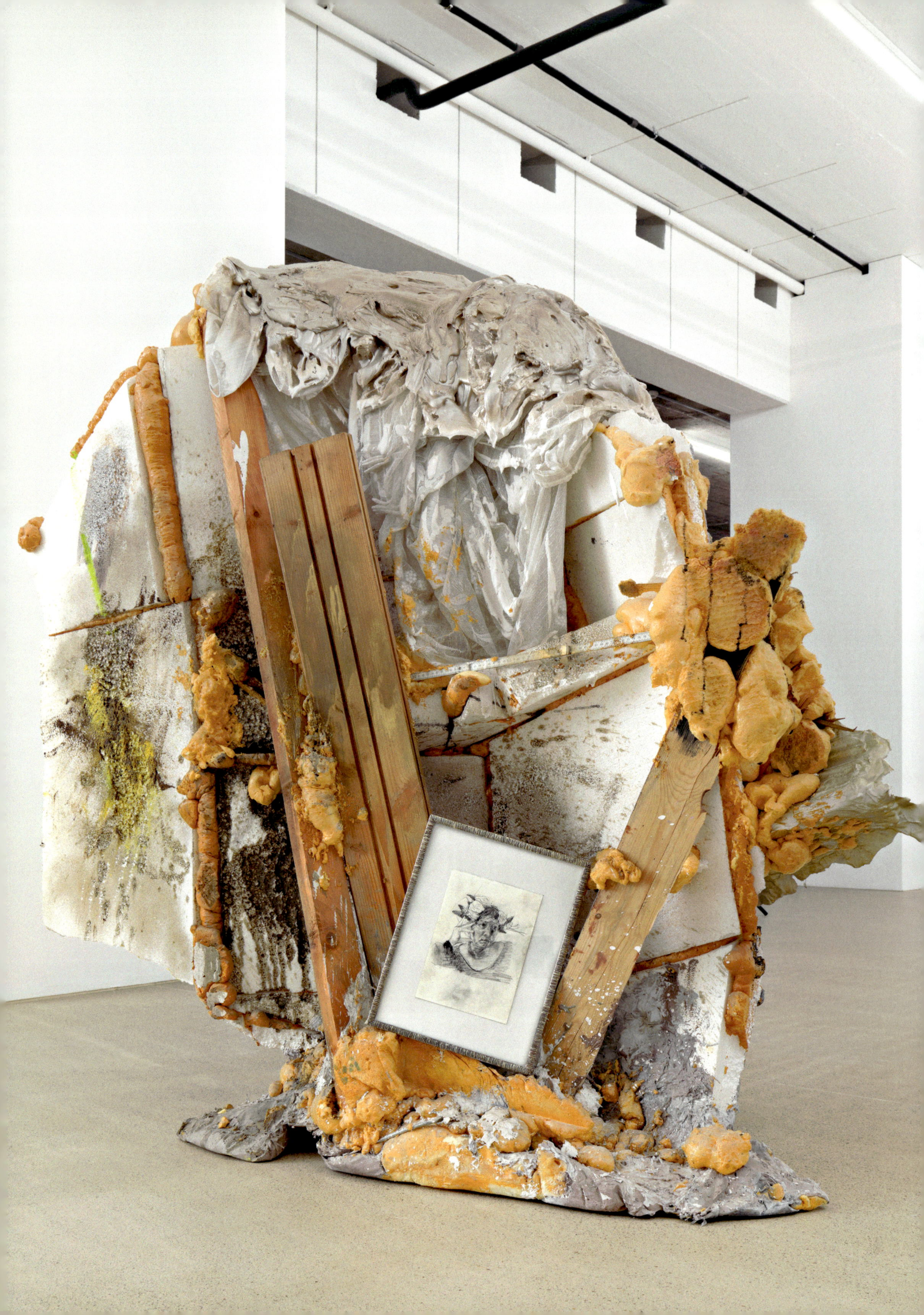

I WANT TO PUT SOMETHING INSIDE MY BODY AND CARRY SOMETHING IN IT. I WANT TO GET INSIDE MY BODY AND GET CARRIED IN IT, I'D LIKE TO GET BURIED IN IT, PUT MY HEAD IN IT AND GET IN IT, I'M NOT SCARED OF IT
2010

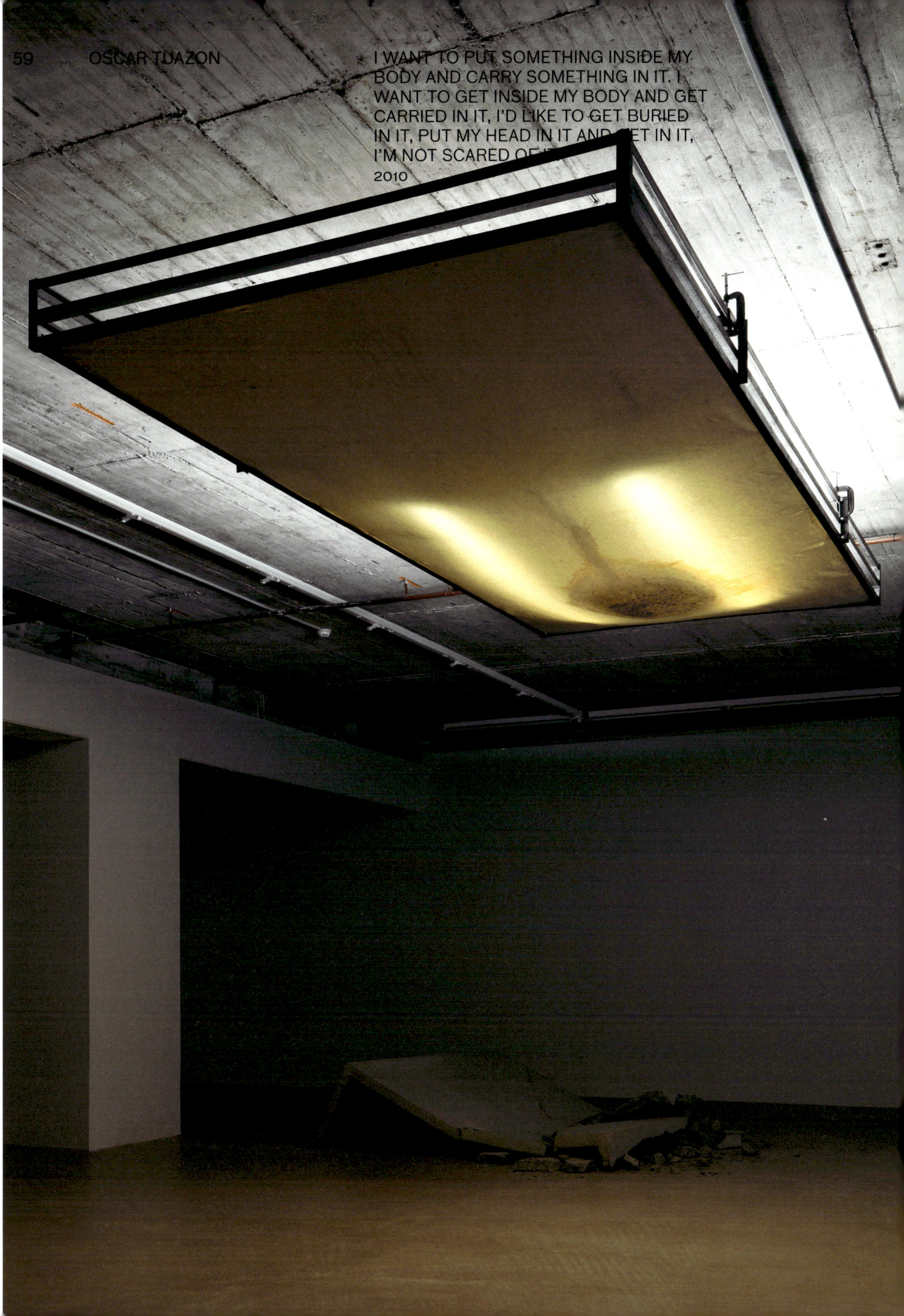

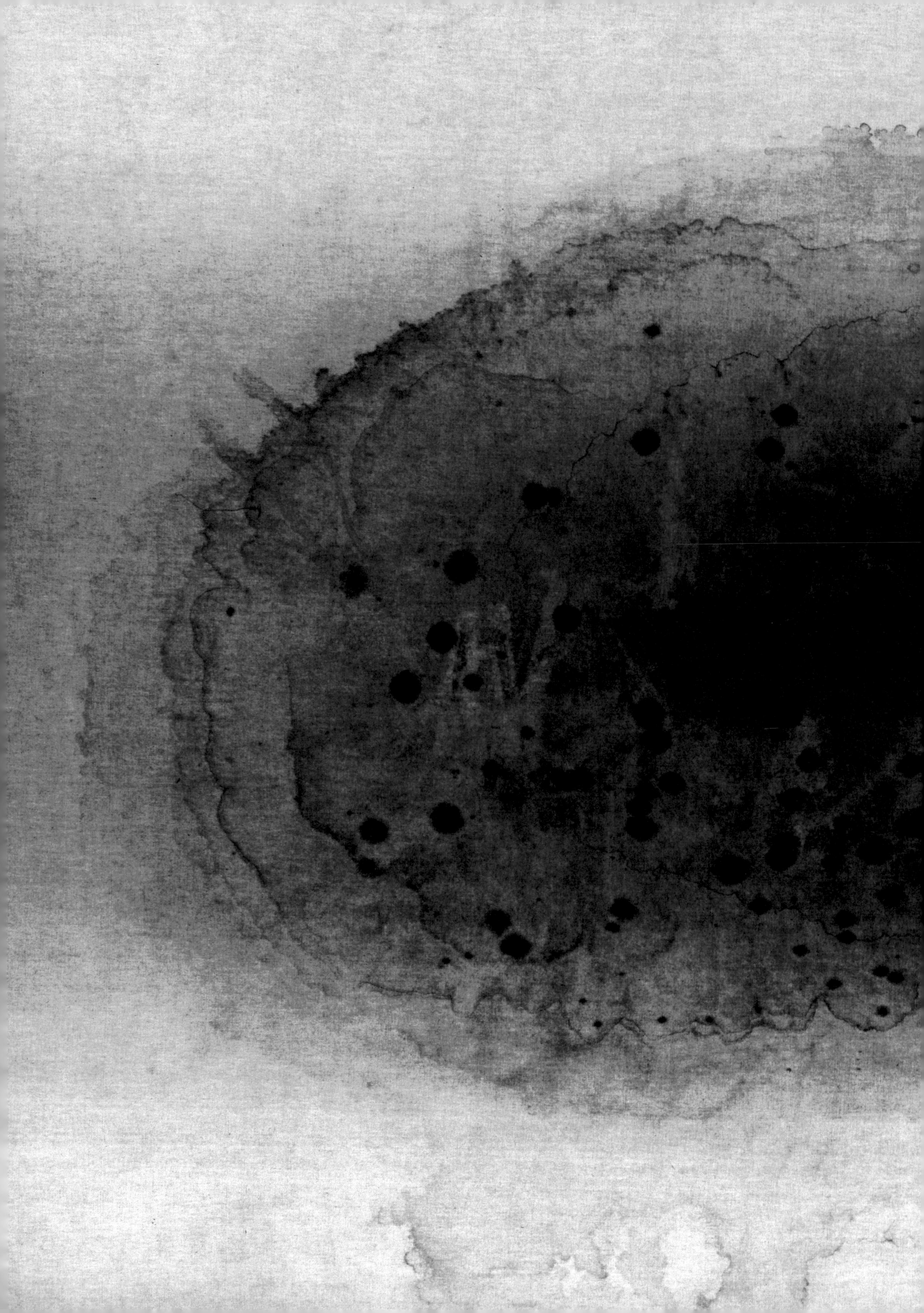

I WANT TO PUT SOMETHING INSIDE MY BODY AND CARRY SOMETHING IN IT. I WANT TO GET INSIDE MY BODY AND GET CARRIED IN IT, I'D LIKE TO GET BURIED IN IT, PUT MY HEAD IN IT AND GET IN IT, I'M NOT SCARED OF IT.

2010

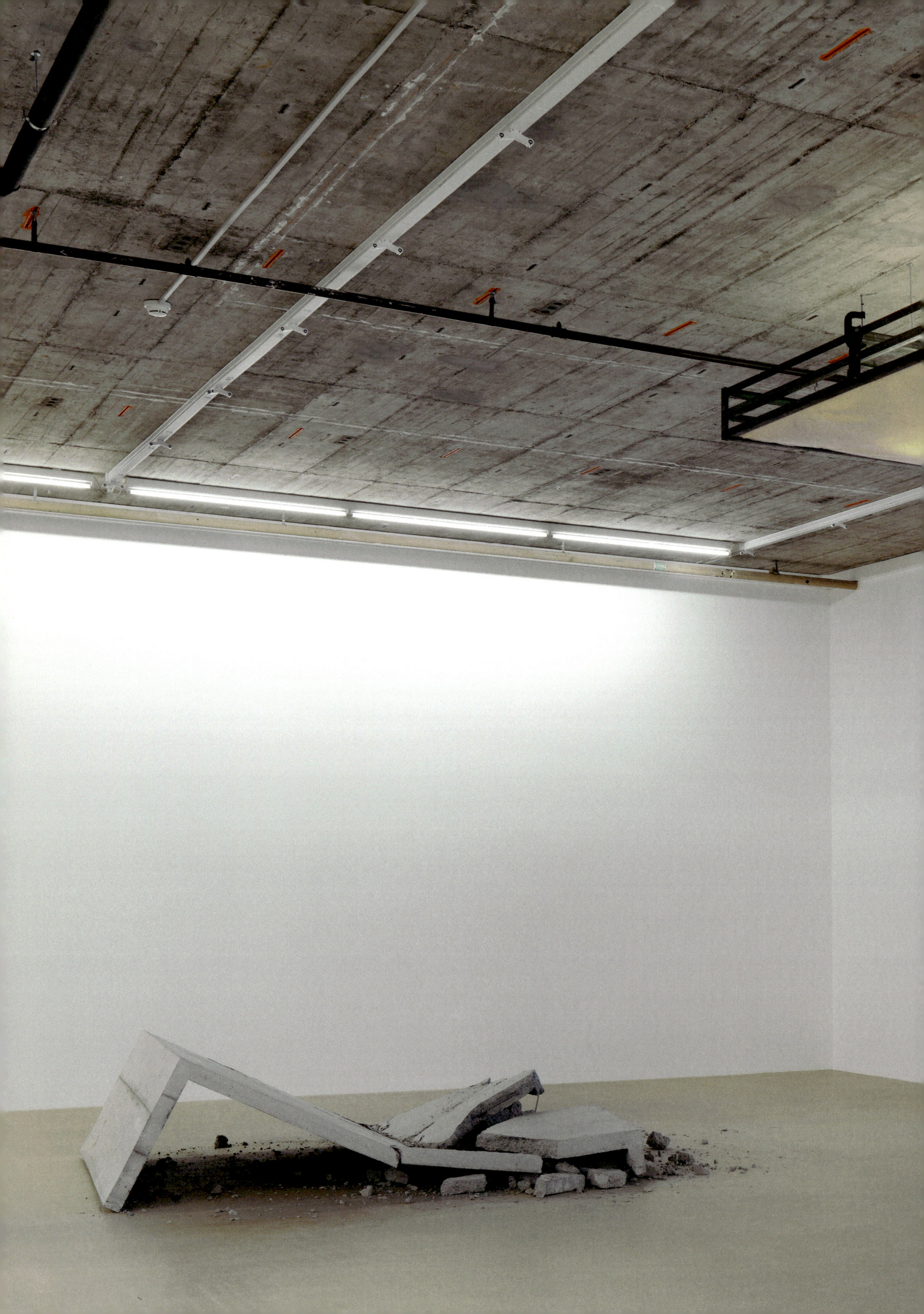

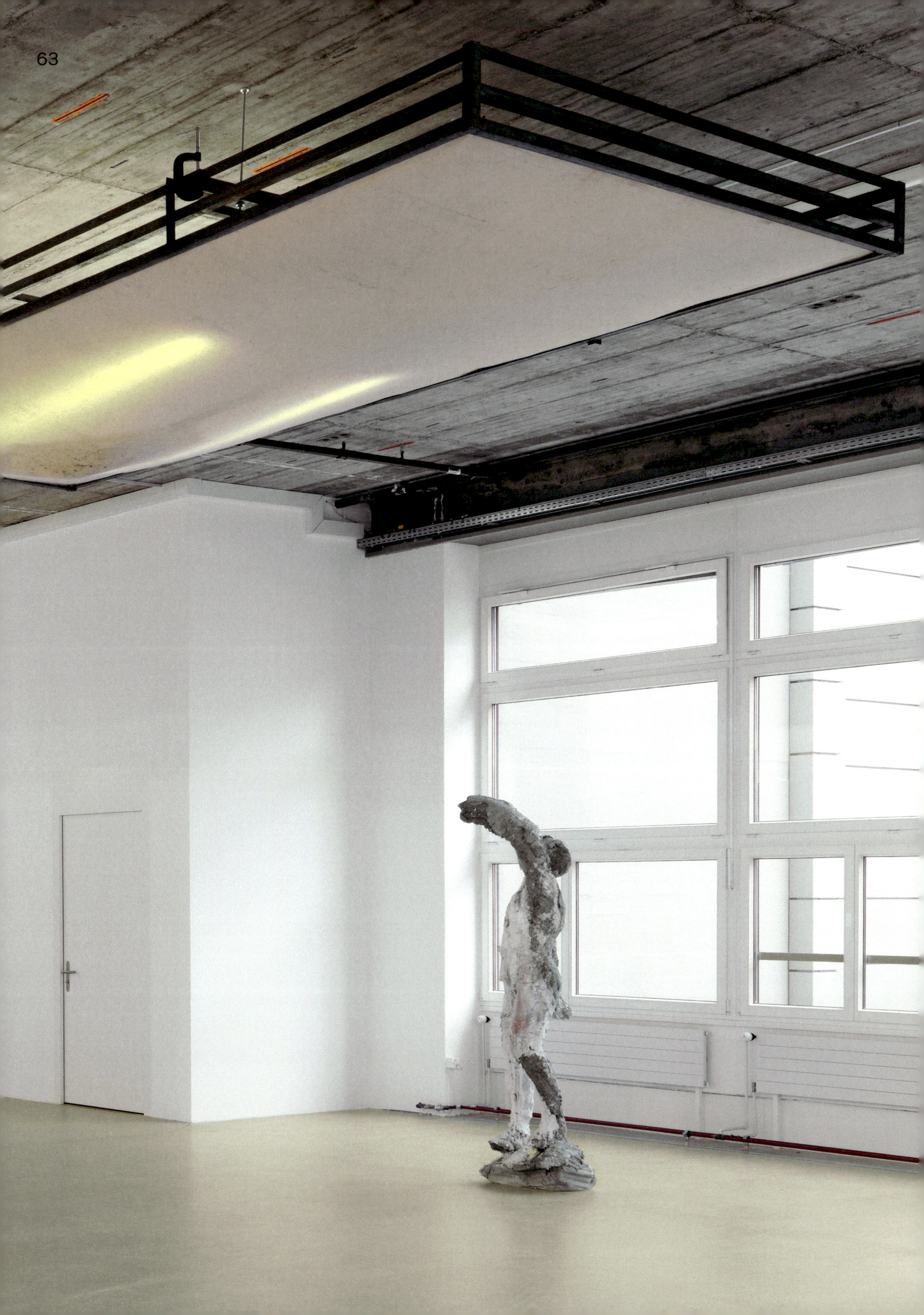

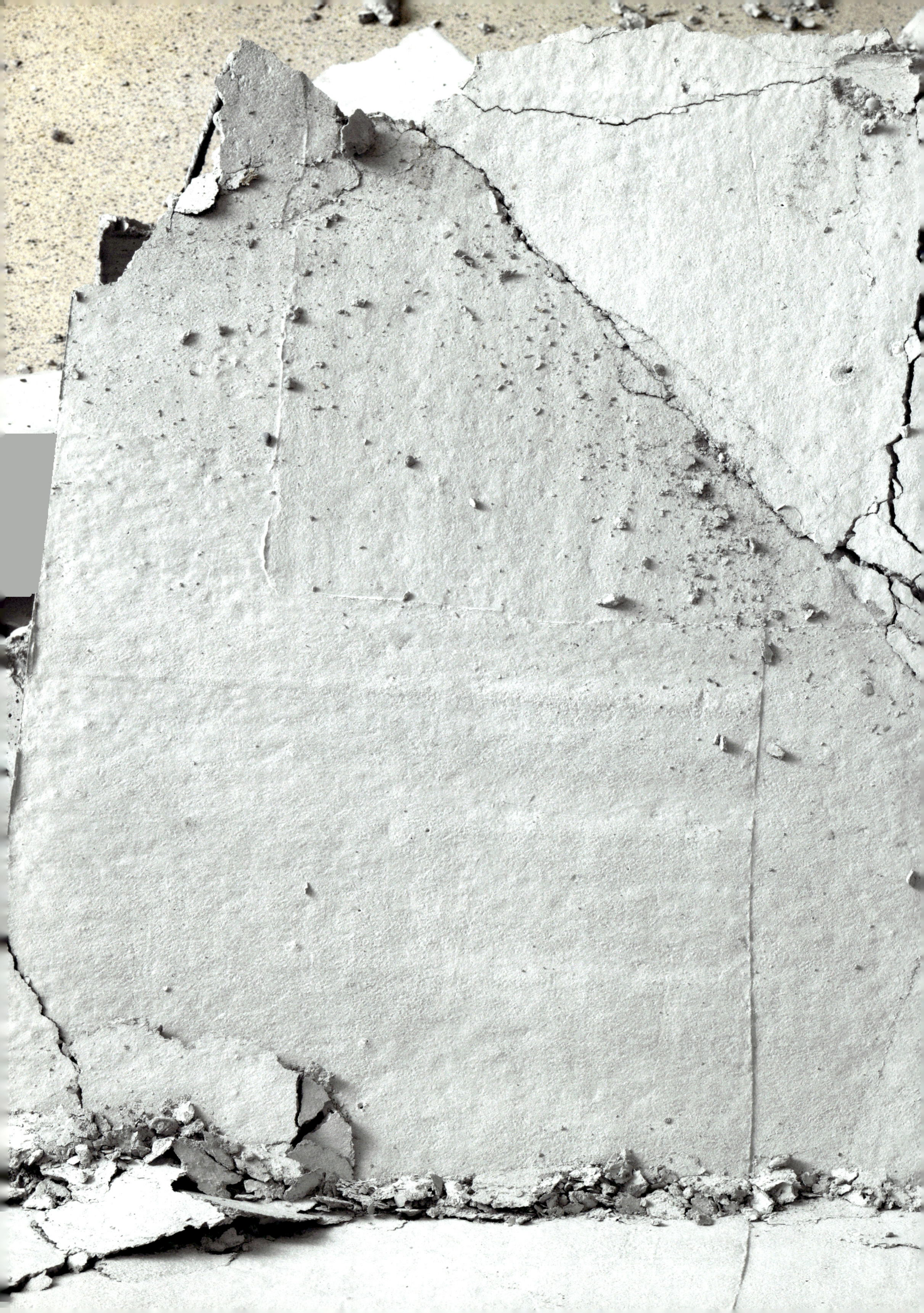

I USE MY BODY FOR SOMETHING, I USE IT TO MAKE SOMETHING, I MAKE SOMETHING WITH MY BODY, WHATEVER THAT IS. I MAKE SOMETHING AND I PAY FOR IT AND I GET PAID FOR IT.
2010

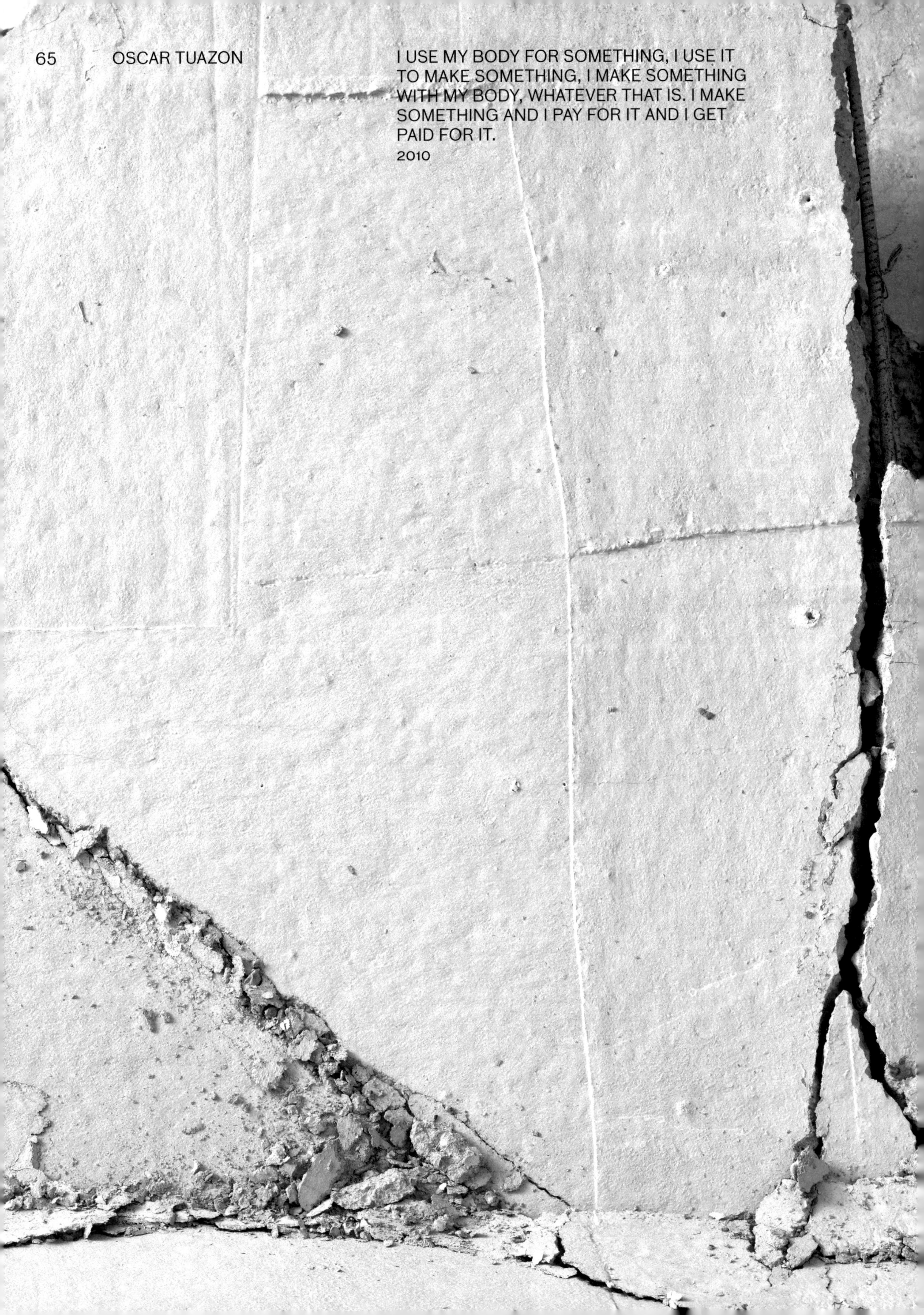

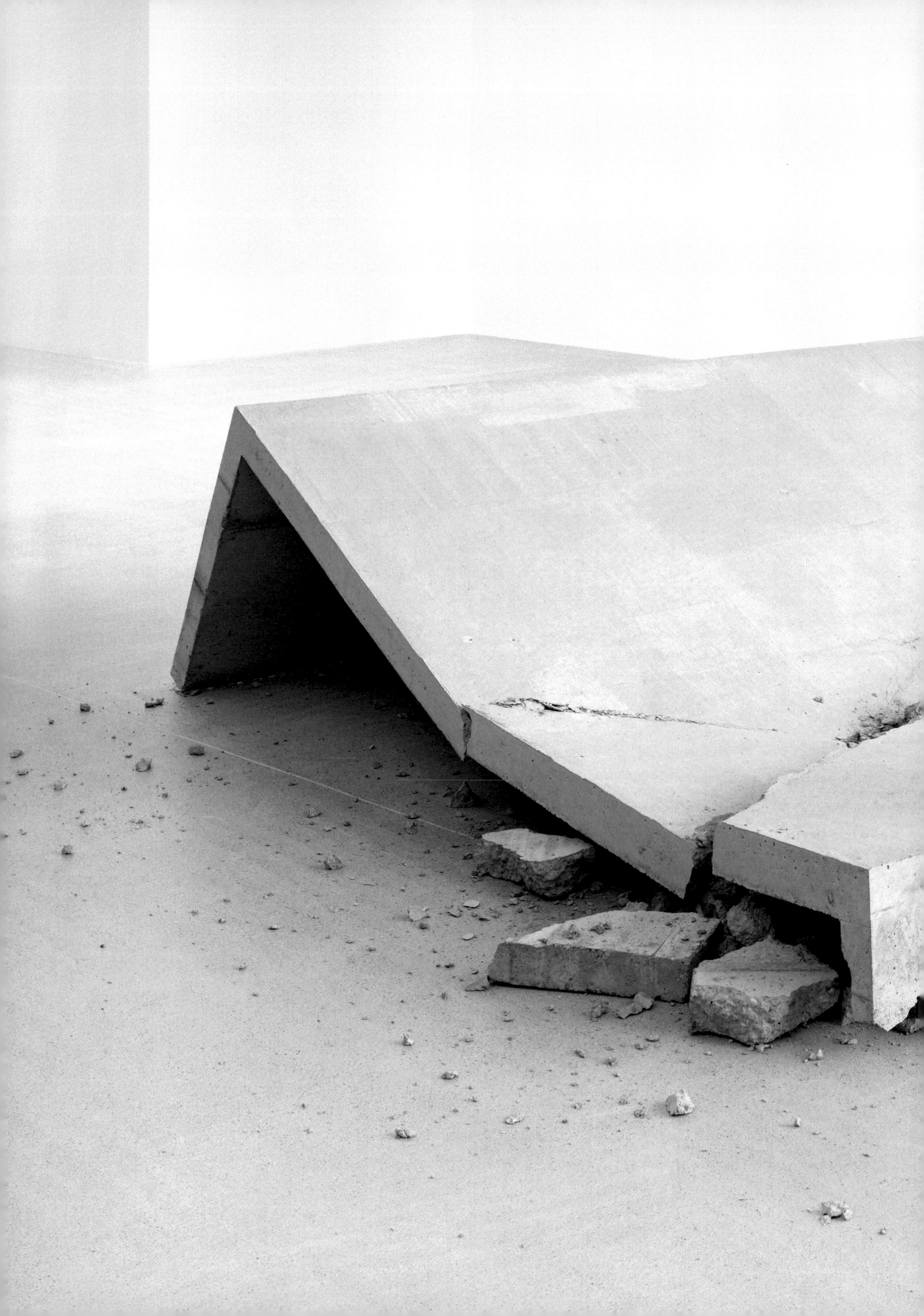

OSCAR TUAZON

I USE MY BODY FOR SOMETHING, I USE IT TO MAKE SOMETHING, I MAKE SOMETHING WITH MY BODY, WHATEVER THAT IS. I MAKE SOMETHING AND I PAY FOR IT AND I GET PAID FOR IT.

2010

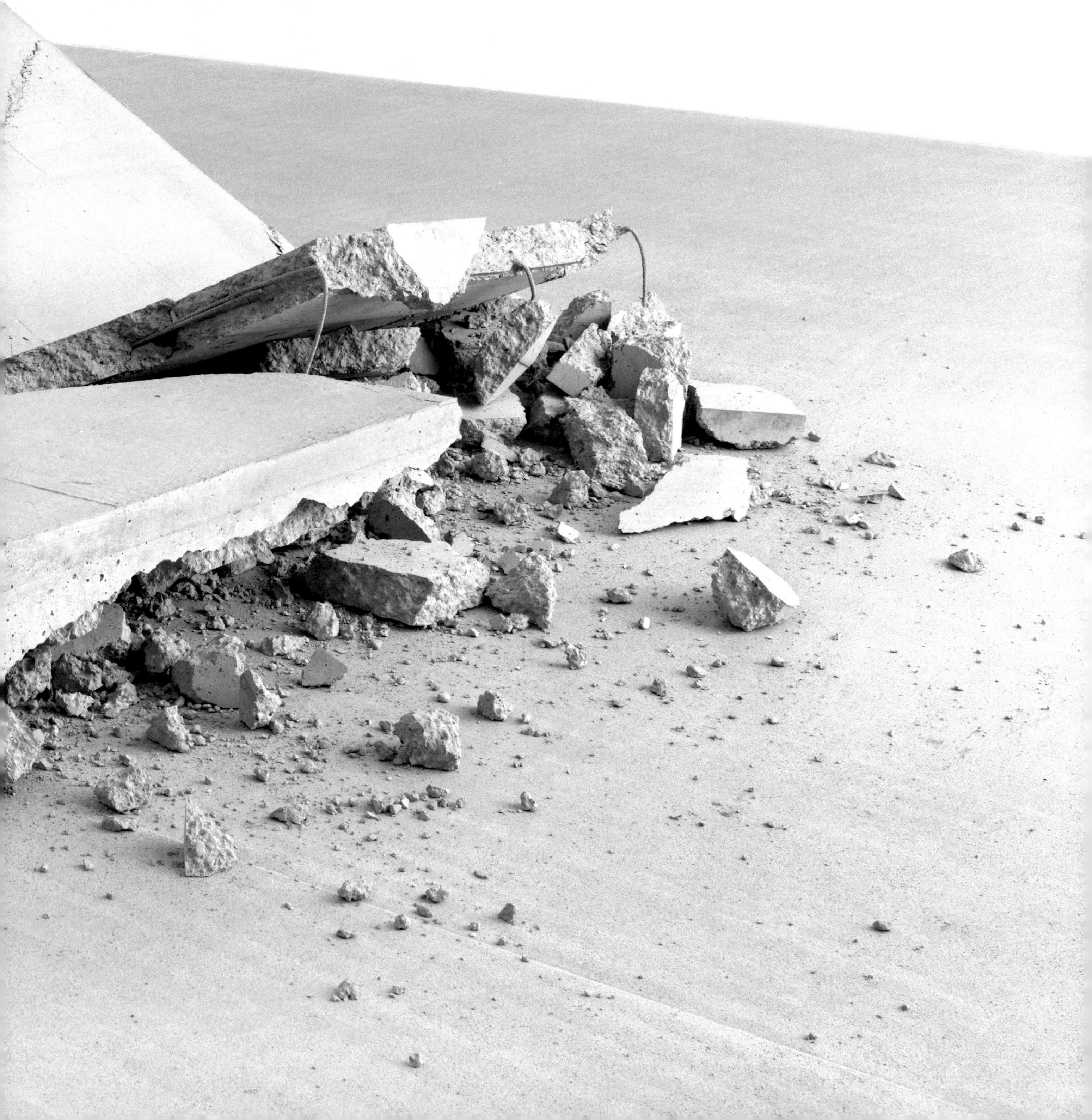

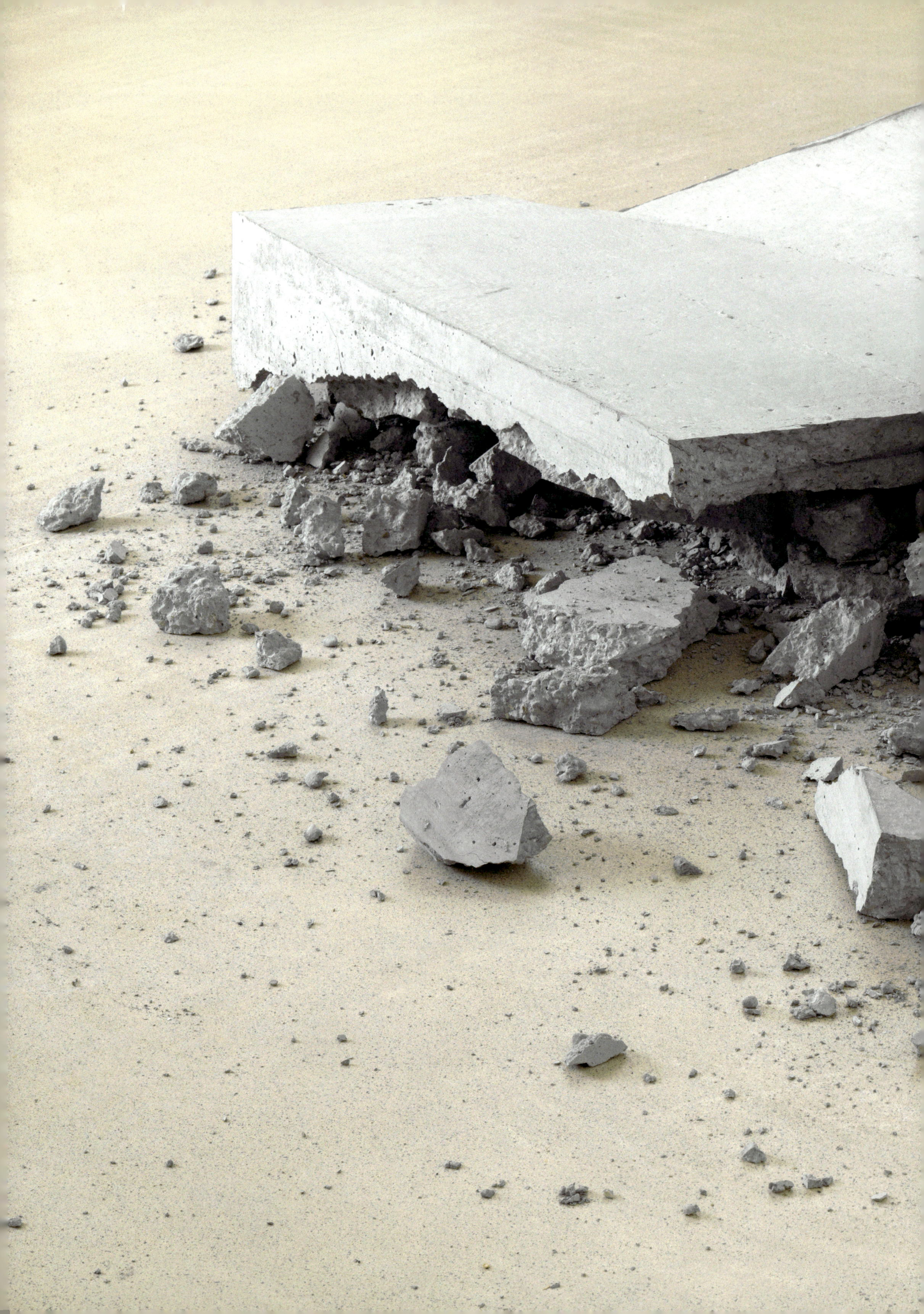

HEIKE MUNDER / THOMAS D. TRUMMER

Displaced Fractures

I

Das Widerstreben liegt in der Natur des Menschen und wahrscheinlich in jeder kulturellen Aktivität. Es bildet bei genauer Betrachtung sogar den Kern des Kulturellen. Wer sich widerspenstig zeigt, ist nicht nur aufmüpfig, sondern in besonderer Weise kulturell aktiv. Vor rund achtzig Jahren, um die Wende zum Jahr 1930, erschien in einem Wiener Fachverlag eine Schrift Sigmund Freuds, die dem Phänomen einen Namen gab: Der Titel *Das Unbehagen in der Kultur* inspirierte zahlreiche Modernitätstheoretiker in der Folgezeit zu immer neuen Abwandlungen. Längst haben so unterschiedliche Geister wie Jacob Taubes und Charles Taylor, Judith Butler und Nina Hagen ihre Variationen zum Thema Unbehagen geliefert. Das Original und seine ursprünglichen Absichten drohen im Reigen der Anspielungen verloren zu gehen. Tatsächlich setzte Freud mit seiner Schrift seine jahrelangen Bemühungen fort, die Wechselwirkungen zwischen individueller und kultureller Neurose aufzuweisen. Neu war die These, die bis in die Gegenwart brisant bleibt, dass neben dem herkömmlichen Interesse an der Individualneurose das Projekt einer «Pathogenese der kulturellen Gemeinschaften» Kontur gewann: Nicht nur Individuen leiden unter Repressionen, sondern auch soziale Gemeinschaften. Die Rede vom Unbehagen hatte eine Vorgeschichte, die Freud in Umrissen wohl geläufig gewesen sein muss. Bereits der englische Philosoph John Locke hatte Ende des 17. Jahrhunderts von «uneasiness» gesprochen und glaubte, damit den Antrieb menschlichen Handelns gefunden zu haben. Warum tun Menschen überhaupt etwas und nicht vielmehr nichts? Lockes Antwort baute auf einer Verbindung aus Mythos, Puritanismus und Anthropologie auf: weil ihnen nicht wohl ist dabei. Niemals ist der Mensch eins mit seiner Situation, und ausnahmslos ist er unfähig, wie Lockes Zeitgenosse Pascal schrieb, untätig in seinem Zimmer zu bleiben. Das Unbehagen ist das Motiv allen menschlichen Handelns; es ist die letzte und tiefste Begründung. Freuds Schrift greift diese Geschichte auf, verkehrt jedoch, vom Willensdenker Nietzsche inspiriert, ihre Moral ins Gegenteil. Einerseits ist Kultur eine Verfehlung des Menschlichen, weil sie die eigensinnige Triebwelt abspaltet; zugleich bedeutet sie die Erfüllung des Menschlichen, weil sie die Bewusstlosigkeit dieses Treibens aufweist. Kultur, so Freud, zähmt die Willensbekundungen der Individuen, um sie zugleich zu neuen Widerständen anzufachen. Kultur ist, so besehen, eine aus ihrer eigenen Mitte heraus bedrohte Einrichtung, die sich selbst herausfordert und als zutiefst fragwürdig begreift; Kunst ist nichts anderes als die Auflehnung gegen die eigene Etablierung.

II

Die Kunst besitzt seit jeher ein Sensorium für das Brüchige, Poröse und Fragile des Menschen. Die Bruchlinien des Menschlichen werden von den Künstlern dieser Ausstellung jedoch nicht direkt am Körper verhandelt, sondern an stellvertretenden Architekturen. Die Frakturen und Nahtstellen von Gebäuden bilden Metaphern für die Risse im menschlichen Dasein. Der titelgebende Begriff «displaced fractures» verschiebt diesen Gedanken zurück auf den Körper. Er entstammt der Medizin und bezeichnet das Phänomen, dass sich Bruchstellen von Knochen an anderer Stelle als an dem Ort der Hauptbelastung zeigen. Eine Verschiebung findet statt, Ursache und Wirkung trennen sich, weil Energien wie Symptome an fremder Stelle sichtbar werden. Weiter äussert sich dieser Gedanke in der Psychologie, wo es den Begriff des «displacement» gibt. «Verschiebung» bedeutet hier Übertragung, Verdrängung oder Sublimierung ebenso wie auch einen psychischen Abwehrmechanismus, um bedrohliche Tendenzen, die sich aus Trieben und Wünschen ergeben, zu bewältigen.

Die Installationen, Rauminterventionen und Skulpturen dieser Ausstellung arbeiten auf unterschiedlichen Ebenen mit dieser Verschiebung von Symptomen. Es dominiert dabei ein Spannungsfeld zwischen formverweigernden und monumentalen Gestaltungen, zwischen subjektiven und rational-formalen Gesten. In dieser Analogie zum Begriff «displaced fractures» bieten die an sich stabilen, jedoch auch der Zeitlichkeit unterworfenen Materialien des Bauens Projektionsflächen, auf denen sich Befindlichkeiten und Fragen nach dem Dasein ausagieren lassen. Schon bei flüchtigem Blick wird klar, dass Widerwille, Gegenstreben und energische Widerspenstigkeit zur Debatte stehen. Diese drücken sich in kommunikativen und skulpturalen Formbildungsprozessen aus, in denen die Übergänge von Materialzuständen und skulpturalen Dimensionen sichtbar werden. Alles liegt real vor uns und lässt unsere verschüttete Erfahrung und die Sensorien dafür, was Material ist und wozu Material symbolisch dienen kann, neu aktivieren. In der Übertragung von subjektiven Fragestellungen unserer Zeit auf das vermeintlich Feste zeigt sich in diesem Skulpturendiskurs das Prekäre der Gegenwart und wird greifbar. Das Formverweigernde, oft

Formlose, in dem schon Rosalind Krauss und Yve-Alain Bois ein Synonym des Verdrängten erkannten, wird in der Ausstellung zu einem der zentralen Themen. Die ausgestellten Werke zeigen die Strukturen des Architektonischen genauso wie die Spuren des Persönlichen. Es sind präzise Haltungen, in denen sich die formale Zuspitzung konkretisiert. Besonders der dynamische Einsatz von Farben und das Benutzen freier Formen prägen diese Eingriffe. Sie bezeugen die Anwesenheit des Menschlichen, um letztlich durch die freie und trotzige Handhabe die Verletzlichkeit der Jetztzeit und der Erinnerung anzudeuten.

III

Allen Werken gemeinsam ist das Einnehmen eines Raumes, eine voluminöse Besetzung, und der Hang, über Objekte subjektive Zustände abzurufen. Im Werk von Phyllida Barlow wird dies exemplarisch sichtbar: In ihren Arbeiten türmen sich rohe Materialien zu dichten Form-Clustern auf. Zum Teil zu Behausungen gebündelt, zeigen sie stets eine rohe physische Präsenz, die lange Zeit nicht nur der glatten Ästhetik des Minimalismus, sondern genauso der in den 1980er Jahren gängigen polierten Ästhetik eines Jeff Koons oder Haim Steinbach entgegenstand. Bei Barlow ist Kunst Präsenz und Konfliktplatz, grosse Architektur und einfaches Modell, monumentale Form und subjektive Inschrift zugleich. Begriffe wie «Existenz» und «Gefährdung», «Ich» und «Anderes», «Befindlichkeit» und «Dasein» werden in die Aktualität gebracht. Barlows Skulpturen sind trotz ihrer Massivität dennoch immer körperlich und damit anthropomorph. Es sind Formfindungen zwischen urbanem Requisit und autonomer Gestalt, zwischen Architektur und Oberfläche. Wir sehen abgeschlossene, in sich ruhende Skulpturen, in denen auf menschlicher Erfahrung aufbauende Spannungsverhältnisse mit jenen des Materials parallelisiert werden. Man kann vielleicht von einer Neupositionierung der individuellen Subjektkonstruktion innerhalb des skulpturalen Diskurses sprechen, die Skulptur wieder thematisch werden lässt, indem Kategorien wie Grösse, Gestalt, Form und Formlosigkeit freigelegt werden. Alle diese Begriffe werden radikal befragt, wobei die hier besprochenen Künstler und Künstlerinnen eine Individuation im Gegenständlichen suchen, um persönlichen und allgemein menschlichen Bedingungen, Leben und Lebenswillen im Werk eine entsprechende Gestalt zu geben.

IV

Oscar Tuazons Werk verhandelt das Spannungsverhältnis von Architektur und Natur, das sich im Zerfall des öffentlichen Raums zeigt. Die Essenz dieser Auseinandersetzung überführt er mittels einer reduzierten architektonischen Sprache in den Ausstellungsraum und benutzt dazu einfache Baumaterialien, die er in ein physisches Spannungsverhältnis zueinander stellt. Die rechteckige Skulptur mit dem signifikanten Titel *I want to put something inside my body and carry something in it. I want to get inside my body and get carried in it, I'd like to get buried in it, put my head in it and get in it, I'm not scared of it.* (2010), aus einem Metallrahmen bestehend, in den eine mit Wasser gefüllte Plache gespannt ist, hängt knapp unter der Raumdecke. Diese Struktur wirkt zweckdienlich und dennoch fehl am Platz, weil es in einen Ausstellungsraum installiert wurde, um durch blosse Anwesenheit zu irritieren. Stets verkeilen sich verschiedenartige Elemente theatralisch und lassen eine Bühnensituation im Raum entstehen, die den Blick auf Details lenkt, die sonst nicht sichtbar sind. Tuazon lässt im Ausstellungsraum eine zweite innere Struktur wachsen, wobei zwei Ebenen gegeneinanderstehen: jene des Inneren, die sich einnistet, und jene des Äusseren, die ummantelt. Um die Brüchigkeit des Daseins aufzuzeigen, bedarf es der Übertragung in das Material. Am deutlichsten wird dies in einem schweren Tisch aus Beton mit dem poetischen Titel *I use my body for something, I use it to make something, I make something with my body, whatever that is. I make something and I pay for it and I get paid for it.* (2010). Der Tisch knickt an seinem Standbein ein, zerbricht, zerfällt zu Schotter und Sand und hält sich nur auf einer Seite kärglich aufrecht. Sein bröckelndes Material ist industriearchäologischer Rest, mithin Bestandteil einer alltagstypischen Architektur und ein unlebendiger Körper, der stellvertretend für einen lebendigen steht. An Modellbauten, die hier für die Analogisierung von Ding und Ich stehen, wird die Metamorphisierung des Gegenständlichen erprobt. Denn es gilt, die Beschädigung zu zeigen, den augenscheinlichen Zerfall der Setzung, den Widerstand des Materials dem eigenen Zugriff gegenüber, um Affektivität und physische Objektivierung sichtbar werden zu lassen. Was im Material angedeutet ist, wird im Titel wiederholt und elaboriert. Das eigene körperliche Tun wird eingebunden in den alltäglichen Kreislauf kapitalistischer Wertschöpfung und Verwertung. Hier verdichten sich Körperlichkeit, Subjektivität und Gesellschaft zu einer poetischen, aber auch lakonisch-widerständigen Darstellung sozialer Gefüge und ihrer ihnen innewohnenden Konsequenzen. Manche dieser künstlerischen Verdichtungsorte scheinen daher wie Schmerzsammelstellen des Ichs, andere wie entleerte Ruinen kollektiv abgespalteter Sehnsucht. Um eine solche Unfertigkeit, Unentschiedenheit und damit auch Möglichkeitsform zu erreichen, wie es im Werk von Tuazon aufscheint, braucht es den Willen zum Widerstand gegen die eigene Zielwahl. Darum das auffällige Seinlassen der Dinge in einer künstlerischen Arbeitsweise, die prozesshaft ist und die Eigendynamik des Materials zur Geltung bringen möchte.

V

Ein derartiger Umgang mit Material kann als Impuls verstanden werden, der die Kräfte, die den verwendeten Stoffen innewohnen, aktiviert. In den Werken von Klaus Winichner dient das Material dazu, seinem Bewusstsein eine Form nach aussen zu geben, damit es eine dreidimensionale Ausdehnung erlange. Über das Aufhäufen von Stoffen bringt er des Weiteren das Ruinöse des Jetzt zur Geltung. In verschiedenen Gattungen wie Skulptur, Gemälde und Zeichnung verbindet Winichner das menschliche Porträt – seines oder aus seiner Umgebung – mit dem skulpturalen Diskurs, wobei er in seiner Auseinandersetzung mit der Skulptur oftmals industrielle Baumaterialien oder Bauschutt verwendet. Die sinnbildlichen Porträts entstehen nicht nur durch Figuration, sondern durch fragmentarische Architekturen, die das Menschliche repräsentieren. Es sind abstrakte Assemblagen, die aus teilweise vom Künstler bearbeiteten Matratzen, Büchern, Blumentrögen und amorphen Materialien zusammengesetzt sind. Diese oft raumfüllenden skulpturalen Konglomerate wirken wie Hinterlassenschaften des menschlichen Daseins. Charakteristisch in dieser Auseinandersetzung um die Form ist ein «terror perpetuus», eine fortdauernde Unruhe und innere Erregbarkeit, die das fertige Kunstwerk nicht in die Autonomie verheissende Freiheit entlässt. Jeder Abschluss, jede Vollendung würde den Sieg entweder der Substanz oder der formenden Kraft bedeuten. Charakteristisch will Winichner beides vermeiden – auch die Überlegenheit seiner eigenen Hand. Eine Beherrschung des Materials wäre nichts anderes als die Prozesshaftigkeit einer Kunst, das lebendige, widerständige Geschehen zu einem unbefriedigenden Endpunkt zu führen.

VI

Winichners Werk steht in Bezug zur alten, gleichsam vorsokratischen Skulptur. Es geht um Statik, bildhauerische Kraft, Selbstständigkeit, Autorität und Realismus. Die abgegriffenen und verstaubten Bücher, die Winichner auf Flohmärkten erwirbt und die sich häufig der klassischen Figur widmen, geben eine Ahnung davon, wie sehr er das eigene Tun in eine sowohl bildhauerische wie auch intellektuelle Tradition eingeschrieben sieht. Sie sind in diesem Werk Kommentare auf die lange Geschichte der Plastik, deren Rolle als Standbild und öffentliches Denkmal, ihren Nutzen zur Repräsentation und Ehrfurchtsbezeugung. Ganz anders verfährt Ulrich Rückriem: Handwerkliche Präzision und ein ausgeprägtes plastisches Bewusstsein bestimmen sein von Monumentalität und Formalismus geprägtes Werk. Er nimmt Ideen und Vorgehensweisen der amerikanischen Minimal und Concept Art auf, wobei er jedoch ein eigenständiges Werk schafft. Geschlossene Steinblöcke werden zersägt oder mit Bohrungen versehen, um an Haarrissen, Schnittkanten und Bruchlinien Erinnerung und Geschichtlichkeit skulptural ablesbar zu machen. Der Prozess der Arbeit und das vorhergehende Konzept dazu stehen für Rückriem dabei im Zentrum. Was sich im Gewaltakt des Schneidens, Brechens und Bohrens anzeigt, gilt auch für die Sprache und ihre Bedeutung. Wer sich anmasst, diese stille Volumen zum Sprechen zu zwingen, hat ihre Eigenart sinnwidrig zu Verständnis gebracht.

Rückriems Skulpturen finden bis heute ihre Platzierung auf vielen öffentlichen Plätzen – sie sind längst Bestandteil nachkriegsdeutscher Identität geworden. Oft als Mahnmal oder Denkmal konzipiert, sprechen diese Steine von einer Geschichte gesellschaftlichen Handelns – um dabei vollkommen erstarrt im Weg zu liegen. Tatsächlich entsteht die ästhetische Kraft dieser Skulpturen allein durch die Anwesenheit des unbehaglich Kraftvollen. Der Widerstand des Steins bleibt sichtbar und körperlich erfahrbar.

VII

Kilian Rüthemann setzt sich in seinen Arbeiten mit den architektonischen Eigenschaften eines Ausstellungsortes auseinander. Die Ästhetik seines Werks ist bestimmt durch das Freilegen von Strukturen und der Suche nach dem Labilen und Fragilen im scheinbar Feststehenden. Im Versuch, den Räumen eine bisher ungesehene Poetik zu entlocken, greift er zu brachialen Mitteln – etwa wenn er auf einer Treppe einen zusätzlichen Betonboden ausschüttet, der das Begehen wesentlich unbequemer macht. Rüthemann betreibt Materialstudien, die Widerständigkeit hervortreten lassen und somit auch erforschen. Die Form gehorcht bei Rüthemann einer strengen Organisation. Das ungehemmte Vorwärts gibt es bei ihm nicht, dafür aber kinetische Momente und damit auch Verschiebung und «displacement». Für das Istituto Svizzero in Rom hatte Rüthemann 2009 einen Sarkophag aus Schaumstoff entworfen, der im Aussenraum ausgestellt wurde und der auch im migros museum für gegenwartskunst zu sehen sein wird. Die Verwitterung nimmt dem Material die einheitliche Farbe, lässt ihn wie ein antikes Erbe erscheinen. Rüthemann spielt hier mit der Wirkung der Erosion des Materials. Zugleich wird damit das Werk aus der Autorität des Erschaffers entlassen. Bemoosung und braune Feuchtigkeitsschäden sind Wirkungen des Wetters und zeichnen das Objekt. Das Material, das in die Selbstständigkeit entlassen wird, bildet eigensinnige Reaktionen. Das Grab ist Inbegriff der Kultur, der Anwesenheit und Glaubensfähigkeit von Menschen. Folgerichtig scheint aus dem Kunststoff Natur zu werden, das zeitgenössische Objekt wird so zum sinnbildlichen Relikt der altehrwürdigen heroischen römischen Geschichte.

Wie Rüthemann erprobt Emilie Ding Materialverhältnisse in einer minimalistischen Sprache. Ihr Arbeiten ist den Kunstvorstellungen Rüthemanns durchaus verwandt. Was bei Rüthemann das Spiel mit der Spannkraft des Materials ist, das ist bei Ding die Wertschätzung und der Einsatz der Kante. Am Zuschnitt zeigen sich die Dinge, die den Diskurs des amerikanischen Minimalismus fortsetzen. Ding platziert markante Formelemente, *Erased* (2008–2010), in denen sich stets eine Gebrauchsfähigkeit andeutet, auf dem Ausstellungsboden. Es sind Betonstücke, die – gewinkelt und mit stählernen Bolzen versehen – wie Scharniere, Stützelemente oder Versatzstücke von Architekturen aussehen. Nicht nur die Verbindungen fehlen – auch ihre Funktion bleibt unerklärlich. Anordnung und Zuschnitt dieser Blöcke bilden eine Auseinandersetzung mit formalen Diskursen. Ding verbindet hier einen Diskurs über die menschliche Existenz – disparat, vereinzelt, bedroht – mit einer technischen Debatte, wobei Existenz und Individualität überstiegen und infrage gestellt werden. Das geschieht durch die massive Materialität und Grösse der Betonskulpturen wie auch durch ihre angedeutete, nicht enden wollende Serialität. Die ursprüngliche Aggressivität der Betonskulpturen wird neutralisiert, indem sich die einzelnen Objekte scheinbar natürlich in den bestehenden Raum einfügen und damit den Diskurs auf einer abstrakt-geistigen Ebene erst möglich machen.

VIII

Architektur, so wäre zu zeigen, entsteht, wenn Objekte raumumschliessende Grössenordnungen erreichen und ebenso betret- wie bewohnbar sind. Im Unterschied zur Skulptur ist Architektur begehbar, vermittelt Schutz, Umhausung, Deckung. In ihrem 16-mm-Film *Palast* (2004) zeigt Tacita Dean Aufnahmen vom «Palast der Republik». Ohne eine Gesamtansicht des Berliner Gebäudes zu vermitteln, konzentriert sich Dean auf seine Oberflächenphänomene, seine sinnlich-poetische Erscheinungsqualität. Spiegelungen in getönten Scheiben, goldschimmernde Reflexionen und das warme Licht der Abendsonne stehen im Kontrast mit der aufragenden und stolzen Erscheinung der Domkuppel in unmittelbarer Nachbarschaft. Dean filmt einen Palast, dessen Zerstörung kurz bevorsteht und heute schon vollzogen ist. Das DDR-Gebäude wird nach Senatsbeschluss durch die Rekonstruktion des Wilhelminischen Berliner Stadtschlosses ersetzt. Dean, wie viele andere, ist zwiespältig gegenüber einem sich neu erhebenden Herrschaftsanspruch. In Deans Betrachtung klingt eine präsumptive Trauerarbeit an, die in langsamen Bilderfolgen entfaltet wird. Das Wissen um den zukünftigen Verlust und um geschichtsmächtige Entscheidungen erzeugt jenes charakteristische Unbehagen, das nicht die Kultur qua ihrer Existenz sich zuschulden kommen lässt, sondern durch die undurchschaubare Macht einer Entscheidung, die – um Neues herzustellen – das Alte rekonstruiert, modifiziert und dem Jüngeren vorziehen muss. Das Gebäude hat ein Verfallsdatum. Darin ist es einem Bewusstsein ähnlich, welches sich selbst im Modus der Verfallenheit wahrnimmt. Das Motiv des Widerwillens tritt hier als Nostalgie auf, solange es sich nach einem Vorwärts richtet, welches sentimentalisch das Jetzt noch erinnert. Es tritt auf als Empörung, wenn es sich gegen eine Zukunft richtet, die unausweichlich ist. Die Bewertung von kultureller Geschichte als politischem Zeichen setzt Dean jedoch nicht als lautstarkes Demonstrationswerk, sondern als stille Elegie um.

IX

Die explosive Kraft der Widerspenstigkeit tritt am Deutlichsten im Werk von Klara Lidén zutage. Architektur ist eine Ordnungsmacht, an deren Funktionieren oder Scheitern sich die Künstlerin reibt. Sie zementiert das Sittliche und Übliche, verdeckt Leidenschaften und Menschliches. Anders als bei Dean ist sie bei Lidén nicht Behausung und Schutzraum, sondern ein entfremdeter Horror Vacui. Lidén nimmt den öffentlichen Raum durch seltsam deplatziert wirkende körperliche Handlungen ein, wenn sie sich tanzend in eine U-Bahn begibt oder einen «Moonwalk» in den Strassen New Yorks aufführt. In ihrem Werk *Position 0310* (2010) – einer Reihe von vier Videos – klammert sich die Künstlerin wie ein Tier an öffentliche Säulen oder Gasrohre. Sie hält still in Totenstarre. Allein der Verkehr rundum sagt dem Videobeschauer, dass es sich nicht um Standbilder handelt. Irritation und Aufbegehren gegen Regulierungen des öffentlichen Lebens sind dabei stets kennzeichnend. Lidén fertigt Installationen aus vorgefundenen Materialien wie Karton oder abgerissenen Plakatpapieren an. Die Zusammenstellungen ähneln den historischen Déchirures und sprechen die Sprache der Auflehnung gegen Material und Umwelt. Anti-autoritär, appellativ, unbeirrbar die Gelegenheit zum Widerstand ergreifend, stemmt sich die Künstlerin gegen die Superiorität des Seienden, des vermeintlich Realen. Das Unheilvolle der modernen, urbanen Welt erprobt Lidén am eigenen Körper.

X

Derzeit macht sich eine aufgestaute Ausdrucksenergie gegen morsche Versachlichungstaktiken Luft, der in dieser Ausstellung Rechnung getragen wird. Nicht die Dinge *an sich*, sondern *für sich* sprechen lassen – das ist die Reformforderung der Gegenwart. Es geht weder darum, über eine Eingemeindung der Kunst in die Wissenschaften deren Ansehen zu steigern noch über sorgfältige Sinnlichkeitsdrainagen den Wert der Worte anzuzeigen, sondern andere, vielfältigere und brennende Produktionsenergien zur Entladung zu bringen. Kunst möchte Entrüstungsgebärden setzen, Widersprüche zeigen, vielleicht sogar Ding- und Selbstbeschädigung forcieren, auf jeden Fall eine Zuspitzung im Entscheidungsfall suchen. Expressionistische Höhen und quälerische Tiefen, Grosses und Kleines, Soziales und Elementares, Selbsterhaltung und -entäusserung werden aufgerufen, jedoch nicht im Ausgleichsbestreben, sondern im dramatischen Wettstreit. Folgerichtig findet sich in den Skulpturen, was begrifflich im Widerwillen nicht deutlicher gesagt werden könnte. Wer baut, der bezieht den Zerfall ein, wer aufrichtet, den Niedergang, wer auffaltet, die Erosion des eigenen Strebens. In den Arbeiten spiegeln sich Brüchigkeiten, Risse und prekäre Zustände, Mut ebenso wie Resignation, Wehrhaftes und Schwäche-Eingeständnis, Gestaltungsdrang und Trümmererfahrung. Relikte klassischer Bildhauerei werden zu einem unbewusst-bewussten Zeichen, das unsere eigenen Assoziationen und Befindlichkeiten mit den Zusammenhängen und Entitäten unserer Welt in eine bodenständige Abhängigkeit bringt.

KARSTEN HARRIES

Vom Widerwillen gegen Architektur oder Die Antinomie des Seins

Der Titel bedarf einer Erklärung: Wie ist dieser Widerwille gegen Architektur zu verstehen? Eine erste Antwort gibt schon der Titel dieser Ausstellung: *Displaced Fractures – Über die Bruchlinien von Architekturen und ihren Körpern* und die Werke der hier vertretenen Künstler: Immer wieder kommt es zu Eingriffen in und Angriffen auf die vorgegebene Architektur. Was sich hier zeigt, ist ein gerade heute weit verbreitetes Unbehagen an Architekturen aller Art.

Warum aber ein solches Unbehagen? Träumen wir nicht alle von einem behaglichen Zuhause? Ist es nicht Aufgabe der Architektur, uns diese Welt wohnlich einzurichten? Und gilt das nicht auch von den Begriffsarchitekturen, die uns Sprache und Vernunft bauen? Kant meinte, die menschliche Vernunft sei ihrer Natur nach architektonisch. Warum dann dieser scheinbar unnatürliche Widerwille gegen Architektur, dieser Zug zum Zerbrechlichen, dieses Spiel mit Rissen und Brüchen, gerade in unserer Zeit, die den Dekonstruktivismus zur akademischen Mode werden liess – einer Mode, die sich von der Philosophie schnell auf die Geisteswissenschaften und die Kunst, überraschenderweise sogar auf die Architektur ausbreitete. Richtungweisend war hier die Ausstellung *Deconstructivist Architecture,* kuratiert von Mark Wigley und Philipp Johnson, die das Museum of Modern Art in New York 1988 veranstaltete. (1) Der Katalog sprach vom «Aufkommen einer neuen Gesinnung, fasziniert von den Möglichkeiten, Architektur zu infizieren, zu unterbrechen, zu vergewaltigen, zu untergraben». Dieser Gesinnung entspricht eine gegen die tradierte Architektur gerichtete Architektur, eine Anti-Architektur also, die in der heutigen Architekturwelt, in Theorie und Praxis, durchaus eine beachtliche Rolle spielt, so zum Beispiel im Werk von Frank Gehry, Zaha Hadid, Peter Eisenman, Daniel Libeskind, Rem Koolhaas, und Coop Himmelb(l)au, den in jener Ausstellung gefeierten Architekten. In diese Richtung geht auch die Arbeit der hier ausgestellten Künstler.

Haben wir es nur mit einer vielleicht bald vorüberziehenden Mode zu tun? Warum gerade heute? Das heisst aber auch: nicht nur heute! So ist es Kain, der die erste Stadt erbaut haben soll, und das erste Werk der Architektur, das die Bibel erwähnt, ist der babylonische Turm. Schon hier spüren wir etwas vom Widerwillen gegen Architektur, der zwar besonders zeitgemäss zu sein scheint, aber eine Geschichte hat, die zeigt, das ihn etwas nährt, das uns Menschen als Menschen bedrängt.

Von Anfang an begleitet ein gegen sie gerichteter Protest die Architektur. Das Paradies hatte kein Haus nötig: In diesem Garten waren Adam und Eva schon zu Hause. Nun verlor uns der Sündenfall, dieses den Menschen befreiende Erwachen unserer Vernunft, diese Heimat. Aber erlaubt uns nicht eben diese Vernunft, für das Verlorene Ersatz zu schaffen? Und so träumten schon Bacon und Descartes von einer Wissenschaft und Technik, die es uns erlauben würden, den uns verwehrten Weg ins Paradies dennoch zurückzugehen. Dies blieb der Traum der Aufklärung, und diesem Traum verdankt auch unsere Welt ihre Gestalt. Gibt es eine vernünftige Alternative?

Aber wird die Vernunft hier nicht überfordert? Der Lehre des babylonischen Turms folgend, dass kein menschliches Wollen uns unsere wahre Heimat einräumen kann, versetzten so Maler wie Hans Baldung Grien oder Albrecht Altdorfer die Geburt Christi in irgendeine fantastische Ruinenarchitektur: Ist eine Ruine nicht ein passenderer Ort für die Geburt des Erlösers, der der Zeit ihren Stachel, der Hölle ihren Sieg nehmen soll, als die Architektur, die uns unsere Vernunft baut?

Die Überzeugung, dass das Haus, das uns die Vernunft gebaut hat, ein wirkliches Wohnen nicht erlaubt, hat den von Nietzsche proklamierten Tod Gottes überlebt. Etwas tief in uns ist unzufrieden mit den geistigen und gebauten Räumen, die uns unsere Vernunft eingeräumt hat, erfährt Angriffe auf diese Architektur als Befreiung. Und solche Unzufriedenheit fühlt sich angesprochen vom Zerbrechlichen und Brüchigen, fühlt sich zu Hause in Ruinen, die uns das «mysterium tremendum et fascinans» der Natur, des Raumes und der Zeit, erfahren lassen. Bedeutsam ist der Entschluss, Ruinen nicht nur zu malen, sondern zu bauen. Ein frühes deutsches Beispiel ist die Magdalenenklause im Nymphenburger Park (1725–28) mit ihren Rissen und ihrem abgebröckelten Putz. Gerade das 18. Jahrhundert, das Zeitalter der Aufklärung, liebte solche Ruinen. Wie es der Dekonstruktivismus und wie es diese Ausstellung zeigt, hat das Ruinöse seine Anziehungskraft behalten. Zeigt sich hier so etwas wie das schlechte Gewissen unserer von der architektonischen Vernunft gestalteten Lebenswelt?

Dazu ein paar Worte aus dem gegen die «90-grädigen Ecken von Wien» gerichteten Ausstellungs-Pamphlet des 2000 verstorbenen Wiener Malers und Architekten Hundert-

1 Philip Johnson, Mark Wigley, *Deconstructivist Architecture*, New York 1988.

wasser: «Dass man 1920 das Trottoir und die Hauswände glatt macht, war notwendig, doch 1957 ist es Wahnsinn, den ich nicht begreife. Die Bombenwürfe von 1943 waren perfekte automatische Formenlehre, die gerade Linie und deren leere Gebilde sollten zerquetscht und zermörsert werden, wurden es auch. Im Anschluss daran hätte normalerweise ein Transautomatismus einsetzen sollen ... Doch man baut Würfel, Würfel! Wo bleibt das Gewissen...» (2) In dieser zugegeben rhetorisch übertriebenen und verspielten Bejahung der Zerstörung von Architektur durch die Bomben des 2. Weltkriegs ist der Widerwille gegen Architektur, besonders gegen die funktionale Architektur des 19. und 20. Jahrhunderts, offenkundig. Hundertwasser versucht, uns zu einem natürlicheren Leben zurückzurufen: So lesen wir im «Verschimmelungs-Manifest», das er 1958 in der Abtei Seckau sprach: «Wenn sich an einer Rasierklinge der Rost festsetzt, wenn eine Wand zu schimmeln beginnt, wenn in einer Zimmerdecke das Moos wächst und die geometrischen Winkel abrundet, so soll man sich doch freuen, dass mit den Mikroben und Schwämmen das Leben in das Haus einzieht und wir so mehr bewusst als jemals zuvor Zeugen von architektonischen Veränderungen werden, von denen wir viel zu lernen haben.» (3) Hat uns unsere Vernunft nicht uns selbst entfremdet? Hier kehrt sich der Widerwille gegen Architektur gegen den Rationalismus. Ihn nährt ein Heimweh, das in Rissen und Brüchen, Rost und Schimmel, Spuren des verlorenen Paradieses findet.

Aber den Widerwillen gegen Architektur nährt auch ein entgegengesetztes Fernweh, dass Gebautes nicht der Natur, sondern der Freiheit öffnen will. Ein gutes Beispiel bietet das Werk von Lebbeus Woods. Woods hat der vielversprechenden Karriere, die ihm seine Mitarbeit mit dem Architekten Eero Saarinen eröffnet hatte, den Rücken gekehrt, um sich als «Anarchitekt» zu betätigen, sich ein Wort aneignend, das wir zuerst bei dem englischen Architekten Robin Evans finden – ein Wort in dessen Namen dann Gordon Matta-Clark, der – wie mit einem Beil – ein verwahrlostes Haus aufspaltete, 1973 in New York eine Künstlergruppe um sich versammelte. Und sind nicht auch die hier ausgestellten Künstler Anarchitekten?

Woods ist ein Schöpfer von Raumfantasien, die die uns vertraute Architektur angreifen, indem sie zum Beispiel fantastische Gebilde in sie eindringen oder polypenartig umarmen lassen. Heute sind solche Fantasien nicht unerwartet: Hat Bataille uns nicht gelehrt, Architektur mit den uns unseren Platz anweisenden Stimmen von Priestern, Königen, Bürgern, Kapitalisten, und Polizisten zu verbinden? Hier ist es nicht das Denken an die allzu oft vergewaltigte Natur, die den Widerwillen gegen Architektur nährt, sondern eine Freiheit, der die Technik bislang ungeahnte Möglichkeiten eröffnet hat. Ist es uns heute nicht möglich, uns eine Umwelt zu schaffen, die ganz anders unseren dauernd sich ändernden Nöten und Verlangen entspricht als die allzu fest eingeräumte Umwelt, die unser Erbe ist? Die Utopien, die solche Möglichkeiten versprechen, müssen den Ruf nach einer ortsgebundenen Architektur, die das Primat der Natur oder das der dem Körper und somit der Schwere unterworfenen Lebenswelt protestlos anerkennt, als unerträglich rückwärtsblickend ablehnen, allzu bereit, sich mit leblosen Imitationen der Platz und Ort stiftenden Architektur einer nicht zu wiederholenden Vergangenheit zu begnügen. Und so nennt sich Woods einen Feind der Schwerkraft und erklärt ihr den Krieg. Ihrem arroganten Anspruch, sein Leben zu beherrschen, stellt er seinen eigenen Anspruch entgegen, ein freier, autonomer, sich selbst bestimmender Geist zu sein.

Woods steht mit diesem Anspruch durchaus nicht allein. In seiner Kriegserklärung kommt ein Verlangen zum Ausdruck, das schon die Aufklärung kennt. So zeigt sich uns schon Ledoux mit seinem sphärischen Haus als Feind der Schwerkraft. Der Enthusiasmus, mit dem die Architekten der Aufklärung gerade die Kugel aufgriffen, ist im Grunde derselbe Enthusiasmus, der in dieser Revolutionszeit die ersten Ballons grüsste. «Die Luftbälle sind», so Helmut Reinicke, «die erste Erfindung, an die sich der Begriff einer Weltrevolution knüpft. Der Ballon fährt in den Himmel – als Zeichen, dass die Vernunft auf der Erde um sich greift. Eine solche Revolution ... hat dieses Subjektive, dass die Menschen sich finden, sich selber ein menschliches Gepräge geben wollen; diese Subjektivität ist das Göttliche der Religionen. Der Angriff auf diese ist die grösste Vermessenheit und dadurch Befreiung. Das Luftschiff ist eine derart praktische Vermessenheit: der Mensch

2 Hundertwasser, «Verschimmelungs-Manifest gegen den Rationalismus in der Architektur», in: Ulrich Conrads, *Programme und Manifeste der Architektur des 20. Jahrhunderts*, Berlin, Frankfurt am Main, Wien 1964, S. 149.
3 Ebd.

hat gezeigt, dass er über Grenzen schreiten kann. Er hat damit die Allmacht der Götterwelt eingeholt.» (4)

Verwandte Ideen sollten die architektonische Praxis der Moderne mitbestimmen. So forderten Architekten wie Theo Van Doesburg, Le Corbusier oder Mies van der Rohe von der Architektur ein schwimmendes oder schwebendes Aussehen. Das Gebaute sollte, soweit es die Konstruktion erlaubt, der Schwerkraft zu widersprechen scheinen. Computer Aided Design erlaubt es heute dieser Forderung, auf ungeahnte Weise zu genügen. Eine Geisteshaltung, die die Menschen von allen platzanweisenden Architekturen befreien möchte, findet hier ihren Ausdruck. Der sich in immer wieder andere Bilder kleidende Traum vom verlorenen Paradies will nicht verschwinden. Aber gerade solche Achitekturen reizen zum Widerspruch. Träumen wir nicht alle, wie Gaston Bachelard meinte, von einem gemütlichen Haus, das wirkliche Geborgenheit verspricht, von einem natürlicheren Leben, von der Heimat, die uns in der Erinnerung manchmal ruft und die es doch so nie gegeben hat, wenn wir auch vielleicht in einem Bauernhof des 18. Jahrhunderts deren Metapher erfahren. Dem Traumhaus entspricht die Traumstadt, gedacht vielleicht im Bilde von Messkirch, mit schattigen Erkern, verträumten Madonnenbildern an den Häuserecken, rauschenden Brunnen. Es ist dies ein Traum, der auch heute noch immer wieder unser Bauen und Wohnen mitgestaltet. Beispiele sind leicht zu finden, auch in Amerika. So versucht heute ein so erfolg- und einflussreicher Architekt wie Robert Stern diesen Traum mit Projekten wie *Celebration* in Florida Wirklichkeit werden zu lassen. Und ebendiesem Traum dient auch der, rein finanziell betrachtet, vielleicht erfolgreichste Maler im heutigen Amerika, der sich selbst so bezeichnende «Painter of Light», Maler des Lichts: Thomas Kinkade. Nicht nur zeigt er uns in seinen Bildern immer wieder Glück versprechende Häuser, wie wir sie vielleicht in Weihnachtsgrüssen erwarten. Ein Bauunternehmer verspricht jetzt sogar, diesen Traum Wirklichkeit werden zu lassen und so den Traum vom eigentlichen Wohnen zu erfüllen.

Kitsch ist relativ harmlos, solange es bei hübschen Bildern bleibt, in die Menschen, denen ihre Wirklichkeit nicht genügt, sich von Zeit zu Zeit flüchten können. Aber Kitsch verliert seine Harmlosigkeit, wenn er versucht, die Wirklichkeit zu umarmen – so, wenn Architektur Kitschvisionen in gebaute Architektur übersetzt. Und Kitsch wird wirklich gefährlich, wo er zu einer das Leben formenden Macht wird. Was hier zu kurz kommt, ist unsere Freiheit. Heimweh droht alles Fernweh und damit unsere Menschlichkeit zu ersticken.

Nun ist Freiheit oft schwer zu ertragen. Und ebendies führt zu Träumen von einer uns unseren Platz anweisenden Architektur. Solch Träumern versprach einst der Kitsch-Künstler und Architekt Adolf Hitler, sie von der Last ihrer Freiheit zu befreien: «Die Vorsehung hat mich zu dem grössten Befreier der Menschheit vorbestimmt. Ich befreie den Menschen von dem Zwange eines Selbstzweck gewordenen Geistes, von den schmutzigen und erniedrigenden Selbstpeinigungen einer Gewissen und Moral genannten Chimäre und von den Ansprüchen einer Freiheit und persönlichen Selbständigkeit, denen immer nur ganz wenige gewachsen sein können.» (5) Wie es uns auch die ästhetische Praxis so mancher Kunst- und Architekturschule jener Jahre zeigen kann, war dies kein vereinzeltes oder eitles Versprechen. Auch Nietzsches Traum von einer Gesellschaft stiftenden Architektur ist ein Traum von architektonischer Praxis als Errichten eines neuen babylonischen Turms. Dem Bauhaus war dieser Traum nicht eben fremd. Heidegger träumte ihn – auch er, wie der Nationalsozialismus, an das griechische Vorbild denkend. Und war es nicht von Anfang an Aufgabe der Architektur, nicht nur dem Körper, sondern auch der Seele Obdach zu geben und dem Menschen seinen Platz anzuweisen? Ist es nicht diese ethische Funktion, die die Architektur über alles bloss funktionale Bauen erhebt?

Angesichts solcher den Menschen ihren platzanweisenden Architekturen wird der Widerwille gegen Architektur verständlich. Im Verlangen, Architektur «zu infizieren, zu unterbrechen, zu vergewaltigen, zu untergraben» meldet sich eine Freiheit, die sich weigert, irgendeine vorgegebene Ordnung, sei sie ethisch, moralisch, religiös oder architektonisch, anzuerkennen. So kann es nicht überraschen,

4 Helmut Reinicke, *Aufstieg und Revolution. Über die Beförderung irdischer Freiheitsneigungen durch Ballonfahrt und Luftschwimmkunst*, Berlin 1988, S. 76–77.

5 Hermann Rauschning, «Gespräche mit Hitler», in: *Die Bildenden Künste im Dritten Reich*. Eine Dokumentation von Joseph Wulf, Hamburg 1966, S. 12.

dass dem heute wieder entdeckten Georges Bataille das Gefängnis zum paradigmatischen Architekturwerk werden sollte. Architektur, so heisst es, sperrt ein und verdient es deshalb, zerstört zu werden, auch wenn durch solche Zerstörung Chaos und Bestialität droht. «Es ist evident», so Bataille, «dass Monumente gutes gesellschaftliches Benehmen und oft sogar wirkliche Furcht auslösen.» Die Erstürmung der Bastille wurde ihm zum Symbol dieses Zusammenhangs: «Diese Massenbewegung lässt sich schwer anders erklären als durch die gegen die es beherrschenden Monumente gerichtete Feindschaft des Volkes.» [6] Aber zugegeben, dass monumentale Architektur manchmal gutes Benehmen mit sich bringt. Heisst das auch, dass sie es deshalb verdient, abgeschafft zu werden? Leidet unsere Welt an einem Überfluss von gutem Benehmen? Sollten wir, um einer grösseren Freiheit willen, ins Labyrinth zurückkehren? Ein gegen das eigene, der Welt allzu hörige Selbst gerichteter Hass spricht aus solcher Überzeugung. Wie Bataille so klar erkannte, der Widerwille gegen die uns angeblich beherrschende Architektur wird leicht zum Widerwillen gegen die Vernunft. Freiheit will sich nun auch nicht mehr von der Vernunft binden lassen, wie es die Aufklärung forderte. Gerade dies, meint Denis Hollier, hatte Bataille mit seinem Acephalus zeigen wollen: Wer die Fesseln der Architektur abwerfen will, muss erst seinen Kopf verlieren. «Dieses Erstürmen der eigenen Form fordert in der Tat eine unvergleichlich hinterlistigere Strategie als einfach Zerstören oder Entrinnen. Das Bild des Acephalus, sollte somit als Bild der Selbstverstellung verstanden werden, als negatives Bild eines antimonumentalen Wahnsinns, der die Zerstückelung des Sinns mit sich bringt. Der Maler André Masson zeichnete diese Figur, und Bataille schrieb den dazugehörenden Aphorismus: ‹Der Mensch wird seinen Kopf verlieren, so wie der Zuchthäusler seinem Zuchthaus entkommt.›» [7]

Wie solch ein Erstürmen der eigenen Form aussehen könnte, wurde uns von der französischen Künstlerin Saint Orlan vorexerziert, als sie versuchte, mithilfe von Chirurgie und Psychoanalyse eine juristisch andere Person, das heisst wiedergeboren, zu werden. Heute ist dies mehr als nur ein eitler Traum. Ist nicht auch der eigene Körper Material, natürliche, aber auch unnatürliche Verlangen zu befriedigen? Und eröffnet die Technik heute der Freiheit nicht einen bislang ungeahnten Spielraum? So soll einst die Kunstfertigkeit eines Daedalus – griechisches Urbild des Architekten – es der kretischen Königin Pasiphae erlaubt haben, ihr Verlangen, sich mit einem Stier zu vereinen, zu erfüllen. Saint Orlan treibt ein noch eindeutiger unnatürliches Verlangen. Hier ist es der Traum, wie Gott, Urheber ihrer selbst zu werden. So erklärte diese Heilige Gott zu ihrem Feind.

Aber was ist das für ein Ich, das sich hier bemüht, mithilfe der Technik eine andere Person zu werden? Verliert es nicht jeden Inhalt? Und verliert damit nicht solches Bemühen Mass und Richtung? So wird, was sich als autonomes Handeln ausgibt, zum Spielball allzu zeitgemässer Moden. Hier überschlägt sich die Freiheit, überschlägt sich der Widerwille gegen Architektur und weckt ein Heimweh, das uns zurückruft.

Wir sind Amphibien. Immer wieder lockt uns das Versprechen der Schlange «Eritis sicut Deus» und kostet uns irgendein vemeintliches Paradies. Und immer wieder lockt uns auch das verlorene Paradies. Das Widerspiel von Fernweh und Heimweh bestimmt unser Dasein und lässt sich nicht dialektisch aufheben. Dieses uns in entgegengesetzte Richtungen ziehende Widerspiel nährt den Widerwillen gegen Architektur. In diesem Widerspiel spiegelt sich die Antinomie des Seins.

Aber wie ist diese Antinomie zu verstehen? Das Wort «Antinomie» lässt an Kants vier Antinomien denken und daran, was seine Antinomien beweisen wollten: die Notwendigkeit, ein jedes Ding in zweierlei Bedeutung zu verstehen, als von unserem Begreifen abhängige Erscheinung und als Ding an sich. Die Antinomien versuchen somit, eine in unserem alltäglichen, vernunftbestimmten Umgang mit den Dingen übergangene Tiefendimension aufzureissen. Aber warum ist der Verlust, wenn er überhaupt als ein solcher verstanden werden darf, existenziell bedeutsam?

Wenn ich hier von einer Antinomie des Seins spreche, denke ich nicht nur, nicht einmal zuerst an Kant, sondern an Heidegger. Nicht, dass Heidegger von einer Antinomie des Seins spräche! Doch verwickelt ihn und uns sein Seinsdenken in eine solche Antinomie. Wichtig ist hier nicht Heidegger: Unser Denken verwickelt sich in irgendeine Variante dieser Anti-

6 Denis Hollier, *Against Architecture*, Cambridge (Mass.) 1989, S. ix. Zitat: Georges Bataille, «Architecture», in: *Œuvres Complètes*, 12 vols., Paris 1971–88, 1: S. 171–172.

7 Ebd., S. xxi.

nomie, wenn immer es versucht, dem Sein ein Haus zu bauen, das ihm den gehörigen Platz anweist. Ein jedes solches Begreifen greift zu kurz. Was Not tut, ist, Dinge in ihrer konkreten Dinglichkeit zu erfahren, die uns von unserer Vernunft, und das heisst auch, die von unserer Sprache erbaute und eingerichtete Welt aufzureissen, aufzubrechen, sodass Risse und Brüche uns einen Kontakt mit der Wirklichkeit finden lassen, den uns unser alltäglicher Umgang mit allzu bekannten Dingen und Personen immer wieder verbaut. Solcher Kontakt ist Bedingung eines uns Menschen wirklich gerecht werdenden Daseins. Und doch kann «Kontakt finden» hier nicht «begreifen» bedeuten: Die Wirklichkeit lässt sich so wenig begreifen, wie das verlorene Paradise sich wiedergewinnen lässt. Was dies verbietet, ist das Wesen unserer Vernunft.

Doch was soll das Gerede von der Antinomie des Seins?

In *Sein und Zeit* spricht Heidegger von der Abhängigkeit des Seins, nicht des Seienden, vom menschlichen Dasein. Ein merkwürdiger Satz! Gibt es Seiendes ohne Sein? Wie kann Heidegger auf der Abhängigkeit des Seins vom menschlichen Dasein bestehen und dann die Abhängigkeit des Seienden bestreiten? Widerspricht Heidegger hier nicht sich selbst? Im Humanismusbrief finden wir seine Antwort: «Nur solange Dasein ist, ‹gibt es Sein›? Allerdings. Das bedeutet: Nur solange die Lichtung des Seins sich ereignet, ereignet sich Sein dem Menschen. Dass aber das Da, die Lichtung als Wahrheit des Seins selbst, sich ereignet, ist die Schickung des Seins selbst.» (8) Aber das Sein, das es nur gibt, solange es Menschen gibt, ist schwer zu verstehen als das Sein, dessen Schickung wir unser Dasein verdanken. Zwei Seiten des Seins oder Seinsbegriffe stossen hier aufeinander, wobei Heidegger zuweilen zwischen Sein und Seyn unterscheidet. Dieser scheinbare Widerspruch ist Ausdruck der Antinomie des Seins. Ihn gilt es zu verstehen.

Einen Schlüssel gibt uns Heideggers Bestimmung der Sprache als Haus des Seins. Um für uns zu sein, müssen die Dinge im Haus des Seins, das heisst in der Sprache, ihren Platz finden: «Kein ding sei wo das wort gebricht», wie Heidegger es bei Stefan George lesen konnte. Die Metapher weiterdenkend, können wir fragen: Aber ist das Sein in diesem Haus wirklich zu Hause?

Dazu ein Bild, das uns Wittgenstein zur Erklärung der Sprache der Wissenschaft in seinem *Tractatus* (6.341) gibt: «Denken wir uns eine weisse Fläche, auf der unregelmässige schwarze Flecken wären. Wir sagen nun: Was für ein Bild immer hierdurch entsteht, immer kann ich seiner Beschreibung beliebig nahe kommen, indem ich die Fläche mit einem entsprechend feinen quadratischen Netzwerk bedecke und nun von jedem Quadrat sage, dass es weiss oder schwarz ist. Ich werde auf diese Weise die Beschreibung der Fläche auf eine einheitliche Form gebracht haben.» Die leere Seite steht hier für den Raum alles Möglichen. Sie ist ein Bild unserer Freiheit. Nur ein Teil dieses Raumes ist besetzt: Die Flecken stehen für das Wirkliche. Sie könnten auch anders sein. Es gibt unendlich viele mögliche Welten. Aber lassen sich die Flecken im Bild je adäquat mithilfe der geometrischen Netze, die uns unsere Vernunft knüpft, beschreiben? Dann müssten diese eine entsprechende Form haben. Nehmen wir aber an, die Flecken wären unregelmässig aus Kreisfragmenten gebildet. Eine vollständige Beschreibung mit einem geometrischen Netz würde dann die unmögliche Quadratur des Kreises bedeuten. Unser Sehen übersteigt hier eine Vernunft, die das gesehene Verhältnis als Verhältnis zweier ganzer Zahlen darstellen möchte. Schon die Griechen bestürzte die Erfahrung der Irrationalität der Welt. So soll die Pythagoreer ihre Entdeckung der Irrationalität der Wurzel von 2 zutiefst beunruhigt haben. Zuerst soll man versucht haben, diese traurige Entdeckung geheim zu halten, und der unglückliche Mensch, der dieses Geheimnis dann doch verriet, soll im Meer ertrunken sein. In der Begriffsarchitektur, in der man sicher zu wohnen glaubte, zeigte sich ein Riss.

Kehren wir zu Wittgensteins Bild zurück. Lädt es uns nicht ein, die abgebildete Wirklichkeit als die Reichweite der Logik und im *Tractatus* heisst das auch der Sprache übersteigend zu denken? Die Wirklichkeit lässt sich nicht ins Haus, das ihr unsere Vernunft baut, einsperren. Die Wirklichkeit erfahren heisst Transzendenz erfahren.

Aber auch dies gilt: Alles, was uns irgendetwas bedeuten kann, muss sich sagen lassen. Und gilt das nicht auch für die Wirklichkeit? Die Vernunft, und das heisst auch die Sprache, baut dem Sein das Haus. So verstanden, übersteigen Logik und Sprache die Wirklichkeit. Der Mensch ist das immer schon irgendwie aus der Wirklichkeit herausgefallene, sie trans-

8 Martin Heidegger, «Brief über den ‹Humanismus›», *Gesamtausgabe*, Bd. 9, Frankfurt am Main 1976, S. 336.

zendierende Wesen. Das bedingt unsere Freiheit. Die Antinomie des Seins gehört zum Wesen des Seins. Das war es, was schon die Pythagoreer so bestürzte.

Bei Stefan George allerdings ging die Bestürzung in die umgekehrte Richtung:

So lernt ich traurig den Verzicht:
Kein Ding sei wo das Wort gebricht.

Auf was muss der Dichter verzichten?

Auf ein wortloses Verstehen der Dinge? So viel müssen wir zugeben: Was uns begegnet, was wir erkennen, sind immer nur sprachlich vermittelte Erscheinungen. Aber das zwingt uns, an die sich unserem Begreifen notwendig entziehende vermittelte Wirklichkeit zu denken. Nietzsche wusste um den mit dieser Vermittlung verbundenen Wirklichkeitsverlust: «Jedes Wort wird sofort dadurch Begriff, dass es eben nicht für das einmalige ganz und gar individualisierte Urerlebnis, dem es sein Entstehen verdankt, etwa als Erinnerung dienen soll, sondern zugleich für zahllose, mehr oder weniger ähnliche, das heisst streng genommen niemals gleiche, also auf lauter ungleiche Fälle passen muss.» (9) Mit diesem Verlust des Einzigartigen erkaufen wir die Möglichkeit, die Wirklichkeit unserer Vernunft zu unterwerfen, dem Sein ein Haus zu bauen. Aber ist dieses Haus ein Käfig? Wird damit Wahrheit zur Lüge? Diese Frage setzt eine «Wahrheit» voraus, die sich unserem Begreifen entzieht und an der wir dennoch, was wir gewöhnlich Wahrheit nennen, messen und ungenügend finden. Der Antinomie des Seins entspricht eine Antinomie der Wahrheit. Diese Antinomie zerreisst immer wieder alle Versuche, dem Sein sein Haus zu bauen.

Im Kunstwerk-Aufsatz spricht Heidegger vom Welt und Erde trennenden Riss und fordert von der Kunst das Aufreissen dieses Risses. «Welt», so verstanden, und Sprache sind verwandte Begriffe: Das Eröffnen einer Welt im Kunstwerk räumt den Raum ein, in dem Dinge und Menschen ihren Platz finden müssen, um für uns zu sein. «Erde» dagegen nennt hier den sich unserem Begreifen immer wieder entziehenden und doch in unserer Erfahrung der Einzigartigkeit einer Person oder eines Dings uns in Anspruch nehmenden transzendenten Grund unseres Wohnens. Nur solche Erfahrung kann unserem Leben einen Sinn geben. Die architektonische Vernunft ist wesentlich nihilistisch. So ist gerade heute der Widerwille gegen Architektur der Anfang eines Bemühens, das uns von unserer rechnenden Vernunft zu fest gefügte Haus aufzureissen, Transzendenz hineinwehen zu lassen.

9 Friedrich Nietzsche, «Über Wahrheit und Lüge im aussermoralischen Sinne», in: *Sämtliche Werke. Kritische Studienausgabe,* hg. von G. Colli, M. Montinari, München, Berlin, New York 1980, Bd. 1, S. 879–880.

HOLGER BIRKHOLZ

Der zerrissene Tempelvorhang
—
Anmerkungen zum Sprung in der Schüssel

Die Zeit ist aus den Fugen:
Schmach und Gram,
Dass ich zur Welt,
sie einzurichten, kam!
(Hamlet I 5)

Verschiebungen, Brüche und Ruinen sind in ihrer Zeichenhaftigkeit ein strukturelles Thema der Kunst. Sie verweisen auf die Spanne, die sich zwischen Vergangenheitsbewusstsein und Zukunftsperspektiven erstreckt: Die Gegenwart ist so etwas wie ein Einschnitt zwischen beiden Blickrichtungen. Von uns aus geht der Blick zum einen zurück und greift aus Spuren und Erinnerungen das auf, was in der Gegenwart als sinnvoll erscheint und unsere Identität bestimmt. Zum anderen trägt die Entscheidung für eine Fokussierung auf bestimmte Inhalte der Geschichte ein Verantwortungsbewusstsein in sich, das in die Zukunft weist. In Zustimmung oder Ablehnung wird das «Erbe» der Vergangenheit zum Standpunkt, von dem aus es gilt, nächste Schritte zu unternehmen. Immer geht eine solche Bestimmung mit der Auseinandersetzung mit Idealen einher, mit vergangenen und künftigen. Ruinen können kaum ohne Moral betrachtet werden; sie erweisen sich als Dreh- und Angelpunkt gesellschaftlicher Anschauungen. Als inhaltlicher Referenzpunkt für die Fragen nach der «displaced fracture» soll hier ein Bild aus der Kulturgeschichte dienen: der im Augenblick des Todes Christi zerreissende Tempelvorhang. Das Thema selbst ist Verschiebung – es führt in die Religionsphilosophie. Zudem enthält es ein «displacement», einen Bruch, der verschiedene Symptome metaphorisch miteinander verschränkt.

Tempelvorhang

Die erste und unmittelbarste Reaktion auf den Kreuzestod Christi ist das Zerreissen des Vorhangs vor dem Allerheiligsten im Tempel von Jerusalem. Drei der vier Evangelien nennen beide Ereignisse in einem Atemzug und setzen sie ursächlich zueinander in Beziehung (Neues Testament, Matthäus 27, 51, Markus 15, 38, Lukas 23, 45). Dem körperlichen Tod folgt ein Zeichen auf dem Fuss, das auf die Göttlichkeit des soeben gestorbenen Menschensohnes verweist. Beispielhaft sei hier Markus zitiert: «Da stiess Jesus einen lauten Schrei aus und verschied. Und der Vorhang des Tempels zerriss in zwei Stücke von oben bis unten» (Mk. 15, 37–38). (1)

Die Verbindung zwischen Gott und den Menschen, die durch die Menschwerdung Gottes in Jesus Christus manifest wurde, zerreisst. Der zerrissene Vorhang steht für das Ende des alten Bundes. Er ist das sichtliche Zeichen des nicht mehr in seinem Tempel weilenden Gottes.

Im Neuen Testament gibt es einige Andeutungen auf eine Analogie zwischen dem Körper Jesu und dem Tempel. (2) Christus selbst äussert sich bei Johannes folgendermassen (Joh. 2, 19): «Brecht diesen Tempel ab und in drei Tagen will ich ihn wieder erstehen lassen.» Die Ausdrucksweise ist sinnbildhaft zu verstehen. Die Zerstörung des Tempels steht für die Kreuzigung und damit den zerstörten Menschenleib des Gottessohnes. Der Wiederaufbau bezieht sich auf die Auferstehung. Eine inhaltlich vergleichbare Stelle findet sich bei Markus: «Siehst du diese grossen Bauten? Kein Stein wird auf dem andern bleiben, der nicht zerstört würde» (Mk. 13, 2).

Christus verweist mit seiner Tempelmetapher darauf, dass das «neue» Reich Gottes eben nicht «von dieser Welt» (Joh. 18, 36), sondern göttlichen Ursprungs sei. So gesehen, kommt im zerrissenen Vorhang auch der Bruch mit der Materialität zum Ausdruck: Sie zerfällt und offenbart die nicht sichtbare göttliche Präsenz. In Jerusalem als dem Zentrum der Welt und dem Allerheiligsten in seinem Tempel steht ein hinter dem Tempelvorhang Verborgenes, das die Strahlkraft besitzt, selbst in unzugänglicher Form oder gerade deshalb Fokus der Religion zu sein.

Der von den Autoren des Neuen Testaments beschriebene Riss hat vor allem auch eine symbolische Funktion: Der Tempelvorhang ist eine zentrale Schnittstelle, eine Membran zwischen dieser Welt und der Welt Gottes. Er trennt den Bereich des Heiligen mit Schaubrottisch, Menora und Opferaltar, der ausschliesslich von Priestern betreten werden durfte, vom Allerheiligsten, in dem sogar der Hohepriester nur einmal im Jahr – an Jom Kippur – Zugang hatte. Rein sachlich betrachtet, konnte deshalb ein Riss im Tempelvorhang lediglich durch die Priesterschaft bemerkt werden. Zum Thema eines öffentlichen Blicks in das Allerheiligste wird der Riss erst durch seine Erwähnung in den Evangelien. Die Erzählperspektive dieser

1 Hier und in der Folge zitiert nach: *Zürcher Bibel, Die Heilige Schrift des Alten und des Neuen Testaments* (Zürich 1954), Berlin 1960, *Das Neue Testament,* S. 73.

2 Vgl. Pfarrer Ralf Krust, Predigt zum 10. Sonntag nach Trinitatis über Joh. 2, 13–22 (http://www.predigten.de/predigt.php3?predigt=916).

Bibelstellen ist auktorial. Sie folgt einer übergreifenden, nicht an einen Standpunkt gebundenen Sicht des Erzählers. Einem Beobachter von Christi Kreuzestod wäre es unmöglich gewesen, beide Ereignisse, den Tod und das Zerreissen, zugleich wahrzunehmen, da sie nach biblischer Topografie weit voneinander entfernt stattfanden. Beide Momente unterscheiden sich in der Möglichkeit ihrer Wahrnehmung stark voneinander. Die Kreuzigung selbst ist ein Ereignis, das in der Öffentlichkeit vollzogen wird, um damit ein politisches Zeichen zu setzen. Das Zerreissen des Vorhangs im unzugänglichen Heiligen des Tempels ist eigentlich nicht sichtbar. Als «ausgesprochene» Metapher handelt es sich mehr um ein sprachliches denn um ein wirkliches Ereignis. Allerdings unterscheidet die Bibel nicht zwischen der Handlungsmacht von Worten und Taten.

Der Riss markiert den von der Verschiebung durchquerten Raum. Er ist der Übergang vom Ich zum anderen, vom Betrachter zum Betrachteten. Was dazwischensteht, wird zerrissen, um überhaupt die Möglichkeit zu gewinnen, das andere zu sehen. Die Betrachtung ist ein Zugriff, der es dem Betrachtenden erlaubt, sich das Betrachtete durch den Blick einzuverleiben. Die Verschiebung findet durch Erkennen statt. Das Angesehene bekommt seinen Wert durch die Aufmerksamkeit, die ihm zuteil wird. In der Betrachtung wird das Objekt aus der Kontinuität seiner Existenz herausgelöst, bekommt als Gegenstand klar umrissene Grenzen. Das Objekt verbleibt nicht mehr innerhalb seines Funktionszusammenhangs, sondern bekommt durch meine Betrachtung einen «neuen» Sinn, der abhängt von meinem Verständnis. Dieser sinnstiftende betrachtende Zugriff wird erst möglich, wenn der Vorhang zerreisst. Der ursprünglich in einem Gegenstand angelegte Nutzen kann ihm durch Verschiebung entzogen werden. Er wird in dieser Hinsicht nutzlos. Daneben steht eine Art angedeuteter Nutzen, der durch das Kunstwerk simuliert wird. Diese beiden Aspekte sind wesentliche Grundzüge der in der Ausstellung *Displaced Fractures* versammelten Arbeiten. Als architektonische Versatzstücke, die darauf warten, beim Bau eingesetzt zu werden oder als Fundamente weitere Bauteile zu stützen, liegen die Objekte von Emilie Ding verstreut im Raum. Manchmal erscheinen sie als integrale Bestandteile der bestehenden Architektur und können deshalb leicht übersehen werden. Die «Verbundstücke» ziehen die Aufmerksamkeit auf sich, weil sie nicht erklärbar sind, und werfen die Frage auf, ob und inwiefern sich Zweckdienlichkeit eines Gegenstandes an seiner Gestalt ablesen lässt. Gewindestangen und Schrauben der Betonobjekte weisen auf Verbindungen zwischen den Einzelobjekten hin, lösen diese Verbindungen jedoch nicht ein. Die Verbindungsstücke erscheinen als Zeichen von denkbaren Anschlüssen, deren Funktion sich auf die Optionalität beschränkt.

Die Objekte von Ding erscheinen an ihren Orten seltsam irritierend und vielleicht sogar ein wenig neurotisch, wenn sie sich nicht, qua Institution, durch das Museum als Kunstwerke erklären würden. Auf dieses Deutungsmuster kann Klara Lidén nicht setzen, wenn sie im städtischen Raum vertikale Streben von Pfeilern oder Masten nutzt, um hinaufzusteigen und dort festgeklammert zu verharren. Psychologisch verstanden trägt ihr Verhalten zwanghafte Züge. Diese Sichtweise kehrt sich jedoch um, wenn man die Zwanghaftigkeit der Symptome begreift, die uns selbstverständlich erscheinende Architektur in unseren Städten, die unser Verhalten dominiert.

Einblick in den Körper

Der zerrissene Tempelvorhang ist als Wunde auch Ausdruck von Zerstörung. Er bricht mit der Vorstellung des perfekten Körpers. Er steht für einen nicht freiwilligen Blick ins Innere durch einen Einschnitt, der dem Körper schmerzhaft zugefügt wird. Beim Blick durch die Oberfläche offenbart der Leib sein anderes, verborgenes Sein. Der Blick zeigt, wie er im Inneren aufgebaut ist. Bei Lebewesen fliesst Blut; Muskelfasern, Knochen und Sehnen werden in ihrer lebendigen Form sichtbar. Gebaute Körper zeigen ihre Materialität und technischen Strukturen. Beton oder Holz werden unter der Fassadenstruktur oder unter dem farbigen Anstrich der Oberfläche sichtbar. Gerüste, Stahlträger oder Armierungsstahl kommen zum Vorschein. Die Sicht ins Innere scheint bei uns ein gewisses Bedürfnis zu befriedigen, das darauf zielt, zu begreifen, wie die Form ihre Gestalt zu wahren in der Lage ist. Durch den Riss wird der Blick auf die Konstruktionsprinzipien offenbar.

Im wahrsten Sinne handelt es sich beim zerrissenen Vorhang um eine «displaced fracture». Der Ort der höchsten Belastung ist das Leiden und Sterben des Heilands am Kreuz. Die theologische Dimension offenbart sich aber an einem anderen, dem zentralen Ort der weltlichen Manifestation des Glaubens, einem unzugänglichen Raum, in dem nach alter jüdischer Überzeugung Gott thront. Die Spanne der Erzählung und insbesondere der Erzählperspektive ist so beachtlich wie die Vorstellung, dass dem Sohn Gottes die schmählichste damals vorstellbare Form der Hinrichtung zuteil wird.

Die räumliche Verschiebung zwischen dem Ereignis des Todes und seiner zeichenhaften Analogie im Zerreissen des Vorhangs unterscheidet sich von der Seitenwunde Christi, in der Zeichen und Körper zusammenkommen. Die Seitenwunde wie die Wundmale sind Ausdruck der Versehrtheit des menschlichen Leibes, den Gott in seinem Sohn Jesus angenommen hat. Sie werden in den Evangelien zum zentralen Thema; an ihnen erkennen die Jünger den auferstandenen Christus. Körper, Erscheinung und Versehrtheit werden identisch.

Ein solches Zusammenwirken zeigt sich auch in den Bearbeitungsspuren, Bohrlöchern und Spalten in den Steinblöcken von Ulrich Rückriem. Der Steinblock ist aus dem ursprünglichen Zusammenhang des Felsmassivs gelöst und wird in seiner Vereinzelung gestalthaft. Er wird zu einem wahrnehmbaren Körper durch eine Art Verwundung des Berges. Die technische Realisierung, das Herauslösen sind am Block noch wahrnehmbar. Spuren der Bohrungen, die das Absprengen des Blocks ermöglicht haben, sind zu sehen. Oft ist der Block selbst gespalten. Die beiden gespaltenen Hälften werden von Rückriem trotz ihres Risses als Gesamtblock gestellt, sodass – im Grunde genommen – kein Raum sie trennt. Der Zusammenhalt wird optisch noch gewahrt, doch droht das Auseinanderfallen wie bei einem Sprung in einer Porzellanschüssel, die so gerade noch hält. Dennoch ist der Riss wie eine Fuge deutlich sichtbar und zeichnet den Block als «beschädigt» aus. Die Risse bei Rückriem weisen über den Block hinaus in die materielle Welt, sie sind unendlich fortgesetzt denkbar. Sie werden zu einer Metapher für das Herausgerissensein eines jeglichen Dings aus der Kontinuität. Dieser Philosophie folgend, ist jeder Gegenstand durch Fraktur entstanden.

Klaus Winichner füllt in seiner Arbeit *Untitled* von 2008 solche Risse auf. Spalten und Löcher dreier Matratzen wurden mit unterschiedlichen Materialien verfugt, unter anderem mit Bauschaum, Beton oder Kunstblumen. Der Ausweitung der Risse bei Rückriem stellt Winichner eine ironische Alternative entgegen, die das Problem des Fragmentarischen profan im Hier und Jetzt löst. Die unsachgemässe Ergänzung eröffnet einen neuen, kritisch reflektierten Erzählraum. Sie spricht von einer anderen Art der Nutzung und löst die Blickrichtung auf die Medialität zum Teil wieder auf, indem sie Materialien sprechend einsetzt.

Ruine und Fragment

Unsere Welt scheint auf vielfältige Weise fragmentiert, wenn wir Dinge aus ihr herauslösen. Sie werden erst bedeutsam, wenn wir sie betrachten. Mit Beginn der Moderne rücken auch vorher periphere Dinge ins Blickfeld. Das kündigt sich vielleicht schon 1503 bei Dürer mit dem *Grossen Rasenstück* an – einer meisterhaften Zeichnung von ein paar läppischen Gräsern – und setzt sich heute fort bei künstlerisch gefertigten Objekten, die aussehen, als wären es Betonblöcke, die aus Abbruchhäusern gerissen wurden. Fragmente dieser Art hatte unter anderem Gordon Matta-Clark Anfang der Siebzigerjahre salon- beziehungsweise museumsfähig gemacht.

In solchen Fragmenten gipfeln vielfältige Themen der Kunst- und Kulturgeschichte. Ihre Bewertung als Kunstgegenstände entsteht durch die Möglichkeit der Vereinzelung und dadurch, dass man sie in dieser Form als Spuren, als Relikte eines Grösseren wahrnimmt. Beton, Armierungsstahl und Farbreste sprechen für eine bestimmte durch die Moderne eingeführte Form des Bauens, die mittlerweile ein Alter erreicht hat, in dem sie wieder dem Verfall oder dem Abriss, insbesondere aber auch einem kritischen theoretischen Diskurs preisgegeben wird. So untersucht Kilian Rüthemann die modernistische Architektur der Ausstellungsräume, in denen er seine Arbeiten zeigt. Das geschieht durch rohe Betonverdopplungen von Stufen oder indem er die Deckenstruktur des Oberlichts zerlegt. Auf diese Weise entsteht ein Provisorium, das Fragen an den Raum aufwirft. Wie in einem Forschungslabor werden die Bauteile temporär auf den Untersuchungstisch gelegt. Die Scheiben des Oberlichts werden auf gezielt gesetzte Stelzen gebockt und erhalten dadurch eine grafisch-plastische Form, die – selbst minimalistisch – bestehende Strukturen paraphrasiert und deren Gültigkeit für sich in Anspruch nimmt.

Unsere Gegenwart ist insbesondere bestimmt von den Errungenschaften der klassischen Moderne. Höhepunkte einer rationalistischen Denkweise in Architektur, Design und Kunst sind uns überliefert in den Architekturen Le Corbusiers, den Entwürfen des Bauhaus und Kunstwerken von Schlemmer, Mondrian, Albers und anderen. Insbesondere der sachgemässe Erhalt dieses kulturellen Erbes, das inzwischen deutliche Abnutzungsspuren zeigt, steht dabei im Fokus. Die Komplexität eines solchen Unterfangens zeigt sich unter anderem bei der Restaurierung der Meisterhäuser in Dessau, die schon während der ersten Jahre unter den differierenden Ansichten einzelner Lehrer und Bewohner der Häuser in ihren Bauphasen unterschiedlich fortgeführt oder sogleich wieder umgebaut wurden. Die Frage nach dem gültigen Zeitpunkt und Zustand, an dem sich ein Ideal manifestiert und den man als richtungsweisend für die Restaurierung wählt, wird so wichtig, da sich in ihm wiederum die Wertschätzung in der Gegenwart ablesen lässt.

Dabei stechen die oft nicht so recht miteinander zu vereinbarenden Nähte als Risse oder Verschiebungen deutlich hervor, wie sie immer wieder auch in den Arbeiten von Phyllida Barlow auftauchen. Die grob gekitteten Fugen, unregelmässig verspachtelten Oberflächen oder Keile, die ganze Formen in Schräglage versetzen, machen in ihrer sichtlichen Hilflosigkeit die Brüche umso deutlicher und erheben sie zum eigentlichen Ereignis der Plastiken und Installationen.

Kunsthistorisch stehen sie in der Tradition der Ruinenromantik. Der sehnsuchtsvolle Blick auf verfallene Bauwerke, vorzugsweise Kirchen in der Zeit um 1800, oder angefressene Äpfel barocker Stillleben künden von der Relativität und Vergänglichkeit allen Seins gegenüber der zeitunabhängigen Gültigkeit «ewiger Werte». In barocker Tradition verweisen sie auf die Relativität der irdischen Dinge und setzen dem die Religion oder das Geistige entgegen. Irdischer Prunk verführt. Wenn er Risse oder andere Spuren des Verfalls aufweist, schleicht sich über diese Verfallserscheinungen ein Zweifel an seiner Wertigkeit ein. Metaphorisch gesprochen, sucht der Betrachter hier nach einem Blick durch den Riss. Er zielt auf den Kern der Dinge und sucht darin den Zusammenhalt des Ganzen.

Der Schauer, der einen plötzlich überfällt und aus dem Bewusstsein erwächst, selbst lebendig zu sein und deshalb umso lieber dem Absterben zuzuschauen, verführt uns zum Blick auf Ruinen, wie zum Beispiel Tacita Dean in ihrem Video zum Abriss des Berliner Palasts der Republik. Auch hier schwingt die Forderung nach einer Auseinandersetzung mit den in der Ruine vermittelten Idealen, ihrem Zusammenbruch und ihren Perspektiven mit.

Gerade an zerstörten Werken überraschen immer wieder weltanschauliche Themen. Ideologie wird vor allem in ihrem Scheitern interessant. So wird denn auch die Vollkommenheit eines Ideals, sei es nun architektonisch oder künstlerisch, im Fragment von entscheidender Bedeutung. Die Möglichkeit für diese Umkehrung liegt in einer Art Auflösung des Ideals in seinem zerstörten Zustand. Im Fragment zeigt sich das Ideal als ein Überwundenes. Gleichzeitig ist in jeder fragmentarischen Arbeit das Ideal der Vollkommenheit enthalten. Um einen Gegenstand überhaupt als Fragment erkennen zu können, braucht es eine Vorstellung vom Ganzen. Diese Vorstellung muss nicht zwangsläufig selbst vollständig sein. Es reicht, dass das Fragment Spuren enthält, die darauf hindeuten, dass der Gegenstand an dieser Stelle beschädigt ist und ursprünglich mehr war, als sich an der Bruchstelle erkennen lässt. Einem solchen Bruch gegenüber gibt es zwei korrespondierende Haltungen. Der Bruch kann selbst als sinnvoll genügen oder zu seiner Vervollständigung anregen. Komplettiert wird gedanklich oder materiell. Dabei werden Muster herangezogen, die aus der Erfahrung mit vergleichbaren Dingen erwachsen.

Die künstlerischen Ansätze der Ausstellung *Displaced Fractures* zeichnen sich dadurch aus, dass es sich hier nicht um Ruinen und Architekturfragmente als Readymades handelt – vorgefundene Versatzstücke aus dem Bereich der vergessenen und vernachlässigten Zonen unserer Städte und Architekturen –, sondern um Nachbildungen ihrer Ästhetik. Dieser Ansatz verbindet zwei kunsthistorische Stränge: zum einen die Tradition der europäischen Ruinenromantik und zum anderen das politische Engagement der Künstler aus den Siebzigerjahren. Diese hatten sich in die städtischen Randzonen und Zwischenräume begeben und dort marginalisierte Gesellschaftsformen, Räume und Architekturen beobachtet und analysiert. Durch künstlerische Interventionen wurden sie ins Blickfeld gerückt, mittels Fotografie sichtbar gemacht oder durch gesammelte Fragmente aus diesen Bereichen entnommen, übertragen in die Galerie, aus ihrer Randlage in ein Zentrum kultureller Aufmerksamkeit gerückt.

Die Künstlerinnen und Künstler der Ausstellung *Displaces Fractures* dagegen schaffen mit ihren Plastiken und plastischen Eingriffen in den Raum eher Blickpunkte, vergleichbar den «Folies» in Landschaftsgärten, die spätestens seit dem 18. Jahrhundert auch künstliche Ruinen sein können. Dabei zeigen sich Ruine und Verfall als zwangsläufige Prozesse im Werden und Vergehen der Natur. Die kulturellen Errungenschaften entstehen und vergehen, wie Kulturen selbst Blüte- und Verfallszeiten auf-weisen. Die vorzugsweise in ruinöse Zustände versetzte gotische Architektur erscheint als kulturelle Hochphase des mittelalterlichen Europa. Nach ihrem Verfall wird sie in ihren Überresten zeichenhaft verstanden und so zur Folie für die Gegenwart, die sich an ihnen misst. Darin sind die gotischen Ruinen den zerfallenden Industrieanlagen vergleichbar, die in marginalisierten Zonen unserer Städte allmählich einstürzen, verrosten und von Spontanvegetation überwuchert werden. Sie stehen für die ökonomische Entwicklung der Gesellschaft im Zuge der Industrialisierung. Ihre architektonischen Strukturen sind für heutige Zwecke nicht mehr zu gebrauchen oder ihre Lage nicht ausreichend attraktiv. In dieser Form haben sie inzwischen teilweise eine bemerkenswerte neue Karriere als Kulturstandort gemacht. Mit der Randlage der Gebäude korrespondiert dabei die mit ihnen in die Peripherie gedrängte Kultur.

In Kunstwerken, die den Verfall als strukturelles Prinzip aufgreifen und bildnerisch umsetzen, wird die Destruktion zur Grundlage für die Konstruktion. Das ist in gewisser Weise ein Paradox. Zerstörung wird gleichsam als bildnerisches Mittel verstanden. Diese Sichtweise kann generell zu einer anderen Sicht auf die Materialbearbeitung im Bereich der Skulptur führen. Die Bearbeitung eines Marmorblocks für eine klassische Plastik wäre demnach auch ein Akt der Zerstörung, der den ursprünglichen Marmor aus dem Felsmassiv löst, um ihn zu fragmentieren. Damit wären wir erneut bei Rückriem.

Unsere Identifikation mit dem plastischen Körper führt dazu, dass wir den bildhauerischen Körper als Gegenüber oder Transfiguration unseres Selbst begreifen. Mit dem Prinzip der Übertragung arbeiten auch Ding, Rückriem und Winichner, wenn sie überschaubare Formen schaffen. In ihren Dimensionen oder anthropomorphen Formen nehmen die Arbeiten Bezug auf die als körpereigen empfundene Geschlossenheit. Oscar Tuazon greift die Verbindung zwischen plastischem Prozess und Körper explizit in den Titeln seiner Werke auf.

Architektur wird in ihren herausgebrochenen Fragmenten überschaubar und als Gegenstand individuell und damit eben auch offen für eine anthropomorphe Belebung. Die an diesen Körpern eingeschriebenen Verletzungen werden auch für ihre Betrachter schmerzhaft. Leiden wird dabei ganz klassisch im Sinne eines Mitleidens – Aristoteles würde dabei von «Katharsis» sprechen – nachvollziehbar. Projektion und Verschiebung verbinden sich auf metaphorischer Ebene, wie der Tod Christi sich auf den Tempelvorhang auswirkt und in dessen Zerreissen erst die wahre Dimension des Sterbens Jesu offenbar wird.

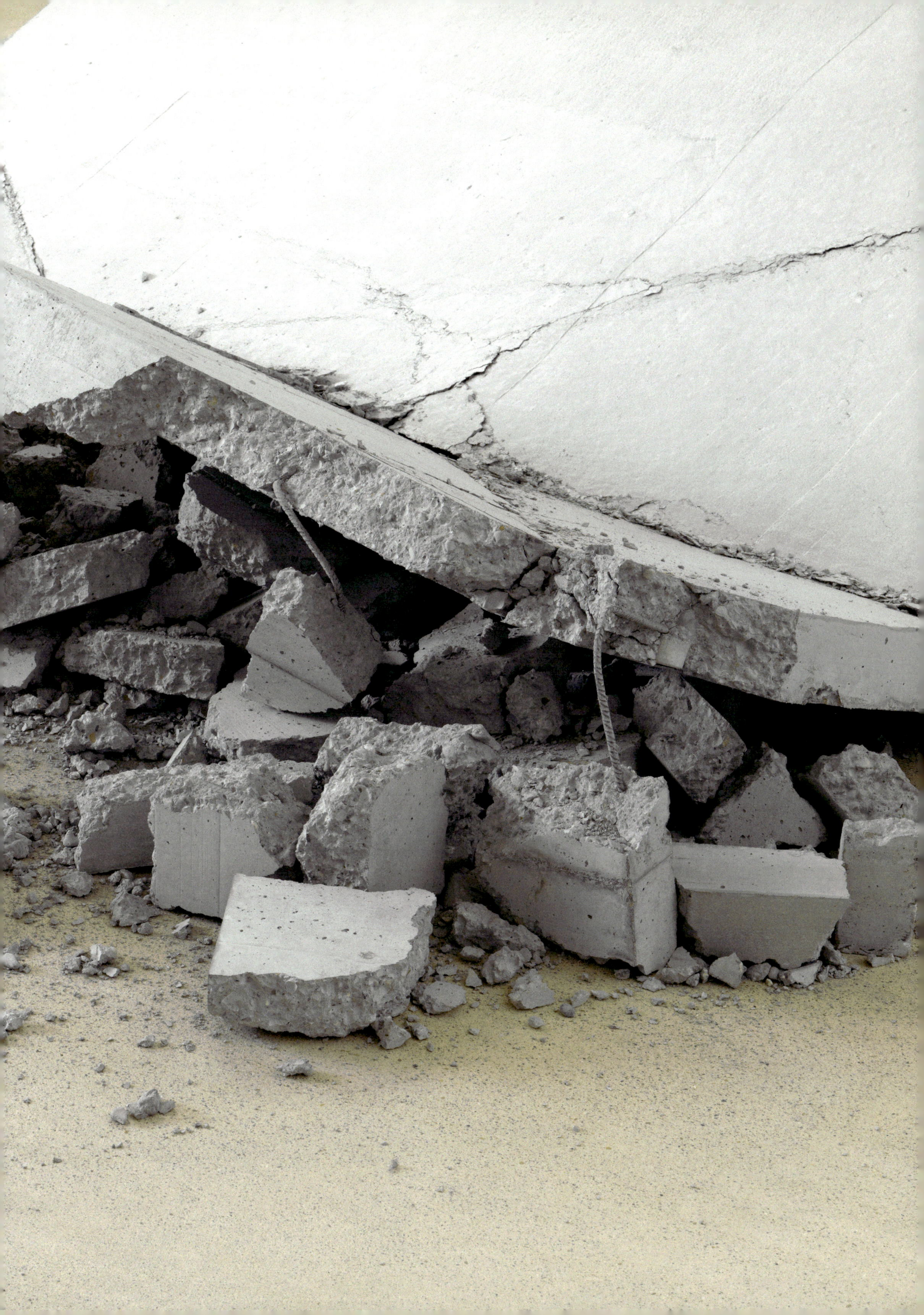

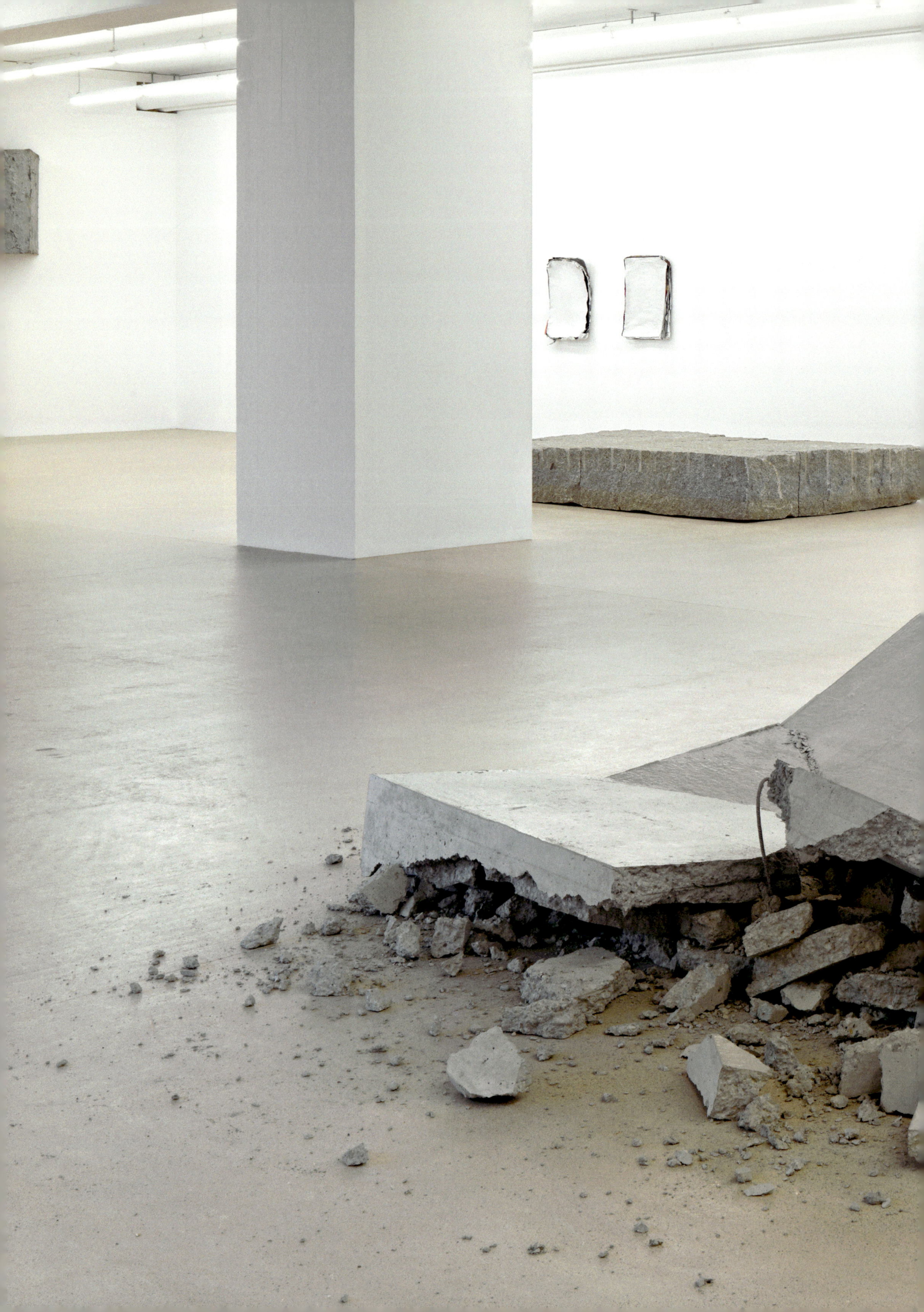

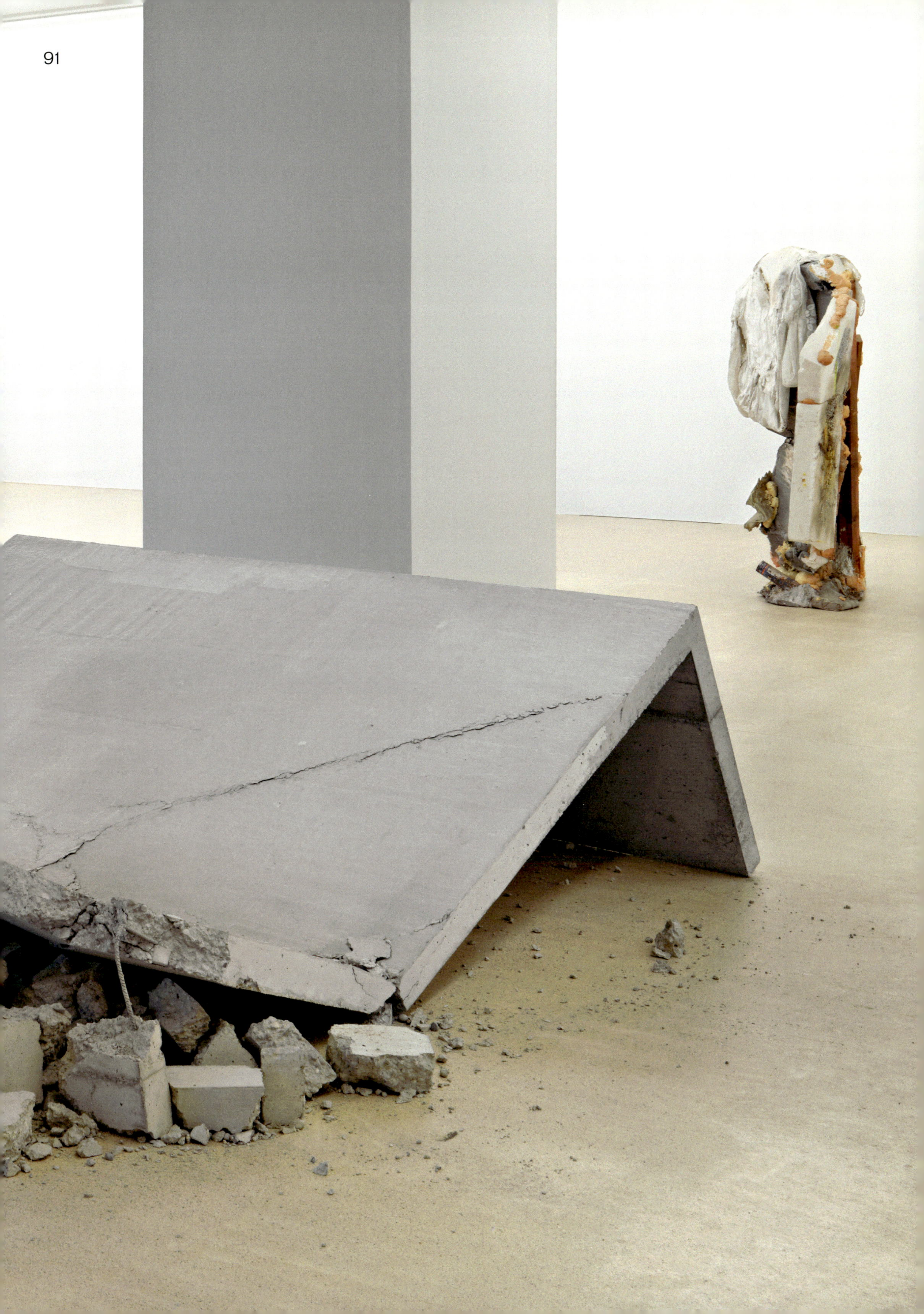

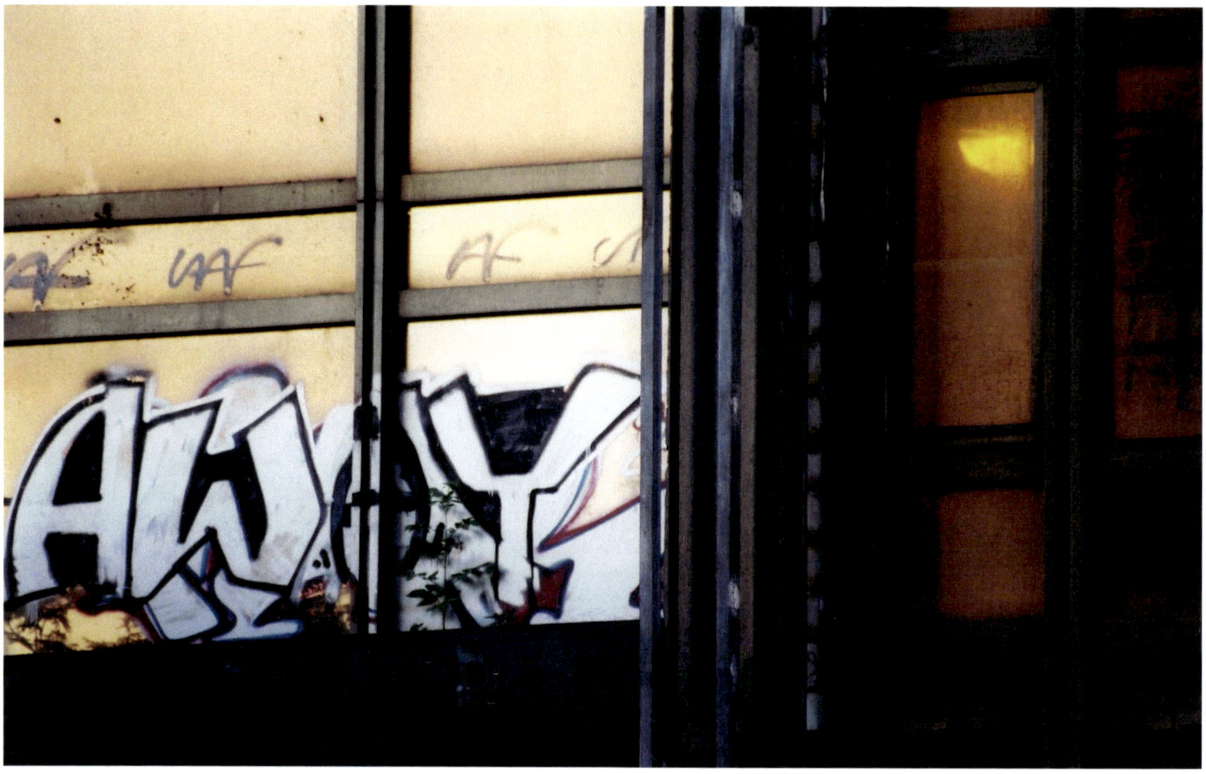

PALAST
2004

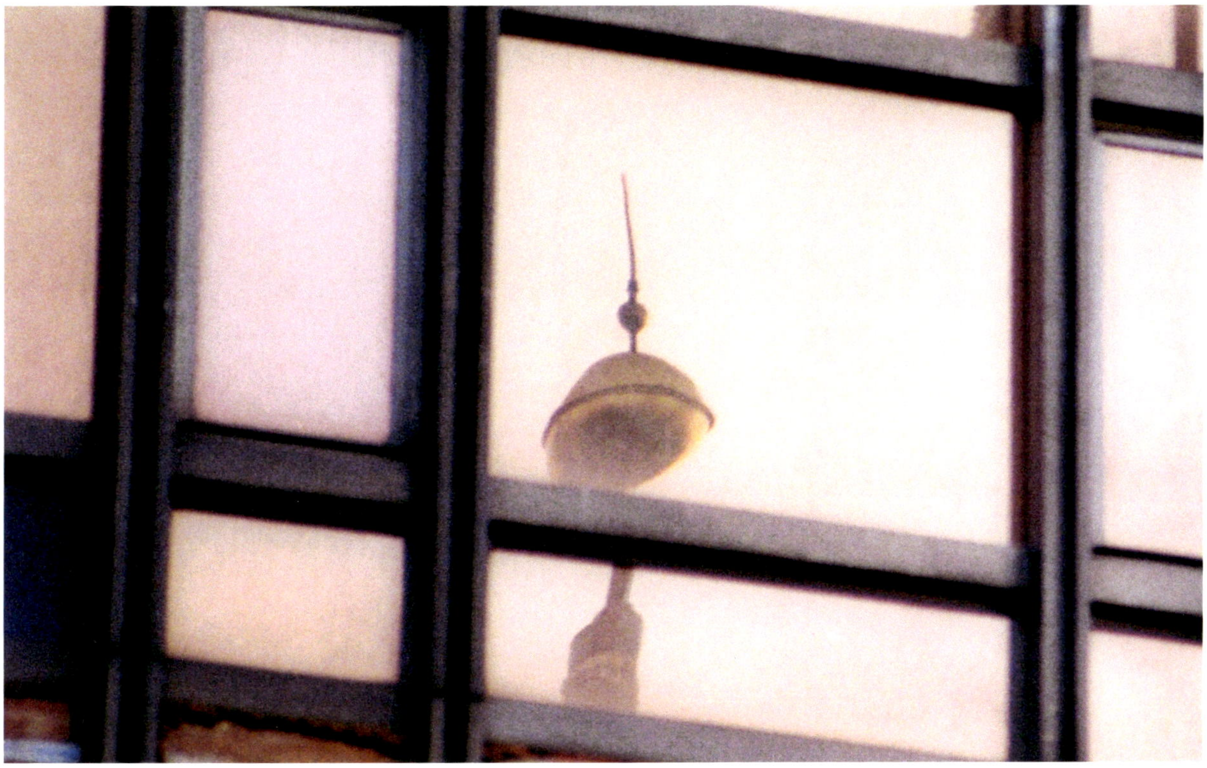

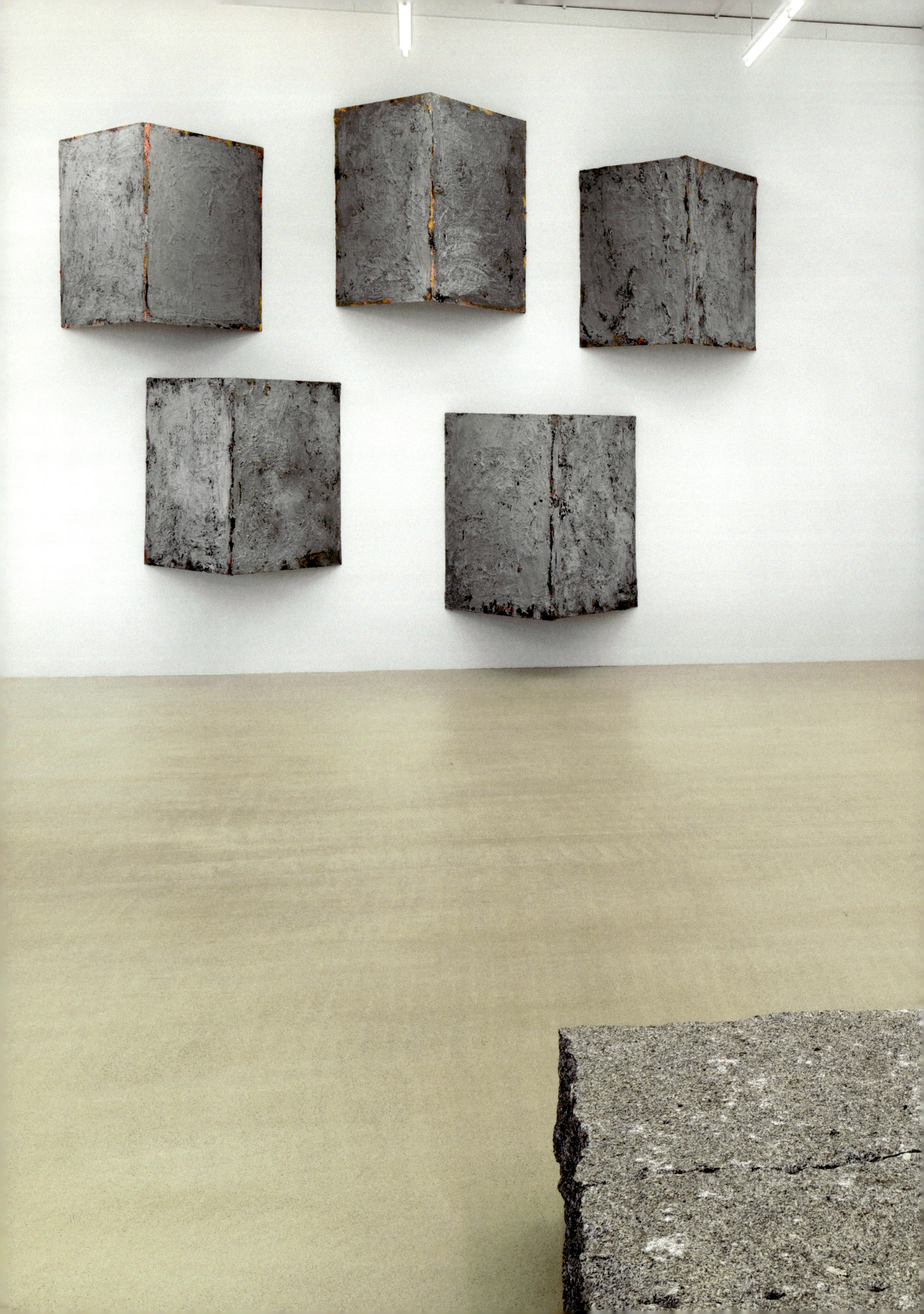

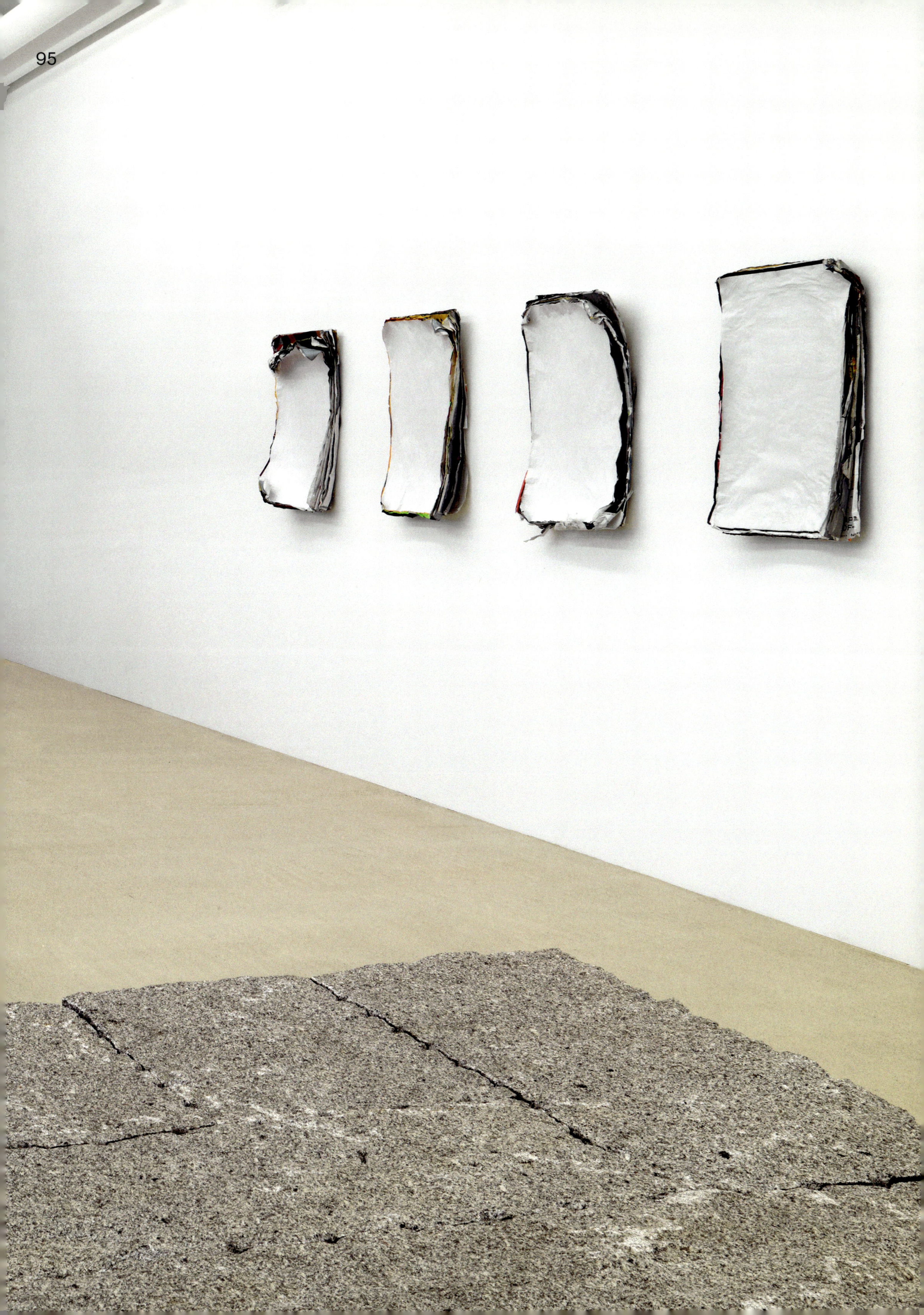

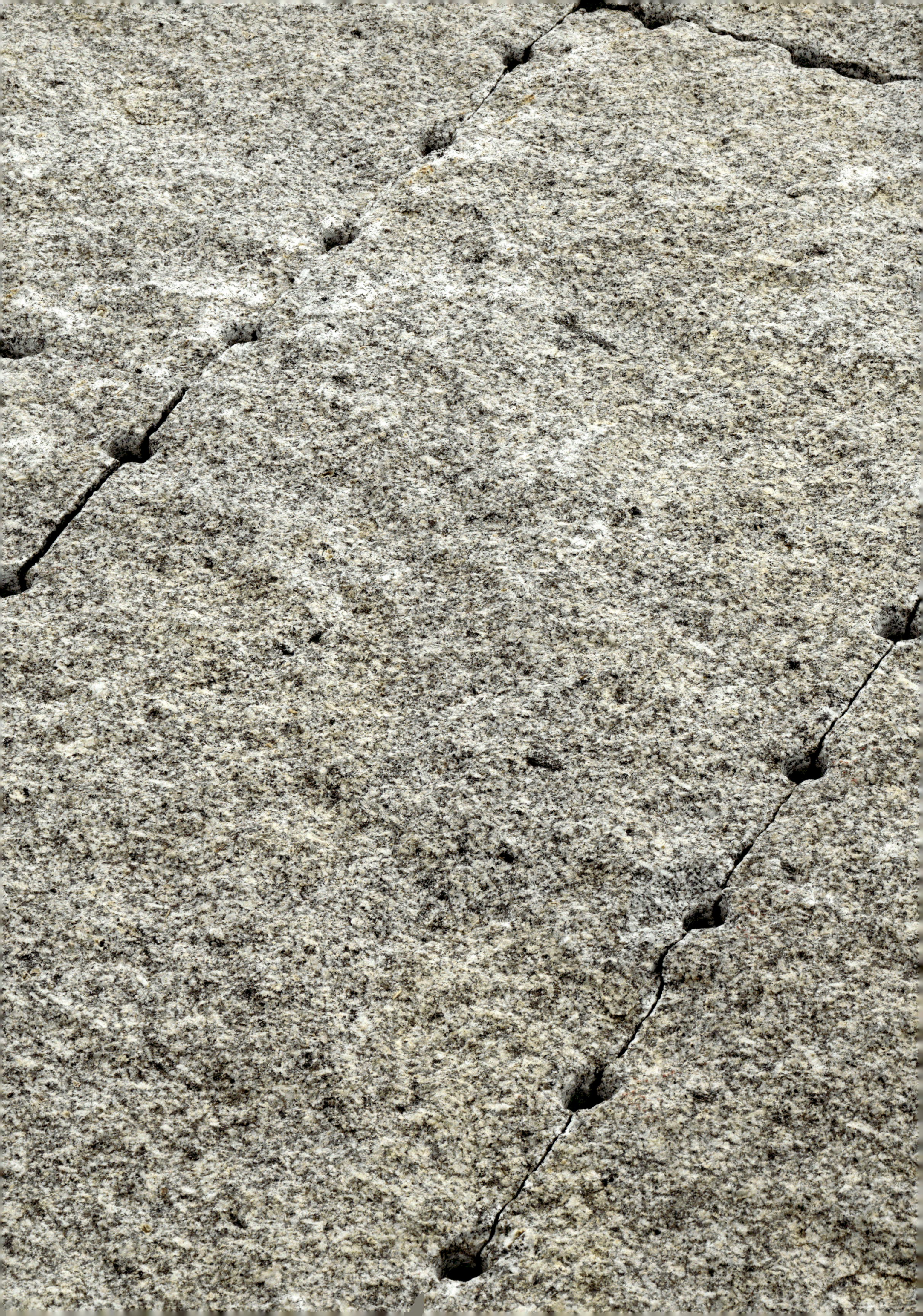

OHNE TITEL (BODENARBEIT)
1990

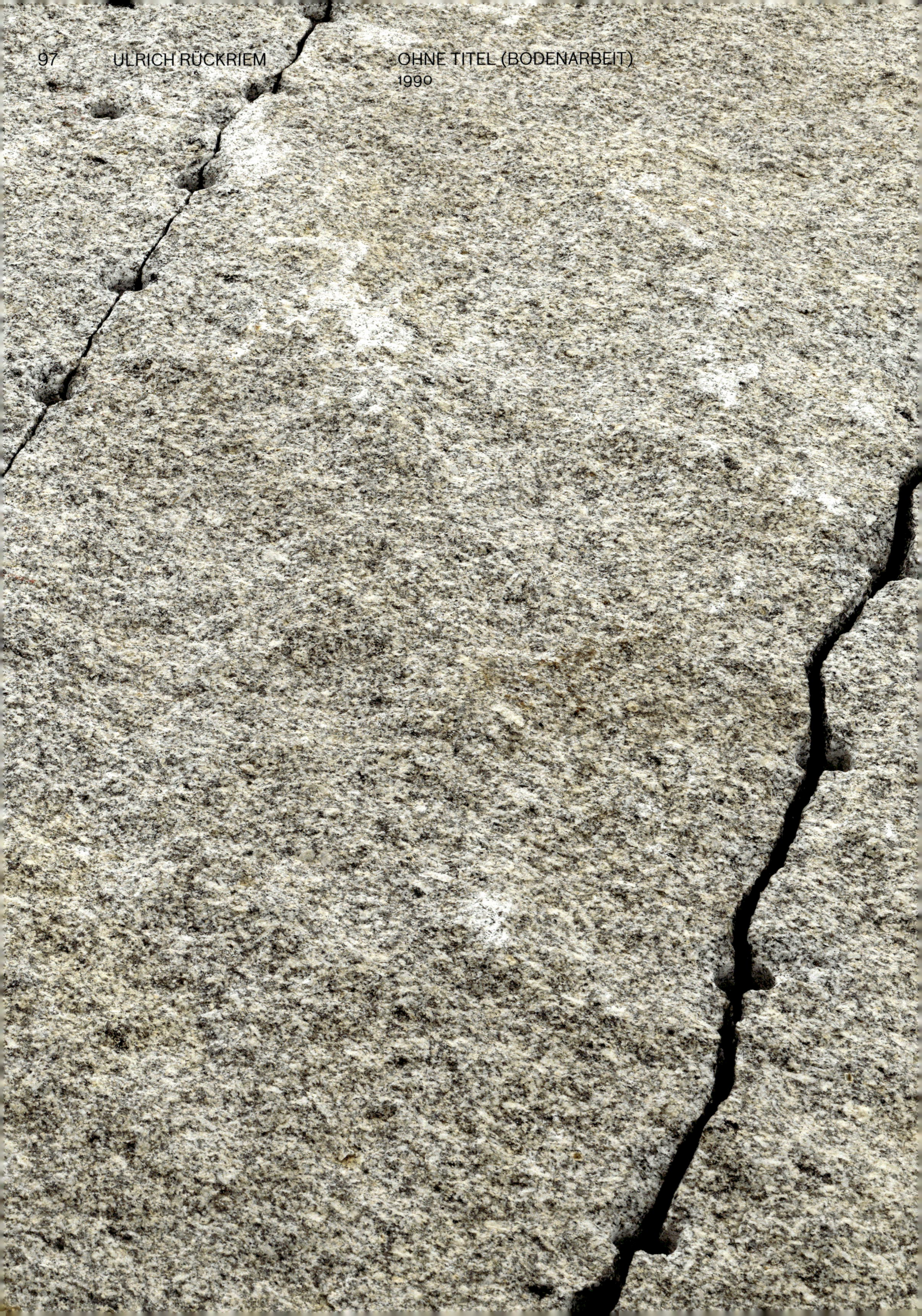

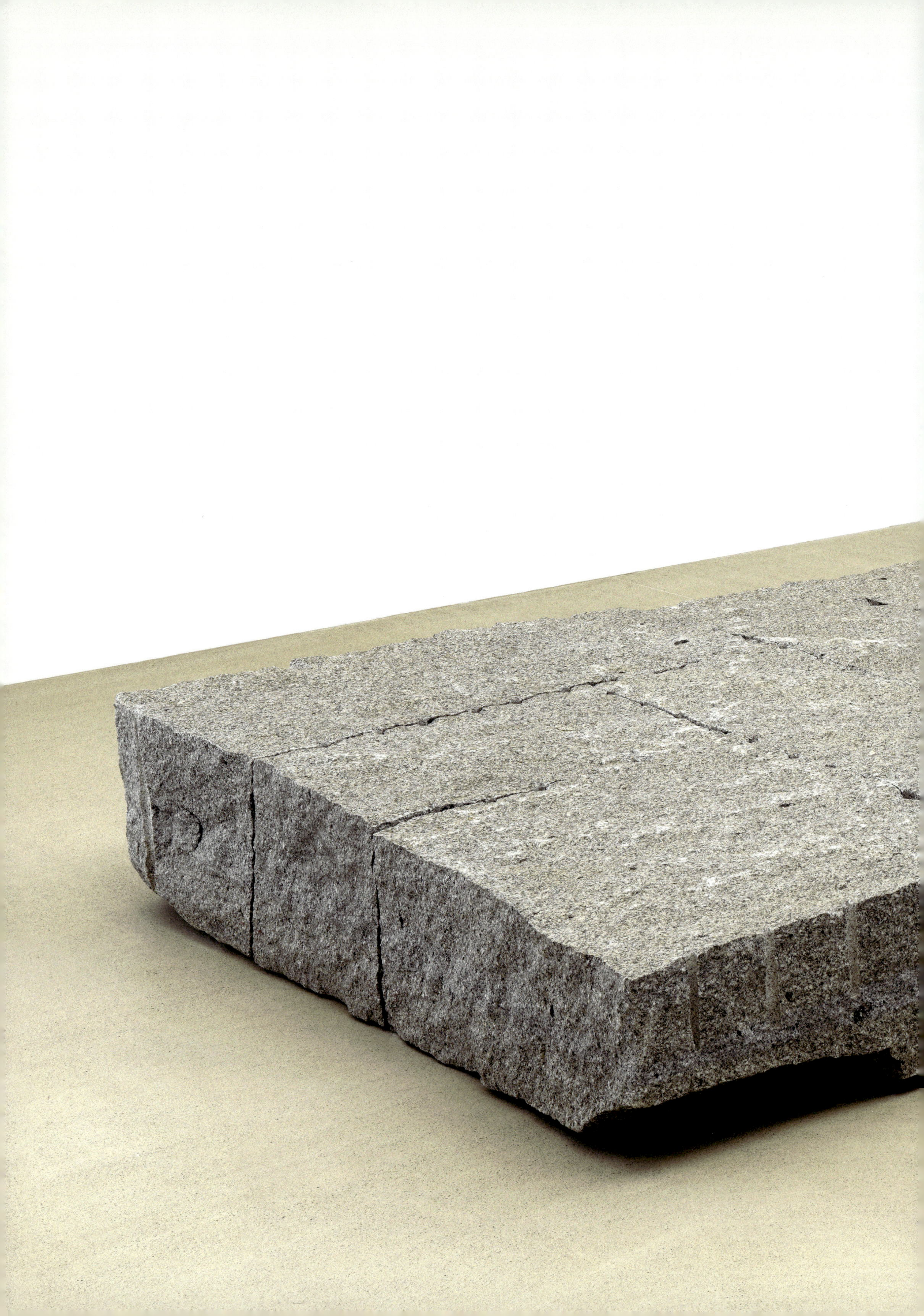

 ULRICH RÜCKRIEM

OHNE TITEL (BODENARBEIT)
1990

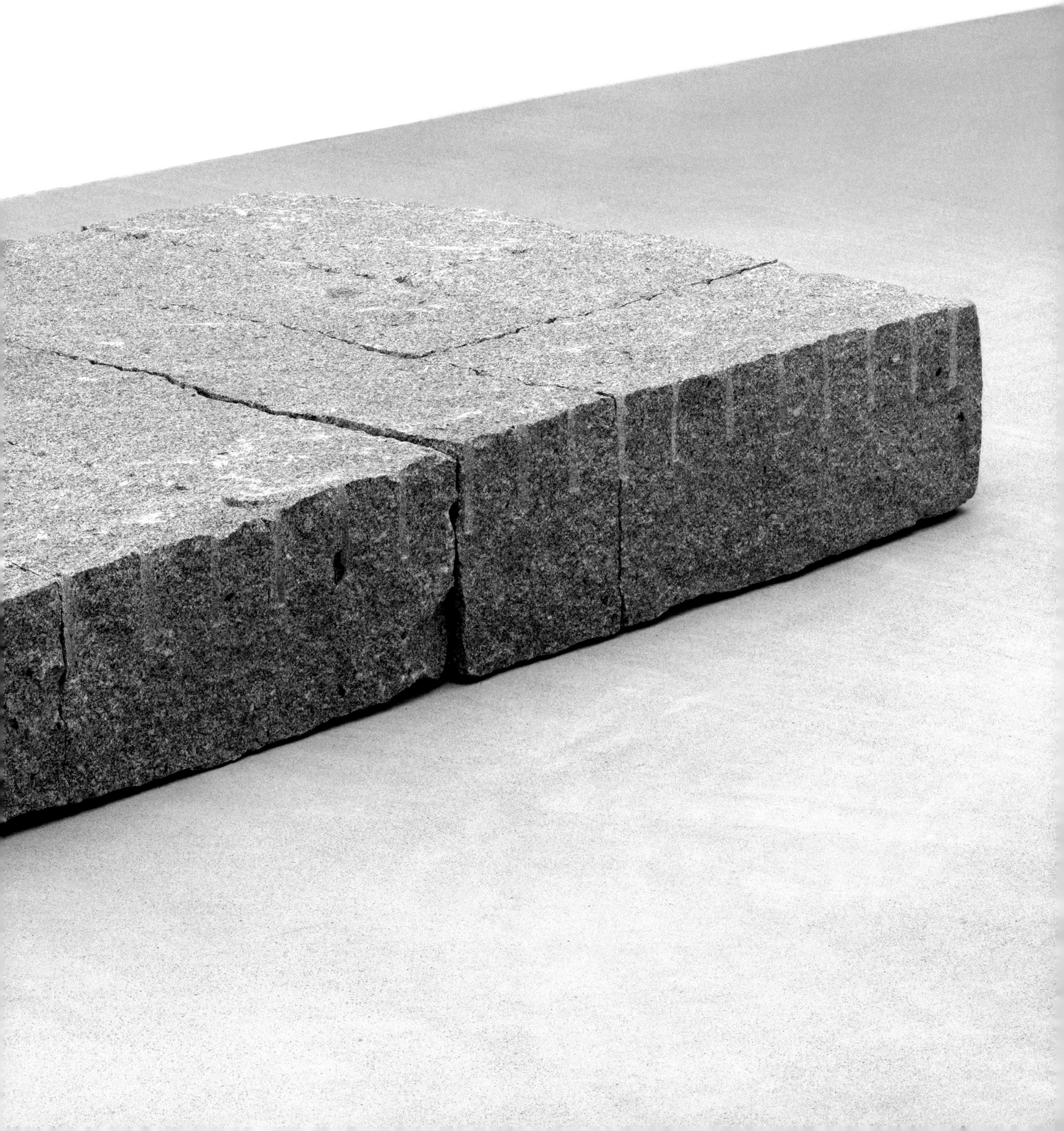

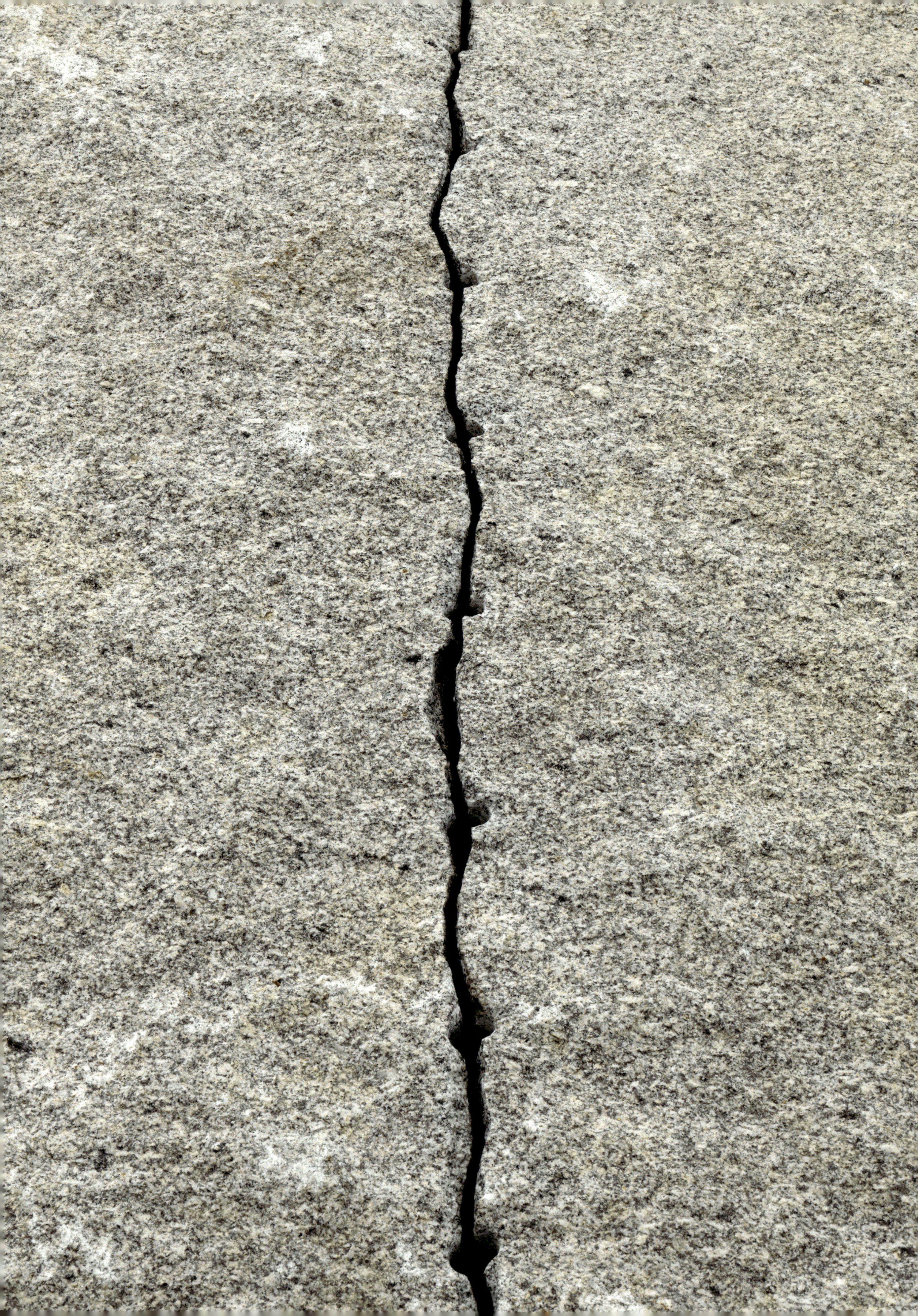

HOLGER BIRKHOLZ

Dr. Holger Birkholz studied Art History, German Philology and Philosophy in Kassel, earning his doctorate in 2002 with a thesis on the term context in art theory and practice. He is curator of Media Installations at the Kassel Documentary Film & Video Festival, and has been a research associate in the Department of Art History at the Dresden Academy of Fine Arts since 2004.

KARSTEN HARRIES

Karsten Harries is the Brooks and Suzanne Ragen Professor of Philosophy at Yale University, New Haven, and has published many works on Heidegger, the philosophy of the Renaissance and aesthetics, especially the philosophy of architecture. Recently published works include: *The Ethical Function of Architecture*, Cambridge (Mass.) 1997; *Infinity and Perspective,* Cambridge (Mass.) 2001; *Art Matters: A Critical Commentary on Heidegger's The Origin of the Work of Art,* New York 2009; *Die Bayerische Rokokokirche. Das Irrationale und das Sakrale,* Dorfen 2009; *Between Nihilism and Faith: A Commentary on Either/Or,* Berlin and New York 2010.

HEIKE MUNDER

Studied cultural studies at the University of Lunenburg. She has been Director of the migros museum für gegenwartskunst Zürich since 2001. She co-founded the Halle für Kunst Lüneburg e.V., which she co-directed from 1995–2001. Previously curated exhibitions include: *Tatiana Trouvé* (2009); *Karla Black* (2009); *Tadeusz Kantor* (2008); *Rachel Harrison* (2007); *Marc Camille Chaimowicz* (2006); *Robert Kusmirowski* (2005); *Yoko Ono* (2004); *Mark Leckey* (2003); *Art & Language* (2003).

THOMAS D. TRUMMER

Studied Art History, Philosophy and Music at the University of Graz. He is Curator of Visual Arts at Siemens Stiftung, Munich. Recently curated shows include: *Walls in the Street*, Muzej savremene umetnosti, Beograd, Serbia (2008); *Endless Sphere*, Center for Contemporary Art, Kyiv, Ukraine (2008); *Repeat Myself When Under Stress*, Museum of Contemporary Art, Detroit (2009); *Several Silences*, Renaissance Society, Chicago (2009); *Actors & Extras*, Brussels, Belgium (2009); *Coral Visual*, Casa de la Cultura, Buenos Aires, Argentina (2009); *The Science of Imagination*, Ludwig Muzéum, Budapest, Hungary (2010); *Artistic Research*, MIT Cambridge, MA (2010)

PHYLLIDA BARLOW

Born 1944 in Newcastle upon Tyne (United Kingdom)
Lives and works in London

Solo Exhibitions
(Selection since 1985)

2011 Kunstverein Nürnberg
2010 *BLUFF*, Studio Voltaire, London; *SWAMP*, V22, London; *STREET*, BAWAG Contemporary, Vienna
2009 *BRAKE*, One in the Other Gallery, London
2008 *STINT*, Mead Gallery, Warwick Arts Centre, Warwick; *STACK, FENCE*, Southbank Centre, London
2007 *RAMP TOWER FLAGS*, Galería Jesús Gallardo, León; *New Sculpture: in the Gallery and Grounds*, New Art Centre, Roche Court, London
2005 *Untitled: demo*, Studio 1.1, London; *SCAPE*, Spacex, Exeter; *SKIT*, Bloomberg Space, London; *Remnants, Dallas, 2003*, MAC, Centre of Contemporary Art, Dallas
2004 *PENINSULAR*, Baltic Centre for Contemporary Art, Gateshead; *BARRIER*, Tannery Arts Exhibitions, London
2003 *Untitled: Dallas*, Dallas Visual Art Gallery; *Remnants*, The Magnet School, Dallas; *Remnants*, Angstrom Gallery, Dallas
2002 *New Sculpture*, Richard Salmon Gallery, London; *FETE*, Phoenix Wharf, Bristol
2001 *Knives in Hens*, Wimbledon Theatre, London
1996 *Recall*, Marshall's Mill, Halifax
1995 *DEPOT*, Museum of Installation, London; *Sculptures for the Library*, Henry Moore Institute, Leeds
1991 *Plantation*, Business Design Centre, London; *Closed (Vigil II)*, RIBA Sculpture Court, London
1990 *Fall*, DEGW Offices, London
1989 *Crowd*, Hermitage Road Industrial Estate, London; *Wallworks*, Smith Jarawala Gallery, London; *Vigil I*, Windsor Festival, Berkshire
1988 *SLOPE*, The Gallery, Halifax
1987 *Oracle*, St. Peter's Churchyard, Cambridge
1985 *Wrecks*, Bayfield, Norfolk

Group Exhibitions
(Selection since 2001)

2010 *Displaced Fractures – Über die Bruchlinien von Architekturen und ihren Körpern*, migros museum für gegenwartskunst Zürich; *Nairy Baghramian and Phyllida Barlow*, Serpentine Gallery, London; *Old Ideas*, Kunstmuseum Basel; *Phyllida Barlow & Fiona MacDonald*, Co Exist Galleries, Essex; *I go to Sleep*, Modern Art, Everynight, London
2009 *The Real, V22 Sculpture Exhibition*, The Almond Building, London; *Collaborators*, ROOM Gallery, London; *Hijack Reality*, Warwick Arts Centre; The Russian Club Gallery, London
2008 *Old Ideas*, Museum für Gegenwartskunst, Basel; *Stuff with Alison Wilding, Laura White, Bettina Buck*, The Almond Building, London; *Prospects and Interiors Sculptors' Drawings of Inner Space*, Henry Moore Institute, Leeds; *STEW*, Art Space Gallery: Michael Richardson Contemporary Art, London; *Entre Muros (Between Walls)*, CAS Gallery, Miami
2007 *Etc...*, Art Project, Copenhagen; *Says the junk in the yard*, Flowers East, London; *An Exploration into Abstract Painting*, Studio 1.1, London; *Rummage Sculptors*, The Winchester Gallery, Winchester; *Jumbo Shrimp*, Woburn Slade Research Centre, London; *Entre Muros (Between Walls)*, Galeria Casa de los Manos, León
2006 *Ebb and Flow*, RAID Projects, Los Angeles; *Wandering Star*, GANA Art Centre, Seoul; *Please Close the Gate: Painted sculpture at Roche Court*, Royal Academy of Art, London
2005 *Sleigh*, Arts & Business, London; *Merveilles du Monde*, Musee de L'Art Contemporain, Dunkirque; *Abb and Flow*, Three Colts Gallery, London
2004 *Love Story*, Danielle Arnaud Gallery, London; *Bird House*, Fieldgate Gallery, London
2003 *Shelf Life*, Studio 1.1, London; *Location, Location, Location*, Albury Arts, Guildford; *The Drawing Auction*, The Drawing Room, London; *The Greatest Show on Earth*, Metropole Gallery, Folkestone
2002 *Harvey's Bodies*, Metropole Gallery, Folkestone; *Neck: Invited Artists*, Royal Academy of Arts, London
2001 *Station to Station*, *Spacex 2*, Exeter Maritime Museum, Exeter; *Mile End Park Sculpture Exhibition*, Mile End Park, London

TACITA DEAN

Born 1965 in Canterbury (United Kingdom)
Lives and works in Berlin

Solo Exhibitions
(Selection since 2004)

2010 *The Common Guild*, Glasgow; *Craneway Event*, Frith Street Gallery, London
2009 Sprengel Museum, Hannover; Musée d'art contemporain de Montréal; *Still Life*, Fondazione Nicola Trussardi, Milan; Marian Goodman Gallery, New York
2008 *In My Manor*, Galerie für Gegenwartskunst, Berlin; *Amadeus*, Marian Goodman Gallery, Paris; *Merce Cunningham performs STILLNESS (in three movements) to John Cage's composition; 4'33" with Trevor Carlson*, Dia Beacon, New York
2007 *Wandermüde*, Frith Street Gallery, London; Hugh Lane Gallery, Dublin; Guggenheim Museum, New York; Miami Art Central
2006 *Analogue: Films, Photographs, Drawings 1991–2006*, Schaulager, Basel; *Human Treasure*, Center for Contemporary Art, Kitakyushu; The National Museum of Art, Architecture and Design, Oslo
2005 *Berlin Works*, Tate St. Ives; *An Aside*, Hayward Gallery, London; Camden Arts Centre, London; The Fruitmarket Gallery, Edinburgh; The Glynn Vivian Art Gallery, Swansea
2004 *Mala Galerija*, Museum of Modern Art Ljubljana, Ljubljana; *Baobab*, Fondazione Sandretto Re Rebaudengo, Turin

Group Exhibitions
(Selection since 2005)

2010 *Displaced Fractures – Über die Bruchlinien von Architekturen und ihren Körpern*, migros museum für gegenwartskunst Zürich; *The Promises of the Past, 1950–2010*, Centre Pompidou, Paris; *Photo Espania: Entre Tiempos*, Madrid; *Haunted*, Guggenheim Museum, New York; *Crash*, Gagosian Gallery, London
2009 *GSK Contemporary 2009: Art of Changing the World*, The Royal Academy, London; Performa Biennial, New York; *Moby Dick*, CCA Wattis Institute for Contemporary Arts, San Francisco; Tirana Biennial; *The Enlightenment*, Dean Gallery, Edinburgh; *Pasaggi, Sicilia La collezione di Riso e oltre*, Museo d'arte comtemporanea della sicilia; *As Long as it Lasts*, Marian Goodman, New York; *From Holbein to Tillmans*, Schaulager, Basel; *Sonic Youth: Sensational Fix*, Malmö Konsthall; *The Quick and the Dead*, Walker Art Center, Minneapolis; *Subversive Space: Surrealism and Contemporary Art*, The Whitworth Art Gallery, Manchester
2008 Folkestone Triennial; *Order. Desire. Light.* IMMA, Dublin; *Where Uses of the Document in Contemporary Art*, ICP Museum, New York; *Porzadki Urojone – so ist es und Andres*, Muzeum Sztuki, Warsaw; *Lost Paradise – The Angels Gaze*, Zentrum Paul Klee, Berne
2007 *Marking Time*, York Art Gallery; *Sea Pieces*, Hamburger Kunsthalle; *Scenes and Sequences*, Kunsthaus Aarau; *Waterlog*, Castle Museum; *On History*, Foundation Santander, Madrid

2006 *Resonance*, Frith Street Gallery, London; São Paulo Biennial; Sydney Biennial; *C'era una volta un re. La Fiaba contemporanea*, Museo d'Arte Contemporanea, Sannio; *Mapping the Studio*, Stedelijk Museum, Amsterdam; *Spool*, Consortium Gallery, Amsterdam; *Constructing New Berlin*, Phoenix Art Museum, Phoenix, Arizona; Berlin Biennial; *Print Run: An exhibition of Prints*, Frith Street Gallery, London
2005 *Universal Experience: Art, Life and the Tourist's Eye*, Hayward Gallery, London; *Here Comes the Sun*, Magasin 3, Stockholm; *Truth universally acknowledged*, Australian Centre for Contemporary Art, Victoria; Venice Biennial; *New Acquisitions*, Museum of Modern Art, New York; *Soul*, Museum Voor Moderne Kunst, Oostende; *Bidibidobidiboo*, Fondazione Sandretto Re Rebaudengo, Turin; *Daumenkino: The Flip Book Show*, Kunsthalle Düsseldorf; *Very Early Pictures*, Luckman Gallery, California State University, Los Angeles; Arcadia University Art Gallery, Glenside; *Universal Experience: Art, Life and the Tourist's Eye*, MCA, Chicago; *Documentary Creations*, Kunstmuseum Luzern; *Some Trees*, Neuer Aachener Kunstverein

EMILIE DING

Born 1981 in Fribourg (Switzerland)
Lives and works in Geneva

Solo Exhibitions
(Selection since 2008)

2010 *Erased*, Salle Crosnier, Palais de l'Athénée, Geneva; *Primitive*, Evergreene, Geneva
2009 Random Gallery, Paris; *Tirants Interstices*, Galerie Praz-Delavallade, Paris
2008 *Le Gros Oeuvre*, Forde, Geneva

Group Exhibitions
(Selection since 2006)

2010 *Displaced Fractures – Über die Bruchlinien von Architekturen und ihren Körpern*, migros museum für gegenwartskunst Zürich; *Triennale de l'art imprimé contemporain*, Musée des beaux-arts, Le Locle; *Of Objects, Fields, and Mirrors*, Kunsthaus Glarus
2009 Centre d'art contemporain, Geneva; *Avalanche*, Manoir de Martigny; *A new Spirit in Lasagnas I et II*, Circuit, Lausanne; New Jerseyy, Basel; *Plattform 09*, ewz-Unterwerk Selnau, Zurich
2008 *Exit/Dark Matter – Black Noise*, Centre national de l'estampe et de l'art imprimé, Chatou; *X*, Galerie 1m3, Lausanne; *Abstraction Extension*, Fondation Salomon, Alex; *Accrochage*, Villa Dutoit, Geneva; *Prix National Suisse*, Kunsthaus Baselland, Muttenz; *Quoi de neuf – Carte blanche à L'Urdla*, L'attrape, Lyon
2007 *SIJANG JEON EUN NEOMU ILEO, HEUNGMIROUN SAMUSIL EUN NEOMUNEUZEO*, Forde, Geneva; *True Stories*, Salle Crosnier, Palais de l'Athénée, Geneva; *Der Tanz der Doppelgänger*, Shark, Geneva
2006 *Black and White*, Duplex, Geneva; *Minigolf*, Circuit, Lausanne

KLARA LIDÉN

Born 1979 in Stockholm (Sweden)
Lives and works in Berlin

Solo Exhibitions
(Selection since 2005)

2010 Galerie Neu, Berlin; Kunstverein Bonn; Serpentine Gallery, London; Art Pace, San Antonio; *Always be Elsewhere*, Jeu De Paume, Paris; Reena Spaulings Fine Art, New York
2009 *Never Come Back*, Kunsthalle Fridericianum, Kassel; *Projects 89*, Museum of Modern Art, New York
2008 *Elda för kråkorna*, Reena Spaulings Fine Art, New York
2007 The Hayward Gallery, London; *Unheimlich Maneuver*, Moderna Museet, Stockholm
2006 *Economy Class*, Reena Spaulings Fine Art, New York
2005 *Dr. 3000*, Reena Spaulings Fine Art, New York

Group Exhibitions
(Selection since 2003)

2010 *Displaced Fractures – Über die Bruchlinien von Architekturen und ihren Körpern*, migros museum für gegenwartskunst Zürich; *Before and After*, Balice Hertling, Paris; *Barbaric Freedom*, Simon Lee Gallery, London; *Fischgrätenmelkstand*, Temporäre Kunsthalle, Berlin; *On Rage*, Haus der Kulturen der Welt, Berlin
2009 *Non-Solo, Non-Group Show*, Kunsthalle Zürich; Massimo de Carlo, Milan; *Political Minimal*, Kunstwerke, Berlin; Nordic Biennial, Moss; Venice Biennial
2008 *After Nature*, New Museum, New York; *Tarantula*, Nicola Trussardi Foundation, Milan; Sydney Biennial
2007 MD 72, Berlin; Kunstverein, Braunschweig; *Beneath the Underdog*, Gagosian Gallery, New York; *Uncertain States of America*, Center for Contemporary Art, Warsaw; Moscow Biennial; *Massive Analogue Academy*, Galerie Christian Nagel, Cologne; *The Perfect Man Show*, White Columns, New York
2006 *Music Is a Better Noise*, P.S.1, New York; *Subito Sera*, Galleria Zero, Milan; *Street Behind the Cliché*, Witte de With, Rotterdam; Berlin Biennial; *Nuevo Estocolmo*, Södertälje Konsthall, Södertälje
2005 *Reena Spaulings – The One and Only*, Haswellediger Gallery, New York; Fotogalleriet, Oslo; *When Humor Becomes Painful*, migros museum für gegenwartskunst Zürich
2004 *I/U/WE*, Färgfabriken, Stockholm; *LTTR Explosion*, Art In General, New York
2003 *Concrete and Imagination*, Urban Art Gallery, Berlin

ULRICH RÜCKRIEM

Born 1938 in Dusseldorf (Germany)
Lives and works in London and Cologne

Solo Exhibitions
(Selection since 1964)

2010 Galeria A arte Studio Invernizzi, Milan; *Granit Bleu de Vire, zugeschnitten*, Staatliches Museum für Kunst und Design, Nuremberg
2009 *40 Bodenreliefs, 3. Variation 2009*, Neue Nationalgalerie, Berlin; *Sculpture*, Bernier/Eliades Gallery, Athens
2008 *Shadows of the stone*, National Museum of Contemporary Art–EMST, Athens
2007 *Wandwerke*, Sprengel Museum, Hannover; Galerie Heinrich Ehrhardt, Madrid; *Ikarus*, Museum Ludwig, Cologne
2006 *The Shadows of the Stone*, Modern Art Oxford; *Die Schatten der Steine*, Figge von Rosen Galerie, Cologne
2005 Boutwell Draper Gallery, Sydney; Neues Museum, Nuremberg Hamburger Kunsthalle
2004 Neue Nationalgalerie, Berlin; Lehmbruck Museum, Duisburg; Zentrum internationaler Skulptur und Quadrat Bottrop; Yorkshire Sculpture Park
2003 Gemeentemuseum, Den Haag
2002 Kunstmuseum Bonn
2001 *New Works*, Royal Hibernian Academy; Gallagher Gallery, Dublin; Inverleith House, Royal Botanic Garden Edinburgh; National Gallery of Modern Art, Mumbai
2000 Neues Museum, Nuremberg; Goethe Institut Vilnius, Lithuania; Halle Kalk, Cologne
1999 Kunstverein Dortmund
1998 Neue Nationalgalerie, Berlin; Piepenbrock Preis für Kultur, Berlin
1997 Stedelijk Museum, Amsterdam
1995 Städtische Galerie im Lenbachhaus, Munich
1994 Ägyptisches Museum, Berlin
1993 Fundació Espai Poblenou, Barcelona

1992 Galerie Durand-Dessert, Paris; Kunsthalle Esplanade, Ingolstadt
1991 Centre d'Art Contemporain, Geneva; Kunstmuseum Winterthur; Serpentine Gallery, London
1990 The Krannert Art Museum, University of Illinois at Urbana-Champaign; The Henry Moore Sculpture Trust, Dean Clough, Halifax
1989 Reina Sofia, Madrid; The Barn, Clonegal
1988 Landesmuseum, Vienna; Donald Young Gallery, Chicago
1987 Donald Young Gallery, Chicago; Kunstsammlung Nordrhein-Westfalen, Dusseldorf; Kölnischer Kunstverein, Cologne; Museum Abteiberg, Mönchengladbach
1986 Kröller-Müller Museum, Otterlo
1985 Staatliche Kunstsammlung, Neue Galerie, Kassel
1984 Städtische Galerie im Städel, Frankfurt; Kamakura Gallery, Tokyo
1983 Centre Pompidou, Paris
1981 Modern Art Museum, Fort Worth
1979 Kunsthalle Bielefeld; Sperone Westwater Fischer Gallery, New York
1978 Museum Folkwang, Essen; Kunstmuseum Bonn; Venice Biennial
1977 Van Abbe Museum, Eindhoven; Galerie Erhard Klein, Bonn
1976 Museum of Modern Art, Oxford
1975 Lisson Gallery, London
1974 Kunstverein Frankfurt; Kunstraum München
1973 Kunsthalle Tübingen; Städtisches Museum, Mönchengladbach
1971 Galerie Konrad Fischer, Dusseldorf; Videogalerie Garry Schum, Dusseldorf
1970 *Steine und Eisen*, Museum Haus Lange, Krefeld
1967 Galerie Ad Libitum, Antwerp
1965 Leopold Hoesch Museum, Düren
1964 Domgalerie, Cologne

KILIAN RÜTHEMANN

Born 1979 in St. Gallen (Switzerland)
Lives and works in Basel

Solo Exhibitions
(Selection since 2004)

2010 *Attacca*, Museum für Gegenwartskunst, Basel; *Walking Distance*, Künstlerhaus Bremen
2009 *Sooner Rather than Later*, Kunsthaus Glarus; *Double Rich*, Istituto Svizzero, Rome; *Open Space*, Kunsthaus L6, Freiburg; *Extra Infra Ordinary*, Galerie Schleicher+Lange, Paris; *Unter 30 VII*, Kunstmuseum Thun; *Heimspiel – Ostschweizer Kunstschaffen*, Kunsthalle St. Gallen
2008 *Außenportal*, Binz39, Zurich; *Masse Critique*, Centre d'Art, Neuchâtel (with Niklaus Wenger); *Echo*, Stadtgalerie, Berne
2007 *Flatland*, Kunsthaus Baselland, Muttenz; *KANTE*, Espace Bellevaux, Lausanne (with Emil Michael Klein); *For a Blank Implies Space*, Torstrasse, Berlin (with Yngve Holen)
2006 *Lust*, Kunststiftung E. Hauser, Rottweil (with Karin Hueber and Dagmar Heppner)
2004 *White Wedding*, Schalter, Basel (with Florian Germann)

Group Exhibitions
(Selection since 2003)

2010 *Displaced Fractures – Über die Bruchlinien von Architekturen und ihren Körpern*, migros museum für gegenwartskunst Zürich
2009 *Fragile Monumente*, Suzie Q Projects, Zurich; Kunsthaus Aarau
2008 Berlin Biennial; *Unter 30 VI*, Kunsthaus Langenthal
2007 *Vrits*, Falknerstraße 4, Basel; *The Trees Bring Forth Sweet Ecstasy*, Ausstellungsraum Klingental; *Poor Thing*, Kunsthalle Basel; *Fireflies*, Nicolas Krupp Contemporary Art, Basel; *Topfloor*, Platform Garanti Contemporary Art Center, Istanbul
2006 *Regionale 7*, Kunsthalle Basel
2005 *Regionale 6*, [plug.in], Basel
2003 *Heimspiel – Ostschweizer Kunstschaffen*, Kunsthalle St. Gallen

OSCAR TUAZON

Born 1965 in Seattle (USA)
Lives and works in Paris and Tacoma

Solo Exhibitions
(Selection since 2007)

2010 *Oscar Tuazon*, Rat Hole, Tokyo (with Gardar Eide Einarsson); *SEX*, Jonathan Viner, London; *My Mistake*, ICA, London; *It was one of my best comes*, Centre d'art contemporain, Pougues Les Eaux; *My Flesh to your Bare Bones*, maccarone, New York; Kunsthalle Bern; *Against Nature*, Künstlerhaus Stuttgart
2009 Centre d'art contemporain, Geneva; *Ass To Mouth*, Balice Hertling, Paris; Dépendance, Brussels; *I Was a Stranger*, Isabella Bartolozzi, Berlin
2008 *A Vow of Poverty*, maccarone, New York; *Dirty Work*, Jonathan Viner, London; *Kodiak*, Seattle Art Museum, Seattle (with Eli Hansen); *This World's Just Not Real to Me*, Howard House Contemporary Art, Seattle (with Eli Hansen)
2007 *Where I Lived And What I Lived For, Module*, Palais de Tokyo, Paris; *I'd Rather Be Gone*, Standard, Oslo; *Oscar Tuazon / Mike Freeman*, Castillo / Corrales Gallery, Paris; *VOluntary Non vUlnerable*, Bodgers and Kludgers, Vancouver

Group Exhibitions
(Selection since 2002)

2010 *Displaced Fractures – Über die Bruchlinien von Architekturen und ihren Körpern*, migros museum für gegenwartskunst Zürich; Bordeaux Biennial; *When do you see yourself in ten years?* Standard, Oslo; *Rehabilitation*, Wiels, Brussels; *The Concrete Show*, Galleria Franco Noero, Turin; *Dynasty*, Palais de Tokyo et Musee d'Art Moderne, Paris; *Free as Air and Water*, Cooper Union School of Art, New York
2009 *Suddenly!* Pomona College, Los Angeles
2008 *27 november– 21 january 2009*, Catherine Bastide; dependance, Brussels; *Transformational Grammars*, Francesca Kaufmann, Milan; *Sack of Bones*, Peres Projects, Los Angeles; *Suddenly*, Cooley Art Gallery, Reed College, Portland; *Rendevous Nowhere*, Centro Cultural Montehermoso Vitoria; *September Show*, Tanya Leighton, Berlin; *Degrees of Remove: Landscape and Affect*, Sculpture Center, New York; *A Town (Not a City)*, Kunsthalle St. Gallen; *Alex Hubbard and Oscar Tuazon*, Contemporary Art Museum St. Louis; *Dragged down into lowercase*, Zentrum Paul Klee, Berne; *You Complete Me*, Western Bridge, Seattle; Contemporary Northwest Art Awards, Reed College, Portland; Kunsthalle St. Gallen
2007 *Exposition No 1*, Balice Hertling, Paris; *Hello Goodbye Thank You*, castillo / corrales, Paris
2006 *The Elementary Particles (The Paperback Edition)*, Standard, Oslo; *Minotaur Blood*, Jonathan Viner, London; Whitney Biennial; *An Open Operation*, Edinburgh College of Art; *The Culture of Fear*, ACC Galerie, Weimar; *Metronome no. 10*, Portland Institute for Contemporary Art
2005 *Baroque Geode*, Sundown Salon, Los Angeles; *Bridges*, University of Colorado, Denver
2004 *Slouching Towards Bethlehem*, The Project, New York; *Human, Fucking Human*, Lofoten International Art Festival, Bergen; *Adaptations*, Fridericianum, Kassel; *Our Mirror*, Lower Manhattan Cultural Council, New York; *Urban Renewal: City Without a Ghetto*, Princeton School of Architecture; *The Subsidized Landscape*, The Center for Architecture, New York; *Sprawl*, Hudson Clearing, New York; *Adaptations*, Apex Art, New York (with Richard Fischbeck)

2003 Wight Biennial, UCLA, Los Angeles, (with Richard Fischbeck); *24/7*, CAC, Vilnius; *Float*, Socrates Sculpture Park, New York; *Totally Motivated*, Kunstverein München (with Gardar Eide Einarsson); *Between the Lines*, Apex Art, New York, (with Gardar Eide Einarsson); *City Without a Ghetto*, Artists Space, New York; *Inscribing the Temporal*, Kunsthalle Exnergasse, Vienna
2002 *Strike*, Wolverhampton Art Gallery; Museum of the White Man, New York and Suquamish, Washington

KLAUS WINICHNER

Born 1967 in Altötting (Germany)
Lives and works in Berlin

Solo Exhibitions
(Selection since 2007)

2010 *Intermezzo Humaine*, Galerie Sandra Bürgel, Berlin; *Erlitten heitere Wellen*, Kleine Orangerie, Berlin
2008 *Nie zeigen was man denkt*, Galerie Sandra Bürgel, Berlin; *Willkommen to reality*, Galerie Sandra Bürgel, Berlin
2007 *Angaben zur Selbstüberschätzung*, Galerie Sandra Bürgel, Berlin

Group Exhibitions
(Selection since 2000)

2010 *Displaced Fractures – Über die Bruchlinien von Architekturen und ihren Körpern*, migros museum für gegenwartskunst Zürich; *Milch der Revolution. Dokumentarischer Teil*, Das illegale Museum Tom Biber, Berlin; *1910 Figur 2010*, Georg-Kolbe-Museum, Berlin; *Captain Pamphile (after the novel of Alexandre Dumas, with 55 artists)*, Galerie Waldkraiburg; Sammlung Falckenberg/Phönix Kulturstiftung, Hamburg
2009 *Diesseits der Alpen: Hunger Jenseits der Alpen: Durst*, Hadlichstrasse 44, Berlin; *Wir verbessern Ihre Arbeit*, Galerie Sandra Bürgel, Berlin; *The Forgotten Bar*, Galerie im Regierungsviertel, Berlin; *Schickeria: High Society*, BDA Galerie, Braunschweig; *Zeigen. Eine Audiotour durch Berlin von Karin Sander*, Temporäre Kunsthalle Berlin
2008 *Die Maße des Werts (the measures of value)*, Hadlichstr. 44, Berlin; Haas & Fuchs, Berlin
2007 *Unsere Affekte fliegen aus dem Bereich der menschlichen Wirklichkeit heraus*, Galerie Sandra Bürgel, Berlin
2006 *Auf den Fluren des Ganges*, Ballhaus Ost, Berlin; *Nach dem Beischlaf ist die Seele traurig*, Courtyard Gallery, Beijing
2005 *Kirchliche Kunst der Neuzeit*, Galerie Antik, Berlin; *50 Jahre Wirtshaus Huber*, Galerie Antik, Berlin; *Erwachendes Denken*, Lichtspielhaus Bayern
2004 *Café Veneto*, Galerie Giti Nourbakhsch, Berlin; *Im sofortigen Eingeständnis falscher Gedanken und Taten liegt unsere wachsende Unabhängigkeit*, Galerie Antik, Berlin
2003 *Die Frau als Gegenüber*, Menschenraum, Berlin; *Albert Schweizer spielt Bach*, Linienstrasse, Berlin
2002 *Garten, 27.9.99*, Pudel, Hamburg; *Der Zauber des Verlangens*, NBK, Berlin; Kunstverein Göttingen; *They are stupid like 'Atomia'*, Maschenmode, Berlin
2001 *Psycho Pillar*, Maschenmode, Berlin; *Circles 5*, ZKM, Karlsruhe; *Melanie*, Mariechef, Karlsruhe
2000 *Macht der Freundschaft und Sympathie*, Montparnasse, Berlin; *Klaus Winichner zeigt japanische Keramik*, Maschenmode, Berlin

PHYLLIDA BARLOW

48–49/50
Untitled: signs
2010
Plywood, timber, cement, scrim, spraypaint, paint, sealant
5 parts: each ca. 125 × 120 × 93 cm

Sammlung migros museum für gegenwartskunst Zürich

3–4/46–47
SWAMP untitled: barrier
2010
Wallboard, color
120 × 1000 × 800 cm

Courtesy of the artist and V22 Collection, London

TACITA DEAN

92/93
Palast
2004
Film (16mm, color, sound)
10:30 min.

Courtesy of the artist, Frith Street Gallery, London and Marian Goodman Gallery, New York/Paris

EMILIE DING

8–12
Erased
2008–2010
Concrete, steel
13 parts: Dimensions variable

Courtesy of the artist and Evergreene, Geneva

KLARA LIDÉN

22–24
Untitled (from the series "Poster Paintings")
2010
Found posters, blank poster paper, wheat paste
Ca. 90 × 62 × 14 cm

Sammlung Boros, Berlin

22–23
Untitled (from the series "Poster Paintings")
2010
Found posters, blank poster paper, wheat paste
Ca. 62 × 86 × 14 cm

Courtesy of the artist and Reena Spaulings, New York

22–23
Untitled (from the series "Poster Paintings")
2010
Found posters, blank poster paper, wheat paste
Ca. 90 × 62 × 14 cm

Private Collection

22–23
Untitled (from the series "Poster Paintings")
2010
Found posters, blank poster paper, wheat paste
Ca. 90 × 62 × 14 cm

Private Collection

18–21
Position 0310
2010
4-channel-video on 4 monitors (color, no sound)
Each ca. 3 min.

Courtesy of the artist and Galerie Neu, Berlin

ULRICH RÜCKRIEM

96–100
Ohne Titel (Bodenarbeit)
1990
Austrian granite
45 × 200 × 362 cm

Courtesy of the artist and Galerie Tschudi, Glarus

KILIAN RÜTHEMANN

16–17
The Truth Will Always Have a Hole in It
2010
Plaster, rendering
297 × 256 × 4.5 cm

Courtesy of the artist and RaebervonStenglin, Zurich

13–16
Ohne Titel (Sarkophag)
2009
Foam
109 × 230 × 126 cm

Courtesy of the artist and RaebervonStenglin, Zurich

OSCAR TUAZON

59–61
I want to put something inside my body and carry something in it. I want to get inside my body and get carried in it, I'd like to get buried in it, put my head in it and get in it, I'm not scared of it.
2010
Welded steel, clamps, canvas, fluorescent lights, water
60 × 495 × 218 cm

Sammlung migros museum für gegenwartskunst Zürich

64–68/89
I use my body for something, I use it to make something, I make something with my body, whatever that is. I make something and I pay for it and I get paid for it.
2010
Concrete, rebar, mesh
Ca. 77 × 450 × 410 cm

Sammlung migros museum für gegenwartskunst Zürich

KLAUS WINICHNER

55–58
Vom Grund und seiner Ursache
2008
Concrete, plaster, varnish, fabric, drawing, various materials
Ca. 180 × 190 × 85 cm

Courtesy of the artist and Galerie Sandra Bürgel, Berlin

52–54
Science Fiction
2009
Concrete, plaster, book
70 × 50 × 30 cm

Courtesy of the artist and Galerie Sandra Bürgel, Berlin

51
Orangenpflückerin
2010
Concrete, plaster, varnish, various materials
230 × 90 × 90 cm

Courtesy of the artist and Galerie Sandra Bürgel, Berlin

This book was published on the occasion of the exhibition *Displaced Fractures – Über die Bruchlinien von Architekturen und ihren Körpern*, December 11, 2010 – February 20, 2011, at the migros museum für gegenwartskunst Zürich.

The exhibition and the publication represent a collaboration between the migros museum für gegenwartskunst Zürich and the Siemens Stiftung.

EXHIBITION

migros museum für gegenwartskunst

Director
Heike Munder

Exhibition Curators
Heike Munder,
Thomas D. Trummer

Assistant Curator
Raphael Gygax

Exhibitions Coordinator & Registrar
Judith Welter

Head of Administration
Catherine Reymond

Administration
Yvonne Brand

Interns
Anna-Lena Gugger, Alena Nawrotzki, Andrea Roca

Technical Manager Exhibitions
Monika Schori

Technical Manager Collection
Roland Bösiger

Technical Support
Gabi Deutsch, Muriel Gutherz, Roman Gysin, Basil Kobert

Reception
Christa Michel, Katharina Rippstein, Mareike Spalteholz, Monika Stalder

migros museum für gegenwartskunst
Postfach 1766
CH–8031 Zurich
T +41 (0) 44 277 20 50
F +41 (0) 44 277 62 86
info@migrosmuseum.ch
migrosmuseum.ch

The migros museum für gegenwartskunst Zürich is an institution of the Migros Culture Percentage.
migros-kulturprozent.ch

Siemens Stiftung

Governing Board
Dr. Stephan Heimbach,
Georg Bernwieser,
Ulrike Susanne Wahl

Director Art & Culture
Michael Roßnagl

Curator Visual Arts
Thomas D. Trummer

Assistant Visual Arts
Judith Pöverlein

Communications
Reglindis Pfeiffer,
Karolin Timm-Wachter

Siemens Stiftung
Oscar-von-Miller-Ring 20
D–80333 Munich, Germany
T +49 (0) 89 636 3 36 10
F +49 (0) 89 636 3 36 15
info@siemens-stiftung.org
siemens-stiftung.org

The Siemens Stiftung, a nonprofit foundation under German civil law, was founded in the fall of 2008 by Siemens AG. The foundation works with projects to strengthen civil society particularly in Africa, Latin America, and Europe. In the US, Siemens Stiftung pursues *AR*, the *Artistic Research* project since October 2010—a cooperation with ACT the MIT program in Art, Culture and Technology with ongoing accumulation till the end of the spring semester in 2011. This initiative goes along with the long-time involvement in fostering education programs in maths and natural sciences that are particulary provided by Siemens Stiftung globally, also in the US.

The aim of Siemens Stiftung is to make a long-term contribution to reducing poverty and improving education. The foundation operates in three areas: It supports enlarging basic services and improving social structures; initiates educational projects; and contributes to strengthening cultural identity. The Siemens Stiftung works in close cooperation with local and international partners as well as in alliance with the other Siemens foundations established by Siemens in Argentina, Brazil, France, Colombia, and the United States. For further information siemens-stiftung.org

IMPRINT

PUBLICATION

Published by
migros museum für gegenwartskunst Zürich & Siemens Stiftung

Editors
Heike Munder, Thomas D. Trummer

Editorial Coordination
Raphael Gygax

Interns
Alena Nawrotzki, Judith Pöverlein

Translations from German
Gerrit Jackson (Texts: Holger Birkholz, Heike Munder / Thomas D. Trummer), Karsten Harries (Own text)

Copy Editing and Proofreading, German
Doris Senn, Bettina Steinbrügge, Judith Welter

Copy Editing and Proofreading, English
Rowena Smith

Photography
Stefan Altenburger Photography

Concept & Graphic Design
Marie Lusa

Intern
Martina Brassel

Lithography
Georg Sidler, Schwyz

Production
Odermatt AG, Dallenwil

Cover
Phyllida Barlow
Untitled: signs
2010

Back Cover
Klaus Winichner
Vom Grund und seiner Ursache
2008

The migros museum für gegenwartskunst and Siemens Stiftung would like to thank:

The artists
Phyllida Barlow, Tacita Dean, Emilie Ding, Klara Lidén, Ulrich Rückriem, Kilian Rüthemann, Oscar Tuazon, Klaus Winichner

The galleries
Galerie Sandra Bürgel, Berlin; Evergreene, Geneva; Frith Street Gallery, London; Marian Goodman Gallery, New York / Paris; Hauser & Wirth; Maccarone Gallery, New York; Galerie Neu, Berlin; RaebervonStenglin, Zurich; Galerie Tschudi, Glarus

The lenders
V22 Contemporary Art Collection

And
Robert Balthasar, Thomas Batt, Holger Birkholz, Giovanni Carmine, Jens Cording, Alice Dietrich, Nicole Dietrich, Dominik Eisenhut, Edelgard Eckert, Anja Funke, Christoph Gantenbein, Joachim Gerstmeier, Karsten Harries, Beate Hentschel, Carin Huber, Brigitte Huck, Andrea Igaz, Ulrich Keil, Kaspar König, Tanya Leighton, Stefanie Mayr, Josef Dalle Nogare, Tom Offerhaus, Marion Piffer-Damiani, Lukas Roalter, Sabine Sailer, Isabella Schneckenburger, Trevor Smith, Victoria Willemer

Printed in Switzerland

Distributed by
JRP|Ringier
Letzigraben 134
CH–8047 Zurich
T +41 (0) 43 311 27 50
F +41 (0) 43 311 27 51
info@jrp-ringier.com
jrp-ringier.com

ISBN: 978-3-03764-177-4

JRP|Ringier books are
available internationally at
selected bookstores and
from the following distribution
partners:

Switzerland
Buch 2000,
AVA Verlagsauslieferung AG
Centralweg 16
CH–8910 Affoltern a.A.
buch2000@ava.ch
ava.ch

Germany and Austria
Vice Versa Vertrieb
Immanuelkirchstrasse 12
D–10405 Berlin
info@vice-versa-vertrieb.de
vice-versa-vertrieb.de

France
Les presses du réel
35, rue Colson
F–21000 Dijon
info@lespressesdureel.com
lespressesdureel.com

United Kingdom and other
European countries
Cornerhouse Publications
70 Oxford Street
UK–Manchester M1 5NH
publications@cornerhouse.org
cornerhouse.org/books

USA, Canada, Asia,
and Australia
D.A.P./Distributed Art
Publishers
155 Sixth Avenue, 2nd Floor
USA–New York, NY 10013
dap@dapinc.com
artbook.com

For a list of our partner
bookshops or for any general
questions, please contact
JRP|Ringier directly at
info@jrp-ringier.com, or
visit our homepage
jrp-ringier.com for further
information about sour
program.